County Governments In Florida

County Governments In Florida

First in a Series on Local Government

Sponsored by the Reubin O'D. Askew
School of Public Affairs and Administration
Florida State University

FRANK P. SHERWOOD

Professor of Public Administration Emeritus
Tallahassee, Florida, 2008

iUniverse, Inc.
New York Lincoln Shanghai

County Governments In Florida
First in a Series on Local Government

iUniverse books may be ordered through booksellers or by contacting:

iUniverse
2021 Pine Lake Road, Suite 100
Lincoln, NE 68512
www.iuniverse.com
1-800-Authors (1-800-288-4677)

ISBN: 978-0-595-48160-6 (pbk)
ISBN: 978-0-595-60254-4 (ebk)

Printed in the United States of America

To

*My beloved wife, Susie, with whom I will celebrate
a blissful 60 years of marriage
on February 14, 2008*

and

*John P. Thomas, a dear friend and former student, who
was Executive Director of the Florida Association of Counties in
1982 when I arrived at Florida State University.
He urged me not to forget the counties. I hope this book
shows I have not.*

CONTENTS

LIST OF TABLES

PREFACE

Counties may be the quiet governmental jurisdiction in the US federal system, but they are not inactive or irrelevant. Created to fulfill the administrative roles of state government at the local government level, counties in the twenty-first century have expanded their services to provide a range of urban services to citizens outside incorporated areas that fifty years ago would have been unheard of in the American states. As Dr. Sherwood discusses in chapter three, counties have a third role, and that is providing area-wide or regional services such as emergency medical services, fire protection, and disaster management. Thus county leaders have become key coordinators in a rich network of horizontal relationships among municipalities, special districts, and other counties as well as among the vertical networks with the state and federal governments.

With property tax reductions passed by the 2007 Florida Legislature, and more tax reduction proposals expected in 2008, Florida counties deserve the special attention this book gives them. Chapters on County Revenue Sources under Home Rule, and Finances and Mandates in the Counties seem particularly timely. Other chapters discuss the institutions and home rule provisions that counties use to set their governance structures, as well as the consolidation efforts and results in Miami-Dade and Jacksonville, and the newer form of county restructuring—charter counties. The charter government experience of three counties—Broward, Volusia and Orange counties—is presented and assessed for lessons in government reform.

Dr. Frank P. Sherwood has graciously made this first-rate publication available as a sponsored book by the Askew School of Public Administration and Policy. It is the first book in a Local Government series by the Askew School of Public Administration and Policy, and it comes in our inaugural year of co-sponsoring the Center for Florida Local Government Excellence (CFLGE), with our partners the Scott Daley Florida Institute of Government, and the Florida City and County Managers Association. It is one of many future products for training, practical applications, research and teaching we plan to make available to local government managers as the Center for Florida Local Government Excellence becomes established.

Dr. Frank P. Sherwood is a well respected and knowledgeable person on Florida government administration, and an ideal choice to write this book. Dr. Sherwood wrote his first book on local government in 1963 and comes to this task with a wealth of local government knowledge. His work on city-county consolidation led to *Papers Prepared by Frank P. Sherwood in Support of the Tallahassee City and Leon County Consolidation,* published in 1992. While serving on the faculty of the Askew School of Public Administration and Policy at Florida State University, Dr. Sherwood was widely consulted by county administrators and state officials on matters relating to local government administration, civil service reform and administrative reorganization. A former Director of the Federal Executive Institute, Dr. Sherwood led many workshops in Florida for local government managers, including topics such as public service professionalism, managerial ethics, and management reform.

The reader will be pleasantly surprised by the liveliness of Dr. Sherwood's writing and his ability to draw helpful conclusions from the detailed descriptive material he covers. Dr. Sherwood began his career as a newspaper writer and publisher in San Diego, California, with the *San Diego Daily Sun,* and few academics have been able to match his fine communicative style of writing.

While at FSU from 1982 to 1995, Dr. Sherwood served as Director of the then Department of Public Administration, and was a unanimous choice by the faculty in 1991 to be named the first Jerry Collins Eminent Scholar in Public Administration. After retiring from FSU in 1995, Dr. Sherwood was again honored for his national stature in, and contribution to, public administration when FSU established a professorship in his name, the Frank P. Sherwood Professor of Public Administration.

It is with great pleasure that I write this short Preface to introduce *County Governments in Florida.* I expect this book to attract a great deal of interest. It should help educate citizens and policy makers understand the hard decisions on revenue, programs and management in Florida county government they will have to make in the decade ahead. It is fitting that this thoughtful resource is published now when it can contribute to the public dialogue that informs important local government decisions in Florida. We are fortunate to have this insightful volume on *County Governments in Florida* by Dr. Frank Sherwood to provide commentary and guidance.

Frances Stokes Berry
Director, and Frank P. Sherwood Professor of Public Administration
Askew School of Public Administration and Policy
Florida State University
July 26, 2007

INTRODUCTION

This book developed out of conversations between Dr. John P. Thomas and myself, beginning in1982 and continuing for the next two years.

John was an old friend and former student who had become the executive director of the Florida Association of Counties. He was in that position when I joined the faculty of the Department of Public Administration at Florida State University in the fall, 1982. At the time my knowledge of Florida and its governments was meager, and John thus became an early and principal resource.

Inevitably, our conversations fastened on the counties of Florida, with which John was basically concerned. One of John's early points to me was that the counties were a particularly important element of government in Florida because so much of the state's population growth had occurred outside the municipalities. John's knowledge about such matters was comprehensive and broad. Before coming to Florida, he had been on the staff of the National Association of Counties, giving him a real perspective.

As we discussed the counties and the substantial public ignorance about their place and role in the scheme of things, it became increasingly apparent that they were the "lost continent" of Florida politics, very much as they had been labeled on the national scene. While there continues to be a paucity of good and easily accessible information about government at all levels in Florida, that is particularly true with respect to local institutions. The cities, while overlooked to a far greater degree than is desirable, have commanded far more public attention than the counties.

Thus, it is not surprising that John and I jointly concluded that a relatively brief and easily read book on county government in Florida was desperately needed. It seemed tragic that no one—the interested and perhaps activist citizen, the inquiring college student, or the venturesome and curious high school pupil—could find much of anything to consult. There were very few learning resources that covered county governments.

John and I decided that we would write a book, and we divided the task as one might anticipate. John was the one with the knowledge and I with the time to do the writing. So it was that the first two years were devoted to his explaining to me not only the structure but the subtleties of county operations. I found the exercise fascinating, not only because it acquainted me with a level of government to which I had been little exposed but also because it enabled me to learn much of what I needed to know about the whole of Florida government.

Just when it was about time for me to translate all I had heard into the pages of a book, John was offered an opportunity to become the executive director of the National Association of Counties. His departure was a tremendous loss for Florida's counties, but it certainly was a fine promotion for him. I had digested a lot of learning but had committed none of it to the written word. And John was gone, consumed by more major problems.

I don't remember ever talking with him about the book again. But it remained alive for me. The incentive to bring the counties to citizen attention was still very much present. As a result, I began the slow process of writing a book. Things went slowly and were fitted among many other duties. Yet, by 1988, I had completed what I felt was a relatively brief, fairly comprehensive analysis of county government at the time. I did not pretend it was the last word in research. I saw it instead as a contribution to citizen education.

The project was completed about four years after John Thomas had left Tallahassee, and I no longer felt we were involved in a joint project. While I owed him a great debt for providing the basic guidance to the enterprise, it would not have been fair to charge him with responsibility for what I had written. And he had no time to make sure the manuscript reflected his understandings and wisdom not only in respect to Florida but to the nation as a whole. It seemed that I had a manuscript in which no one felt ownership except myself.

Frankly, too, John's departure had left me with a waning interest in the counties. I was living in the state capital and was challenged by the many governance dilemmas faced by one of the fastest growing states in the nation.

The result was that the manuscript on Florida's counties came to occupy a place on a shelf, only briefly resurrected when Professor Richard Chackerian embarked on the task of developing a textbook on Florida government and politics in about 1990. The book was published in 1995[1] and included my chapter on "County Government," drawn almost entirely from my earlier manuscript.[2] Since a relatively few years had elapsed since I had completed my book, I did relatively little updating for the chapter. Only in the description of Florida's two major efforts in

---

1   Richard Chackerian, editor, *The Florida Public Policy Management System: Discontinuity and Reform* (Tallahassee, Fl.: Florida Center for Public Management, 1995), 438 pp. A second edition was published in 1998. by Kendall-Hunt (Dubuque, Iowa).

2   *Loc. cit.,* pp. 291-321.

metropolitan reform, in Miami-Dade and in Jacksonville, did I feel really impelled to make sure things were current.

Many years passed. It was ten years after my retirement from the Askew School of Public Affairs and Administration at Florida State University, in 2005, that I felt the time had come to do something about the counties. Though it was nearly 20 years later, no one had yet written a book about this very important unit of local government in Florida. I was much older, with a limited supply of energy, but I still felt a book needed to be published.

My first move was to resurrect the old manuscript, now nearly 20 years old. I made a few cosmetic changes to make it seem a bit more current, and then asked several people knowledgeable about counties to read it and advise me on its general utility. The feedback was that such a volume was still needed and most of the issues raised were still relevant, but the examples and factual information were terribly outdated. It was clear the book would have little acceptance. It was too much of an antique.

The need was obvious. The manuscript had to be up-dated. At that point, I thought it was mainly a matter of inserting new numbers and providing some new illustrations for old problems. I had hoped I could find someone to whom I could give the manuscript and who would, with relatively little effort, produce a publication that would be current. To my great disappointment I could find no one willing to take on the task. Apparently there was no one interested in writing about the counties in Florida, even when a lot of the work had been done.

I had either to take up the task myself or there would be no book. With some misgivings I decided to hang in there, partly because I thought only some simple updating would be required. Was I wrong! While the structure and role of the counties have remained the same, about everything else has changed. One need note only the dramatic increase in the state's population in 20 years, most of which has occurred in the unincorporated areas of the counties, to realize how ludicrous was my notion of a simple, quick update.

What is contained in these pages is a totally different book. Seven of the 11 chapters are entirely new, and the other four have been substantially rewritten. Only the histories of metro reform in Miami-Dade and city-county consolidation in Jacksonville-Duval remain basically the same; and, in the case of Miami-Dade, the history has been an evolving one, culminating in the adoption of the strong mayor form of government in 2004.

What has been most striking in this substantial writing effort has been the role of the Internet. This has not been "rocket-science" research, but it was quite apparent from the outset that a tremendous amount of information had to be acquired in order even to reflect modestly the variety of circumstances that exists in Florida's 69 counties. Nearly 60 of the counties had home pages which I found useful. The data were not uniform, but there was enough that, taken together, there was a far more detailed profile of the counties than I was able to obtain twenty years earlier. In some cases, as in Collier County, the web site provided a detailed and rather complete picture of county operations.

Further, there were sites that were extremely helpful in summarizing the situation throughout the state. The Florida Department of Financial Services, for example, maintains financial information on all the counties. It can be obtained in summary form, which I found sufficient for my purposes, or in more detail. The Florida Department of Community Affairs maintains a highly useful data base on roughly 1500 special districts in Florida; the Florida Association of Counties has considerable summary information on the organization and practices of the counties; and the Florida Legislative Committee on Intergovernmental Relations has substantial analyses and reports on various aspects of local governance. I was particularly helped by its work on mandates.

I do want to note that this has been a one person effort. There has been no one available to do all the fact-checking that would have been desirable. As a result, there is no doubt that errors will turn up at various points. They may result from my personal inadequacies (though I tried my best to check and recheck the data) and also from the materials with which I worked. As I have noted in a couple of places in the book, the numbers just don't add up. My only recourse was to point out the discrepancies I detected. I could not go back and do the original research. Overall, however, I believe the book faithfully reflects the current reality of Florida's counties.

My hope is that this book will prove useful to a number of audiences. Most of all, I envisage it as a resource for those actively engaged in county government. Up to now, there has been no book to which they could turn that provides a fairly complete picture of county governments in Florida. Awareness of the history and current status of these governments should be the departure point for a wise stewardship of one of the foundations of our political system.

Frank P. Sherwood

CHAPTER ONE

THE COUNTY IN THE FLORIDA SYSTEM OF GOVERNMENT

In the late1980's, the *New York Times* reported on the spectacular change that had occurred in the role and significance of counties in Florida. The story was titled, "Counties Acquire New Burdens and Powers." This trend, identified long ago, has simply become more pronounced. The population of the City of West Palm Beach, as a percentage of Palm Beach County, has dropped dramatically since 1960, when it was about 25% of all residents. Nearly three decades later, it was down to about 10%; and in 2005 it stood at about 8%, when the county had 1,265,000 people and the city of West Palm Beach 101,000. In 2005, as in 1987, there were 36 other cities in the county, none as large as West Palm Beach, and 559,000 County residents were living outside a City. That meant that nearly half (44%) were served only by the Palm Beach County government.

"What has happened," commented the *Times* in 1987, "… is that the county government, in effect, has been superimposed over a complex matrix of jurisdictions. These include 37 municipalities ranging from tiny villages to coastal cities such as Boca Raton and West Palm Beach, 20 or so separate special districts … and scores of private residential developments that have never been incorporated but provide such basic services as fire and police protection."[3]

While the *Times* singled out Palm Beach, it was describing a far more general situation in Florida. With the exception of Jacksonville, which consolidated its city and county governments in 1968, the state pattern is one where the counties are by far the dominant government. It is easy to be misled on this point because Florida does not have huge urban governments that rival other parts of the country. Metropolitan Miami, which includes Dade and Broward counties at a minimum, boasts over four million people. But there is no large city government, as

---

3   *New York Times,* June 10, 1987

you will find in New York, Los Angeles, and Houston. The biggest municipality in the vast Florida megalopolis is Miami, with a 2005 population of 386,000, less than one percent of the total.

This institutional circumstance is of vital significance in assessing the role and importance of the counties in Florida. Where citizens in urban settings in other parts of the country created municipalities to serve their requirements and enabled these institutions to grow with the increasing scale of the problems, Florida took a different route. A major share of the state's population (about half in 2005) stayed separate from a municipality; and many of the others lived in very small cities, which were able to provide only a limit number of services.

As the *Times* noted in 1987, the increased tasks imposed on the counties were "… not the result of any formal transfer of powers … it came as new population growth forced the unincorporated areas and smaller governments to turn to the counties for assistance, just as suburban governments once sought help from the central city government for such services as water supply and transportation."[4]

Thus the counties have emerged as highly significant local governments in Florida. The 67 governments comprehend all the land in the state, are by far the largest jurisdictions both in terms of territory and population, have long been assigned significant tasks by the State, and have increasingly been called upon by the citizenry to undertake a widening range of obligations. There was no grand plan. Things occurred because these institutions had the people and the territory.

This reality provides a basic perspective for this book, which proceeds from the assumption that the counties must inevitably perform a wide range of services and functions for Floridians.

The Palm Beach story is not unique to Florida or to the nation. Once referred to as the "dark continent of American government," counties have particularly emerged from the shadows in the last two decades. A reason for the lack of attention, according to Neal R. Peirce, is that they "… tend to be the slowest changing bodies on the intergovernmental scene."[5]

They have been around a long time, James County having been created in Virginia 353 years ago. Yet they have been little chronicled in the media or in academia. Peirce, a well-known columnist on state and local government, reported, "Conrad Joyner, an academician and former official of Pima County, Arizona, discovered that in all the years since James was founded, only one book has ever been

---

4   Ibid.

5   "Remarks by Neil R. Peirce" (Washington, D.C.: Committee on the Future, National Association of Counties, March 13, 1987), typescript, p. 1

written on the history of the American county. The lonely pioneer author, should you wish to honor him, was Sydney Duncomb of the University of Idaho."[6]

I. FLORIDA COUNTY HISTORY

In Florida, the county as an institution of government can boast a history of about 165 years, dating to the time that Andrew Jackson established two counties, Escambia and St. Johns, in the newly-acquired territory of Florida in 1821. What did Jackson expect of these new governmental units? By asking that question, one can develop some sense of the traditional role of the counties and how things have changed over the years.

Origins in Western Europe.

There was, of course, a tradition of such units in Western Europe. In France local jurisdictions known as *contes* existed. In the British Isles similar governments were known as shires. It was within this tradition that the "county" was brought to America by colonists in Virginia, Massachusetts, New York, and Pennsylvania. The manner in which the citizens of each of these colonies organized local governments varied greatly; but in all situations the county was regarded as a subdivision of the larger government. Alexis de Tocqueville's praise for the genius of American government rested in substantial degree on the decentralization the counties brought to the governmental system. While they were subdivisions of the state and bound to observe the over-arching law of the larger jurisdiction, de Tocqueville found that the staffing of these entities by local people provided a grass roots bias to an otherwise big government. As might be anticipated, local control meant high diversity; and the variety persists. In fact, names still reflect the differences. Depending upon ancestry, counties are called county, city, borough, parish, or district.

Virginia settlements consisted of large plantations which were too widely dispersed to relate easily to governmental authority. Thus, in the southern agrarian society, the county became the dominant unit of local government simply because smaller units would not have been effective. In contrast, Massachusetts settlements were necessarily smaller. The rougher terrain led to an agrarian economy supplemented by fishing and shipping. Indians were far more hostile in New England, thus requiring smaller, more dense groupings of settlers. The township form of government, usually comprising an area of 20 to 40 square miles and based on the

---

6   *op. cit.*, p. 5

English parish system, was more suitable to the New England situation. Although the typical Massachusetts township performed many functions, it never achieved the scope of Virginia counties. The township unit continues to exist throughout New England; but, with the exception of Rhode Island and Connecticut, as a subdivision of the county.

The numbers of counties and their status within the larger state governments vary. There are 3,066 counties across the land: Texas has 254, Florida 67, Montana 56, and Rhode Island 0, thus indicating the range of institutional possibilities within a particular state.

Developments in Florida.

Florida's experience with counties roughly correlates with that of other parts of the nation, though its population explosion in recent years has greatly accelerated the emergence of the counties as dominant governmental actors. Andrew Jackson's order of July, 1821, effectively partitioned the Florida territory into two subordinate units, the Counties of Escambia and St. Johns. Escambia encompassed all the land lying between the Perdido and Suwanee Rivers; and St. John's embraced the territory east of the Suwanee as well as all other areas not included in Escambia. The primary functions of the new counties were judicial, with five justices of the peace established in each. Other county officers were also established: the clerk of the court, the sheriff, and possibly additional justices of the peace. In addition, the counties were empowered to grant and recall licenses or commissions for innkeepers, for retailers of liquor of every description, and for keepers of billiard tables. Counties also had the discretion to impose such taxes as might be necessary to carry out the assigned functions.

The following year an Act of Congress established territorial government, vesting legislative power in a council composed of the Governor and 13 other Presidential appointees. This legislative council was the first American body (previously Spain and France had been in power) to exercise direct legislative control over Florida. It is of particular importance to note that the county governments preceded other governmental entities in performing the judicial function and some services.

Florida achieved statehood in 1845 and began to grow rapidly. The 1860 Census showed a population of 140, 427, nearly four times the population 25 years earlier. The post-Civil War 1868 Constitution showed that the counties were increasingly viewed as administrative arms of the state, no doubt reflecting the demand for increased services by a growing population. Counties were delegated responsibilities in education, the judiciary, elections, and general welfare. The 1885 Constitution also revealed an increasing involvement by the State government in local affairs. It authorized the Legislature to create new counties and to alter existing boundaries; likewise, the Legislature was accorded broad controls over municipalities, including the right to abolish them. By the end of the 19th century, the independence of local governments in Florida had been significantly eroded.[7]

Affairs in Florida in the early 20th century were dominated by the economy. A major land boom in the twenties descended into depression in the thirties. Preparations for World War II benefitted Florida greatly, and many military bases were located within the state. As a result of an expanded economy and the settlement of many war veterans, the population of six counties in the state (Dade, Duval, Hillsborough, Pinellas, Polk and Orange) accounted for more than half the population increase in the forties; and the period was also characterized by markedly increased urbanization.[8]

The population of the state has, of course, grown rapidly since then, particularly in the central and southern parts. The original two counties were partitioned into 67. The growth in numbers of counties was particularly rapid between 1920 and 1925, when 22 were created. The four largest counties in the state inevitably appear where Florida's population concentrates, in the south and central parts of the state. The two largest are in the Miami-Ft. Lauderdale area, Dade and Broward. The third and fourth most populated are in the Tampa-St. Petersburg area, Hillsborough and Pinellas; and the two smallest are Liberty (2005 population 7581) and Lafayette (2005 population 7971). As might be expected, the populations of the Counties differ greatly in their composition. Gadsden County in the Panhandle is majority black; Holmes and Pasco Counties, on the other hand, possess little diversity, with only a small percentage of their populations black. Certainly these widely diverse communities require substantial discretion to enable them to respond to the unique requirements of their respective populations.

Major State Changes

As the term of Governor Millard Caldwell was ending in 1948, the neglect of the local governments in Florida was becoming very evident. They had neither the Constitutional powers nor the resources to provide the services an expanding population required. The 1885 Constitution, designed to address political and economic conditions of another era, was clearly out of date. A proliferation of single purpose districts, created to meet specific service needs in the urban areas,

---

7   Nixon Smiley, *Yesterday's Florida* (Miami: E.A. Seeman Publishing Co., 1974), p. 4
8   Charlton Tebeau, *A History of Florida* (Coral Gables: University of Miami Press, 1971) p. 431

suggested the generally chaotic condition which prevailed. As might be expected, interventions by the Legislature were frequent, intended for the most part to put the State in charge of local matters.

A major reform of Florida government occurred in 1968 when a new Constitution was adopted. Among many changes, an attempt was made to return control of local affairs to the cities and counties. Local jurisdictions were provided substantial freedoms to meet community needs without reference to State requirements. But the reform failed to address the highly important problem of resources to support the assumption of additional service responsibilities. Restrictions on the taxing authorities of cities and counties remained; and the problem of money has continued to plague the local governments of Florida.[9]

II. COUNTIES IN THE FEDERAL SYSTEM

While the concern in this study is with the counties of Florida, it is always important to conceive of any jurisdictional unit in the United States as functioning within an inter-governmental mosaic. Clearly, the two most significant elements of the system with which the counties must deal are the State as the dominant partner and the cities as advocates and providers of urban services. Various types of special districts in Florida further confound the number and complexity of governments within the boundaries of a single county. Over-arching the thousands of governmental units in the United States is the national government, whose Constitution has been an important element of societal stability for nearly 225 years.

The relationship of the national to local governments, both county and city, has been roller-coaster-like in the 20th century. For at least four decades there was essentially no contact between the Federal government and the more than 3,000 counties. To the extent that citizens of Florida had contact with their national government, it was in the performance of such direct services as postal service, soil conservation, agricultural extension, veterans' supports, and park and forest maintenance and preservation. It was really not until the '60s that such arrangements were dramatically changed; and, through a wide range of grant mechanisms, both cities and counties became agents of the national government. Further, the quality of these governments was perceived as a matter of national interest, as was most eloquently reflected in the provision for the general sharing of Federal revenues

---

9   *Report on the History and Status of Local Government Powers in Florida.* (Tallahassee: Committee on Community Affairs, Florida House of Representatives, 1972) p. 1.

with other levels of government. That program began in 1972 and continued for 14 years.

In the Reagan period of the '80s, the relationships of the Federal government with other levels were radically transformed. Federal aid to state and local governments was greatly reduced. As a matter of fact, much of what was left were categorical pass-throughs to individual citizens and constituted no institutional source of revenues. At the same time, the counties had not been absolved of responsibilities for managing major parts of a social net for the disadvantaged. Indeed, it could be argued that the effect of the changes of the '80s was to assign even greater burdens to the counties, but without financial supports. Neil Peirce summed up the situation, "Let us be clear about it: we are in the midst of a great sea change in American governance, a period of Federal retrenchment that could itself last two or three decades. That means that the pain and pleasure of revenue raising and then spending will shift significantly to the state and local level."[10]

He continued: "We are in an era of radical transformation in the role of local governments. In the past we had strictly limited expectations of them: to maintain the roads, collect the taxes, keep the poorhouse and the jails, put out fires, enforce codes. The big social service agenda was added in the last generation. And now the demands are escalating further. For survival in today's world, counties must move beyond a caretaker role; they have to think a lot more broadly than groundskeepers."[11]

Peirce's pessimistic view of the relationship between the Federal government and the other units in the system has proved generally correct. A sampling of financial data for 19 counties for 2004 showed that four percent or less of income came directly from the Federal government. Thus, it has become extremely hard to find Federal dollars for programs, even where a national interest is clearly apparent.

III. THE CRITICAL ROLE OF THE STATE: LOOKING UPWARD

Over time, the critical relationship for the counties has been with the State government. The reason is readily apparent: the county is a subordinate unit, a component element of the larger government. In this sense, the county-state relationship is fundamentally different from that of the states and national government, in which each is considered a sovereign entity dealing on essentially equal

10   Peirce, *op. cit.,* p. 11
11   Ibid., p. 12

terms. Where the counties were originally created to serve as agents of the state, it was the states which formed the Federal government to serve their collective interests. Thus the way in which a state will deal with its counties, as well as its cities, is very much dependent on the good sense and wisdom of its leaders, not on any national legal or constitutional foundation.

As has already been observed, the behavior of the State in regard to Florida local governments was particularly capricious prior to the constitutional reform of 1968. The pattern was characteristic of other states in the Southeast, where there was little appreciation of local community autonomy. Special acts were passed to benefit particularistic local interests at the instigation of individual legislators. Such erratic and unpredictable interventions made it virtually impossible for local governments to deal with the problems of their communities. In effect the beauties of decentralization that de Tocqueville had encountered in the early 19th century had substantially disappeared in a morass of legislative interventions dealing with service responsibilities, personnel, and finances.

1968 Constitution

The 1968 constitution was a significant but limited effort to restore autonomy to the local levels of government. It reflected changed attitudes toward many aspects of government in Florida. Within its Article VIII (voted on separately), the Constitution embraced a very different philosophical approach to local government powers and relationships with the State. As will be discussed in much greater detail later in this book, it did adopt the concept of home rule by enabling local governments to engage in a broader range of services. A rather sharp distinction was drawn in the case of counties, however, between charter and non-charter counties. The idea of the charter was introduced in the 1968 constitution and permitted counties with such status the freedom to engage in activities not otherwise prohibited by general or special law. In contrast, the non-charter county was limited in its powers to those specifically granted by general or special law. Further, municipal ordinances were to prevail over the statutes of the non-charter county in cases of conflict. In the charter county the electorate could decide how to resolve conflicts between the two units of government.

1971 Legislation

Subsequently, legislation in 1971 provided a further broadening of home rule in the non-charter counties. It created a code of county powers and repealed numerous provisions narrowing county powers. The scope of the "county home rule governing act" is stated in the following terms: "The provisions of this act shall be liberally construed in order to effectively carry out the purpose of this act to secure for the counties the broad exercise of home rule powers authorized by the Constitution."[12]

Yet there were two ways in which the 1968 Constitution and the 1971 act failed to deal with fundamental aspects of home rule: (a) a retention of tight controls over revenue sources, both in terms of types and amounts; and (b) a continued freedom on the part of the legislature to impose any demands it chose on the counties to perform specific services without providing the finances to do so, *viz.*, the mandate problem.

As a result, counties in particular continue to experience great difficulties in mounting effective responses to community service needs. Aside from the property tax, most major sources of revenue have been pre-empted by the state. The freedoms available to the counties in respect to the various forms of excise taxes are greatly circumscribed by state legislative policy and action. In the case of the property tax, whose administration and utilization is barred constitutionally to the State government, the statewide homestead exemption of $25,000 of assessed value has markedly reduced its productivity. Caps on property tax rates and other procedural requirements have further reduced its utility as a revenue source.

Unappealing as are all the fiscal constraints, the demands by the State that counties perform specified services is perhaps the most irksome. While it appears that county expenditures are determined by the elected county commissioners and thereby assure a degree of public accountability, visibility and accessibility, such is far from the reality. The individual county commissioner finds it difficult to explain that a major share of the county's expenditures are not determined by local county policy makers.

IV. COUNTY CHARTER ACTIVITY
AND LIMITATIONS.

While there is little in the record that suggests that the leaders of the State government have made a significant investment in the institutionalization of county government, it has to be conceded that the counties have taken only limited advantage of the grants of power available under the 1968 Constitution. Nineteen of 67 counties (within which about 80% of Florida's people live) have voted to approve charters, the major vehicle through which home rule is implemented. The four most populous counties in the state (Dade, Broward, Pinellas, and Hillsborough) all have charters.

---

12 *Florida Statutes,* Chapter 125.

The reasons why the other 48 counties have not achieved greater freedoms derive from a number of factors, some rooted in experience and circumstance and some in the continuing problem of relationships with the State. There are clear local inhibitions, the most important of which is the requirement that the charter be adopted by a majority of voters. Florida's experience roughly parallels that nationally, where five of six charter attempts have failed. As a result, the charters that have been adopted have generally been unexciting and unspectacular in their promise of change. With the exception of Dade, Duval, and Volusia counties, well established arrangements have generally remained in place. The ideological populism of Florida has made it particularly difficult to install new forms of leadership through the charter mechanism. Consequently, the charter and non-charter counties do not function all that differently.

Further, the State has done little to enhance the freedoms of charter counties in the key areas of revenue restrictions and mandates. All counties are treated very much the same. Overall, the relationships between the State and the counties are profoundly troubled by the State's failure to support the institutional development of the counties. It is an issue to which this study will return at numerous points.

V. HORIZONTAL RELATIONS WITH MUNICIPALITIES AND SPECIAL DISTRICTS: A RESULTING CRAZY QUILT

The other critical relationship of the counties is with the municipalities, which function as separate and independent units within the geographical boundaries of the county. The county, it must be remembered, was originally created to perform state-wide functions on a decentralized basis, most notably in the administration of justice. Thus every square foot of the state is included in one of the 67 counties. There is no citizen option in respect to the county.

The municipality, on the other hand, originated within a far more voluntaristic framework. Where the shire in England was the forerunner of the American county, the borough was the model for the municipality. Such boroughs were created in response to the shift from rural to urban patterns of life, in which the density of settlement required a much more active government to secure a necessary quality of life. The municipality, then, has a limited territorial mandate; only those who live in an urban circumstance feel the need for the increased services, regulation, and taxes that the city brings.

As we have noted, nearly half of Florida residents live outside cities and essentially rely on the counties to provide local services. Further, more than two-thirds of the populations of 39 of the 67 counties reside in unincorporated territory. Six of the counties are 90% or more unincorporated; 16 are 80–89% unincorporated; and 17 are 70–79% unincorporated. Pasco (2005 est. pop. 406,898) at 90% and Collier (2005 est. pop. 317,788) at 70% are the two largest counties with a high unincorporated population. In contrast, Broward's 31 municipalities cover over 97% of its population. Thus the general circumstance is that the county functions as an agent of State government for all its residents, including those who reside in its municipalities, and also performs as a city government for its many citizens who live outside the incorporated boundaries of a municipality and require urban services.

Even these figures understate the degree of responsibility counties have shouldered for local, largely urban, functions. Of the 411 municipalities in the state, over 150 have no more than 3,000 people and are not large enough to take on the full range of urban tasks economically. Indeed, only 108 cities (including Jacksonville) have populations over 100,000. Because the smaller municipalities cannot function as "full service" units, they typically have various types of service arrangements with the counties in which they are located.

As is to be expected, the county is often the largest urban government within its boundaries. That raises significant questions in respect to political leadership and representation. County commissioners, traditionally residents of the district they represent, must develop a county-wide perspective. It is difficult to relate these broad regional responsibilities to the day-to-day problems of an urban resident, such as those involving refuse collection, stray dogs, land use regulation, and police response times.

Although the unincorporated areas tend to be at the center of the relationships between the cities and their county, tensions between the two local governments have been traditional and long-standing. Originally, they mirrored the classic conflict between the urban and the rural components of the national society. As land was urbanized, it was assumed that the residents on it would either become part of an existing city through annexation or create a new one through incorporation. As the line between urban and rural has become increasingly fuzzy and the counties have provided urban services, the sharp demarcation between the city and county roles has eroded.

What has emerged is a circumstance in which a wide range of institutional options exist. Citizens can avoid higher taxes and increased regulations by choosing to remain unincorporated. Developers, on the other hand, can select from a number of possibilities in determining the governmental future of the large subdivisions which have characterized much of Florida's growth. Indeed, the creation of many of the state's very small municipalities can be explained in terms of pursuit of a special interest, such as zoning, tax arrangements, and separation from a larger, more economically and ethnically diverse governmental unit.

The result has been a crazy-quilt of governments with which counties must deal, within an atmosphere of tension and competition. Only the State has had the power to influence the shape of local government; and the counties have really been bystanders as bizarre configurations have appeared. The boundaries of individual municipal governments follow no particular pattern and leave the county responsible for servicing communities which may have become the hole of the doughnut. The polyglot character of these local institutions has made it very difficult to develop service arrangements that can achieve maximum efficiency.

The two vehicles by which cities emerge and grow in county territory, incorporation and annexation, are controlled entirely by the State, and many of the problems which confront Florida's counties today in rationalizing service arrangements may be traced back to the '50s and '60s, when 93 municipalities were created, substantially of the small, special interest variety. It is also worth noting that more than two-thirds of these governments (66) were established by special acts of the legislature, not under General Law provisions. Prior to a general tightening up in 1974, essentially any group of 25 registered voters could create a city—and they did. Because of the 1974 legislation, the rate of incorporation slowed dramatically in Florida.

With Florida's rapid urbanization (from about 65% in 1950 to nearly 85% in 1986), it was expected that established cities would grow in some degree. Indeed, in the '70s Florida ranked among the top four states in numbers of annexations. The capital city of Tallahassee has been successful in expanding its borders to encompass much of Leon County's urban growth. Uniquely, Tallahassee has remained the only municipality in the County which increasingly added to its population, an estimated 174,781 in 2005. That situation is unique, however, and it is clear that annexation has not kept pace with urban growth in Florida.

The problems of annexation are similar to those found in other parts of the nation. Relatively small groups of homeowners can often be assembled on a voluntary basis to permit annexation. In these cases, however, the consent of the homeowners must be unanimous. For developers, too, this approach facilitates the annexation of property to a city. The more difficult situation occurs in the heavily populated areas, where unanimity on anything is impossible. A majority of voters in both the affected area and in the municipality must approve annexation under this "voluntary" procedure. Because a full service city typically imposes more taxes and more regulations, it has proven difficult to gain the approval of unincorporated residents for annexation. Tallahassee's ownership of major utilities, which also serve unincorporated residents, has enabled it essentially to eliminate tax differentials as an issue in annexation campaigns. Still, there are many recalcitrants; and annexation proposals are framed to include supporters and omit dissidents. As a result, Tallahassee's boundaries are no more orderly and rational than those of other cities.

While counties must take a formal stance that residents of the affected area and of the municipality must decide on these institutional arrangements, it is obvious that they have a major stake in what happens. At the most immediate level, an annexation can result in drastic change in the shape and scale of the county's municipal services. Jobs can be put in peril; economies and efficiencies of operations can be affected; and obviously the expansion of one political institution will have its implications for the other.

As will be discussed in greater detail later, increasing conflict between the cities and the counties has occurred in the planning and zoning area. The issue involves decision-making on land use, where the cities charge that the counties are usurping traditional municipal powers.

Presence of Special Districts

Although it appears appropriate to concentrate on the relationships between the municipalities and the counties, it should not be assumed that all the elements in the local government system have been identified. Special districts form another, highly important set of institutions within the county environment. One of the largest of local governments in the state, the independent school districts, are, of course, a major part of the inter-governmental system. Theirs, however, is a specialized role. Except to indicate their existence and the pivotal role they play in localities, we will consider them outside the frame of interest of this book.

Bypassing the school districts, though, hardly exhausts the subject of special districts. The Florida State Department of Community Affairs has taken on the task of monitoring them through its Special District Information Program. The task is not a modest one because the Department's database shows 1505 districts in Florida. If they were divided equally among counties, which they are not, there would be over 20 in every one of the counties. Those with the largest number of special districts are Hillsborough with 129 and Lee with 93. A total of 1439 operate within a single county; and another 66 engage in activities that span more than one county. The South Florida Water Management District embraces 16 counties.

While special districts will be treated more extensively later in this book, it is important at this juncture to take account of their great numbers and the range of activities in which they engage. There are 58 categories into which the more than1500 special districts are divided in the Department of Community Affairs data base, with community development and redevelopment being by far the most frequent. Fire control, housing, and water management and control are other areas in which the special district is frequently found.

The 1505 special districts are formal organizations, constituted largely by the counties. Significantly, nearly two-thirds of them are "independent." That is, they exist separately from the county and govern themselves. The other third are "dependent," with a structure that is subordinate to the county government. What this means is that there are nearly 1,000 additional local governments with considerable freedom to operate in a particular function or activity.

As if all these districts were not enough, there is still another complication. The counties also create financing structures, often called taxing districts, to make charges for benefits provided a particular part of the population. They furnish important income to the county and often enable it to provide services that would not be possible through the general funding system. The Department of Community Affairs makes an effort to track these kinds of arrangements, but they are so numerous and varied as to make full monitoring difficult. They will be treated as part of our special districts consideration, but they should be more appropriately regarded as purely a financing tool.

With the emergence of municipal service taxation units to serve the unincorporated areas of the county, the need for single purpose, independent districts has been greatly reduced. Legally, the counties now have the power and some financial means to provide many of the services assumed by the independent special districts. Yet there is little likelihood the independent districts will disappear. They are a permanent part of the institutional landscape with which county and city officials must deal.

VI. SUMMARY

The purpose of this first, introductory chapter has been to set a general framework within which to appreciate the role, relationships, and problems of counties in the governance of Florida. Counties are the oldest local government entities in the state, the first two (Escambia and St. John's) having been created by Andrew Jackson in 1821. They are unique institutions for at least two reasons: (a) they cover the entire state, i.e. every resident lives within the boundaries of one county or another; and (b) they have been traditionally regarded as an important vehicle for decentralization by providing for the local management of state-wide policies and services.

Yet, as the inter-governmental system developed over time, these important assets have been weakened by an increasingly dominant and interventionist State government. Counties—indeed, all local government—came to be viewed as dependent agencies of a central government. Demographic changes in Florida have brought scale and diversity to the State, however, once again forcing an emphasis on decentralization.

For the counties, the emergence of Florida as a highly urbanized state has vastly increased tasks and responsibilities, as well as complicating relationships with other local governments. Settlement patterns and voter decisions have not followed the classic political theory that municipalities will provide urban services to the urban population. Approaches within the state both to annexation and to incorporation have complicated service delivery systems and required that counties function as cities, as well as in more traditional roles. The case of Palm Beach County, where the dominant city of West Palm Beach now possesses a population less than one-tenth that of the county, is illustrative of the changes that have occurred. The emergence of about 1000 independent special districts in the state, also created in large part to meet urban service requirements unattended by the state's municipalities and counties, have further complicated the inter-governmental maze within which the counties, as the dominant and encompassing unit, must seek to achieve some order. While the Constitution of 1968 and subsequent legislation in 1971 did recognize the importance of local governments and undertook to provide them some measure of independence, the counties continue to operate under severe constraints. They are of two kinds: (a) restrictions on the types, amounts, and conditions under which revenue can be secured to support needed services; and (b) demands that counties perform a variety of local functions paid out of local revenues rather than State or Federal monies.

There can be little doubt that the counties are destined to play a highly significant role in maintaining and hopefully enhancing the quality of life in Florida. Yet there are many apprehensions about their structural, managerial, and fiscal capacity to meet the challenges with which they are already confronted

In this context, it is highly important to secure an appreciation of the governments that operate within the urban context, which is the life style of 85% of Floridians. Counties are a significant part of this picture; and an appreciation of their role, problems, and possibilities should help to facilitate needed steps toward improved performance.

CHAPTER TWO

COUNTIES AND THEIR ROLES

Perhaps the most significant characteristic of the county is its geographic integrity and scale. The integrity occurs because the county is a subdivision of the State, assuming responsibilities within its boundaries for all the services and supports to which a citizen of the State is entitled. Thus, from the citizen perspective, there is essentially no ambiguity about the nature of the affiliation.

Counties are, typically, the largest units of local government in the nation. In Florida, for example, the 67 counties comprehend a population of nearly 18 million, third largest in the nation, and a land and water area of 58,560 square miles, twelfth greatest. Even Union County, the smallest in the state, covers nearly 250 square miles; three (Dade, Collier, and Palm Beach) have more than 2,000 square miles of land area; and the median size of Florida counties is about 600 square miles. The Florida situation is not unusual.

Urban services have been defined as those services which are furnished to meet the urban needs of densely populated areas rather than general needs of both urban and rural areas. Urban needs in densely populated areas may be divided into three types: physical, social, and economic. The term "urban needs" is not intended to imply that residents of rural areas do not experience the same requirements; rather, the problems are magnified in situations of high population density.

What accounts for the tremendous expansion of county responsibilities? Obviously, as the American society has become urbanized, nearly all governments have had to shoulder new burdens. But such an explanation accounts for only a part of the growth in county obligations. A further reason stems from the growing recognition that the jurisdictional scale and integrity of the counties are far better bases for economy, effectiveness, and equity in the delivery of certain kinds of services. Water, for example, is not particularly influenced by artificial, legalistic boundaries; and the larger the unit, the more likely it is to have the capacity to deal with problems of flood control.

A second explanation for the growth in county responsibilities lies in the confusion that has surrounded the delivery of municipal-type services, as discussed in Chapter One. In the past 25 years, the American population has shifted from a pattern of farm or city living to one in which a major share of the population now lives in semi-urban areas which are unincorporated or parts of extremely small incorporations. Thus, there are municipalities and there are municipalities. Some communities have been incorporated to deliver a full range of urban services; others have been created for a special purpose and have neither the capacity nor the will to meet the urban service needs of their constituents. It has been assumed that other agencies will meet such requirements, most often the county.

Third, the complications of annexation laws, particularly the difficulties of gaining agreement to pay more taxes and submit to more regulation, have forced the counties into delivering a range of municipal services. The counties became, in effect, governments of "last resort." They are the only governments available to meet such needs.

Finally, there has been growing awareness that the American polity has little stomach for radical change in its political institutions. Even though many urban problems now stretch well beyond the boundaries of the municipalities (and, indeed, of many counties), serious obstacles lie in the path of any proposal to create larger, multi-government units in the metropolitan areas. As the largest units of local government (in terms of territory and population) in the American political system, counties have been regarded by many reformers as providing the most feasible avenue to the creation of an area-wide approach to urban problems. In fact, the counties can be considered the key elements in a radical, but generally unrecognized, change in the structure of local government. The conventional wisdom of federalism, to which Americans remain committed, posits many tiers with varied organizational patterns. However, modern transportation and communication, the growth of nationwide economic organizations, the almost nomadic tendencies of Americans, and other factors have contributed to a breakdown in any real dividing lines. The traditional concept of each level of government serving a special purpose and operating independently of other levels has been extensively modified in recent times because of dramatic transformations in our society.

Institutional change in the county, and thus the ability to develop the capacity to meet a growing set of challenges, has been rendered difficult because of its origins. Though the county is a subunit of the State, there has always been an effort to soften this hierarchical "feel" by putting local people in charge of imposing state rules and laws. The counties have been adherents of the "long ballot," which is to say that they tend to elect a lot of people to office. Elections are good for lots of reasons, but they cannot function as tests of competence or of probity.

A recent case in Michigan demonstrates the problems counties in much of the country have in forsaking their traditional style of operation. A man, elected four times as treasurer of Alcona County, was accused of embezzling $186,500 from County investment monies. At the time of the report he was awaiting trial. Thievery, of course, is found in every kind of government, but the comments of the chairman of the County board suggest a deeper organizational problem. The *New York Times* reported on February 18, 2007:

"Mr. Boyat, the County chairman, said the commissioners did not consider it their job to look over the shoulder of a fellow elected official.

"'We're still catching some heat and being blamed,' he said. 'We tell people you elected him like you elected us.'

"The days of trusting one person in Alcona County appear to be over. From now on, two signatures—including the board chairman's—will be required to move County money around.

"'You can't operate on a handshake any more, and that's what it's always been here …'"[13]

Even in the counties of California and Florida, where new responsibilities have been assumed most dramatically and where the changes in doing business are the greatest, there remains a substantial commitment to traditional county thinking.

I. THE THREE ROLES OF THE COUNTIES

As may already be surmised, the major counties have assumed three highly distinct roles, an understanding of which is critical to an appreciation of their place in the firmament of Florida local governments. They are:

a. Traditional activities that are a function of their organizational charter as a sub-unit of the State government.

b. Municipal services provided to the unincorporated area, as well as to the small cities lacking capacity to engage in a full range of services.

c. Area-wide services that tend naturally to fall to the unit of government with the broadest jurisdiction and therefore with the capacity to deal with the largest share of the problem.

Traditional County Role

As subdivisions of the state, the counties are called upon to perform services that every citizen, irrespective of settlement pattern, is entitled to receive. Everyone, for example, should have the protection of the law and access to the

---

13 *New York Times*, February 18, 2007

courts, be he/she a farmer or an accountant in the city. In effect, such traditional services are geography-specific; they are performed without regard for community size or density of settlement. The controlling consideration is residence within the county boundaries, i.e. identification with a geographic location.

It follows that all 67 counties in Florida are engaged in these functions, as a matter of obligation to the State. Yet the diversity in the size, character, and composition of the counties inevitably bring differences in the ways in which such obligations are discharged. In some cases the responsibility is essentially a legal fiction; in others it involves tasks highly critical to the quality of life in a given county. Thus, even though it is appropriate to speak of generalized county responsibilities, their actualization varies tremendously, as between Miami-Dade in the Miami area and Jackson in the Panhandle.

In any case, both Miami-Dade and Jackson are charged with the following kinds of obligations: public health, welfare, judiciary, corrections and jails, secondary roads, vital statistics and other record keeping, elections, tax administration and revenue collection, and extension programs.

For a variety of reasons involving policy choices at the Federal and State levels, the counties have become important elements of a so-called "safety net," conceived as a basic support system for the less advantaged of the society. They have been charged with administering many of the societal entitlement programs that are particularly focused on the health and welfare areas. It is State policy in Florida, for example, that all its citizens are entitled to health care; but the unit of government charged with the realization of that goal is the county, not the State. However, the State has failed to provide the full resources necessary to achieve such a goal.

It is in the performance of these traditional county functions that some of the most serious problems of financing have arisen. As will be discussed in much greater detail later in the book, mandates by the State to perform certain types and levels of service without needed financial supports have placed the counties in a difficult situation. Consequential responses to these kinds of county imperatives are clearly not going to develop easily, partly because there is a tendency to lump all local governments together.

These county functions differ substantially in character and scope from those with which municipalities are charged. Yet the over-simplified view is frequently expressed that counties are simply over-grown cities. The differences between the two types of jurisdictions are perhaps most easily seen at the financial level. The premise in the city is that the scale and quality of its services should be determined by the willingness and capability of its citizens to pay for them. In contrast, a major percentage of the services provided by the counties arise from its traditional state responsibilities, and their quality and scale cannot be set by a community's willingness and capacity to pay for them.

Thus the imperative remains to confront the relationship of the State and the county in securing a collaboration that accepts the legitimacy of the State as a policy source and also recognizes the county as more than a municipal government. In effect, the county's performance as an effective agent of decentralization depends in a major degree on the way in which the State handles its role as centralizer. Again, in this respect, the relationship is much closer than that between the State and the municipalities.

Role in Providing Urban Services

The identification of the county's special niche in the constellation of governments in the United States has been further complicated by an increasing responsibility for the work traditionally reserved to municipalities.

This assumption of urban services has made it impossible to conceive of the county only in its classic terms. Several of America's counties can also be counted among its largest city governments. This is particularly true in the metropolitan areas, where the counties have greatly expanded their range of services to the point that almost every conceivable municipal-type activity is provided. At the same time, it should be pointed out that the expansion into a substantial number of municipal services has involved a limited number of counties. Obviously, the urban phenomenon has impacted some counties much more than others; and much of the distinction drawn between urban and rural counties is framed in terms of involvement in the delivery of municipal services.

All of Florida's major counties perform such functions in some degree. They therefore have a second responsibility as a quasi-municipal government.

There is no "clean" definition of a municipal service, nor consensus at what point the range of offerings is sufficient to qualify a government as municipal. When a government offers only one or a few services, as is the case with Boards of Education, it is more appropriately characterized as a special district. How many functions create a full service, general government is not a matter on which agreement has been achieved.

Over the years some accord has been reached on the kinds of services that are associated with urban, metropolitan communities (See Table 1). It is important to remember that clusters of people, assembled in considerable density, create the imperative for such governmental activities.

Even a brief review of Table 1 makes it apparent that the interdependence of modern American society has thoroughly confused any urban-rural distinctions. Indeed, the Table contains many functions, notably in the social/economic arena, that national and state governments have defined as obligations to all the people, without regard to settlement patterns. It is not surprising, then, that in Florida the sheriff's road patrol has been defined as both a municipal and a county function, depending on the distribution of the population. In other words, everyone is entitled to protection on the roads. The function is defined as municipal when it occurs in an urban setting, traditional county when found in the less densely settled areas.

TABLE 1
SERVICES TYPICALLY PERFORMED BY COUNTIES

Health Services
Mental Health Service
Communicable Disease Control
    and Support
Home Health
Maternal and Child Health
Sanitation Inspection
Developmental Disability Programs

Public Safety and Recreation
Police Patrol
Emergency Medical Services
Fire Protection
Parks
Museums
Convention Centers/Stadiums

Transportation
Road construction/maintenance
Airports
Safety Programs
Mass Transit
Bikeway

Utilities
Sewage Treatment
Solid Waste Collection/
    Disposal
Water
Power

Social/Economic Services
Indigent Legal Defense
Long-Term Indigent Financial
    Support
Emergency Financial Services
    Family Social Services
Day Care
Human Resources Planning

Hospitals
Job Training

Planning and Urban Facilities
Public Housing
Comprehensive Planning
Land Use
Subdivision Control
Zoning
Growth Management Procedures
Open Space Control

Natural Resource Control
Soil Conservation
Flood and Drainage
Emergency Conservation/Control
Air/Water/Noise Pollution Control

In this context of confusion, it is nevertheless important that counties be recognized for their role in Florida as major urban service governments. While the State has provided a substantial degree of freedom, particularly to the charter counties, to engage in the broad array of services listed above, difficulties have persisted in developing the financial bases that have been available to the cities. Recognition of the municipal service role is required in order to honor the traditional theory that urban dwellers should pay fully for the urban services they receive. There is obviously a need to reduce as much as possible the schizophrenia faced by urban counties in Florida, serving all the people in some circumstances and some of the people in others. The charges of "dual taxation" made by residents of the municipalities are in many respects symbolic of citizen failure to understand the organizational implications of the municipal role assumed by many counties. To the extent that the State has inhibited the capacity of the counties to operate as freely as municipalities in financing such services, there is likely just enough reality to the charge of dual taxation to insure its continued presence as a fact of political life.

Regional Role

The complicated world of the counties is confused further by a third and increasingly important role, namely to function as the protector, provider, and advocate for the regional community, of which it is a major part. This is undoubtedly the most ambiguous (and also ambitious) of the three prime roles in which counties are involved; and its emergence is another evidence of the way in which our rapidly changing society is working a transformation on governmental institutions. Though the new role is rapidly developing, its presence has generated little public awareness, largely because the changes are occurring within familiar and relatively unchanging structures and arrangements.

Residents of large urban communities do know, however, that the diligent and timely collection of rubbish is only the tip of the iceberg of the solid waste disposal problem. The U.S. "throw away" society generates a tremendous amount of material that must be disposed somewhere, somehow. Yet no one wants a dump site close to his/her home, both for reasons of aesthetics and economics and also for fear of pollution. Thus the disposal of solid waste becomes a regional problem; and its impact weighs directly on the individual citizen in terms of the direct costs for collection services. These kinds of issues, some of which constitute new responsibilities for governments and others of which are expansions of older ones, have prompted county involvement for a relatively simple reason, namely the county's status as the geographically largest local government.

The situation in Palm Beach County typifies the underlying process that has led the County to assume regional responsibility. There are 37 municipalities in the County. Further, the territory of the County covers 2,023 square miles, extending south to Boca Raton and north beyond Riviera Beach.

While the multiplicity of jurisdictions is one reason for the focus on the county as the appropriate regional unit, both size and special status provide other important advantages. In the case of Leon County, for example, there is a single dominant municipality, Tallahassee. Its territory, however, is only a fraction of the more than 500 square miles embraced by Leon. Further, the City of Tallahassee has relatively little legitimacy outside its own boundaries; Leon County, on the other hand, is a governmental presence over the entire 500 square miles.

The other regional activities in which counties in Florida may engage are: water quality control, air quality control, disaster management, emergency communications, emergency medical services, flood control, law enforcement, drug programs, transit, and growth management.

A review of the list above suggests an important distinction from the traditional county and municipal functions. In each of the latter cases, there are clearly defined geographic boundaries that set the terms of reference for service delivery. The county is responsible, for example, for the judicial system within its territory; and a municipality typically provides fire protection within very formal, geographic limits. But beginning and ending points are not so easy to determine in maintaining water quality. Toxic elements affecting water quality, for example, are very likely to have originated outside the affected area; and the practices in one community may very well produce toxicity in another. Clearly, there is a profound need to deal with the problem on a scale commensurate with its reality. Frequently, the counties themselves are of insufficient scale to satisfy this need; but, more than other local governments, their size does permit at least a partial response.

There is also the financial side to these considerations. As increasing numbers of people share responsibility for the problem and also potentially benefit from its resolution, the need to broaden the incidence of costs and benefits grows. Thus the county's capacity to impose regulations and levy taxes over a broader area is seen as appropriately and equitably distributing the burdens of such regional programs.

The assumption by Dade County of regional responsibilities in the greater Miami reform of the 50's was an early authentication of this role for counties. The Miami-Dade approach of one institution, the municipality, dealing with immediately local matters and another, the county, with regional issues became known as the "two tier" model. Yet, even in this early undertaking, the three roles were still envisioned. Dade continued to perform traditional county functions; it also provided municipal services in the unincorporated area; and it broke new ground in the performance of its role as the regional government for Miami. Among its major obligations is regional growth management. Subsequently, other charters have also included this area of responsibility.

Reasons for Growth in County Service Responsibilities

One way to summarize the three roles of the counties is to examine the reasons why they have come to occupy a more significant place in the local government system. There has been the growing recognition that certain services can be provided best by the larger jurisdiction. Increasing financial resource problems in the municipalities have prompted a move to the county's greater tax base and consequent ability to finance services. Hence, in a variety of areas, the cities have taken the initiative in seeking the transfer of functions to the counties, with attendant responsibility for their financing.

The increased service demands placed on the counties were accompanied by an optimism that their structures and processes could be modernized and improved, much as had happened earlier in the cities. The apparent assumption was that heightened responsibilities could hasten such reforms. In this sense the over-burdening of the counties was viewed as the means of torpedoing long-established, generally anachronistic, ways of doing business. As will be evident throughout this book, the strategy has not particularly worked. Much reform is still needed to enable counties to discharge their very large tasks with effectiveness and efficiency.

II. FLORIDA COUNTIES AND THEIR ROLE RELATIONSHIPS

Florida's counties are characterized by a remarkably uniform organization structure, as will be discussed in detail in the next chapter. This characteristic applies only to institutional arrangements, however, because the demographic and economic circumstances of the counties are remarkably different. These great variations profoundly affect decisions about what each county can and should do, most particularly the extent to which it engages in urban services and assumes regional responsibilities.

On the one hand, there is Miami-Dade County, whose charter was 50 years old in 2007. As previously noted, it has had a mandate to perform traditional county, urban service, and regional responsibilities. If the charter had not established this wide range of tasks half a century ago, they certainly would have emerged in the ensuing years. Miami-Dade has the largest population in the state, estimated at

2,422,075 in 2005; has responsibility for the third largest land area, 1,945 square miles; and raises and spends over $6 billions per year, according to 2004 data.

At the other extreme are the small, rural counties. Lafayette and Liberty counties have populations slightly over 7,000; and Union, with 15,046 people, covers the smallest land area, 240 square miles. That is only about 12% the size of Florida's largest county, Palm Beach.

Arrayed between these extremes are the state's 63 other counties. Because the counties do differ so much demographically and economically, it is important they not be seen as one institutional mass. In order to emphasize these distinctions, we have separated the 67 counties into four categories based on their predisposition to engage in the three roles we have previously identified: traditional county, urban services, and regional leader. The four types are:

a. *Maximum.* Counties whose community circumstances have already prompted them to engage in all three roles to a substantial degree.

b. *Significantly Expanding.* Counties whose demographics are predisposing them to move toward increasing responsibilities in urban services and regional leadership areas, as well as having heightened obligations in traditional areas.

c. *Expanding.* Counties whose pace of change and therefore assumption of more role responsibilities seem somewhat less than the situation in the *Significantly Expanding* counties.

d. *Continuing.* Counties, while growing and changing, that tend to be concentrated on their traditional county obligations.

In making this analysis and assigning counties to different categories, we have concluded that population and its pressures does the most to push counties toward increased responsibilities. Thus, all but one of the counties in the *Maximum* category has a population of more than 500,000.

On the other hand, the percentage of growth in the period 1990 to 2005 did not seem to correlate highly with engagement in the three roles. Many of the smaller, more traditional counties had high percentages of growth, over 70%, but remained relatively small and limited in their activity. Some of the largest, most active county governments, such as Miami-Dade, Hillsborough, Duval, and Pinellas, recorded slower rates of growth percentage-wise, in comparison to the state average.

Density data rather closely tracks population figures, further indicating that the larger settlements with the heaviest density had the greatest imperative to play a variety of county roles. By far the most densely populated is Pinellas County, with 3,291 people per square mile, which is about 3.5 times more people per square mile than the next densest, Broward County, with 1,345. Comparatively, there are eight counties whose density is less than 25 people per square mile, and they are all considered rural.

In general the *Maximum* counties held responsibility for major segments of state land, though there are exceptions. Pinellas, for example, is the second smallest county in the state, encompassing 280 square miles. Franklin County (population 10,845), in contrast, has a territorial mandate almost three time as large as Pinellas. This suggests that the size of the area plays only a modest part in determining the scale of activities in which a county may engage.

Nearly 50% of Floridians live in unincorporated areas. Inevitably, they will receive the bulk of their urban services from the counties, though special districts will also be important contributors. Urbanized counties, as opposed to those which are predominantly rural, will therefore perform many municipal-type services. Broward is a different case, in that less than 3% of the County is unincorporated, and there are 31 cities, of which 26 have sufficient population to provide full municipal services. That relieves Broward of significant burdens, but there are still five towns, one with a population of 34, which may make the county their urban service provider. Jacksonville-Dade, which is a consolidated city and county, is in quite the opposite circumstance. It provides urban services to essentially all the citizens in its jurisdiction. More typically, the *Maximum* counties find themselves offering urban services to at least 30% of their constituents. With nearly a third or more of their citizens regarding the county as their only local government, it is natural for regional leadership to follow.

The degree to which urban services are required will vary from county to county. Thus far the discussion has focused on governments with large urban populations, which, incidentally, is characteristic of Florida. In the rural counties, it is typical that more than 80% of the people reside in unincorporated areas, with a lessened need for urban services. Liberty county, for example, is 88% unincorporated and is in a far different situation from Pinellas. The former is rural and the latter urban.

It can also be argued that a single city in a county might change the dynamics of the roles played by that municipality and the county. Of the eight counties having a single city, only Tallahassee stands out as a real competitor to the dominance of the county. About two-thirds of Leon County residents are citizens of the city and receive the bulk of their services from that source. The city of Perry contains about a third of Taylor county's citizens and is the only other single municipality with a highly significant presence in a county. The other single cities are in small counties and also have relatively slim populations. One county, Wakulla, rapidly becoming a bedroom community for the city of Tallahassee, is 97% unincorporated, with only two very small municipalities. Single cities are much more common in small counties but seem to have little effect on role relationships.

With the caveat that our analysis is at best a modest approximation of the reality, we have classified the Florida counties (excluding Jacksonville-Duval)in the following manner.

Maximum. Eleven counties are identified (ranked in accord with 2005 population estimates): Miami-Dade, Broward, Hillsborough, Orange, Palm Beach, Pinellas, Duval, Lee, Polk, Brevard, Volusia.

Significantly Expanding. The 17 counties in this category are judged the ones most likely to move first to *Maximum* status. They all have populations of 150,000 or more and are ranked in terms of their population size: Seminole, Pasco, Sarasota, Collier, Manatee, Escambia, Leon, Lake, Alachua, St. Lucie, Osceola, Okaloosa, Clay, Bay, St. Johns, Charlotte, Hernando.

Expanding. The 21 counties in this category are moving somewhat more slowly in taking on new roles. Yet the situation is such in Florida that virtually all counties in Florida are feeling great pressure to do more. Populations in this category vary from a high of 141,000 in Martin County and 136,000 in Santa Rosa County to a low of 16,000 in Gulf County and 21,000 in Taylor County. All but Taylor had a higher percentage growth from 1990–2005 than did the state as a whole. The 21 counties in this category (ranked by population) are: Martin, Santa Rosa, Citrus, Indian River, Highlands, Flagler, Sumter, Nassau, Columbia, Walton, Monroe, Jackson, Gadsden, Hendry, Suwanee, Okeechobee, Levy, Hardee, Wakulla, Taylor, Gulf.

Continuing. The final group of 17 counties are most apt to maintain their traditional county functions and least likely to move into urban services and regional leadership roles. Many are rural counties. Eleven of the 17 have populations of less than 15,000 and none has more than 32,000 residents. Fifteen of the 17 are at least 70% unincorporated; and, with the exception of DeSoto County, have a density level of 50 persons per square mile or less. In this group there is a substantial correlation of low population, low density, and large unincorporated areas. The 17 counties (ranked according to population) are: De Soto, Bradford, Baker, Washington, Holmes, Madison, Gulf, Gilchrist, Union, Hamilton, Calhoun, Dixie, Jefferson, Franklin, Glades, Lafayette, Liberty.

III. THE CHALLENGES OF FLORIDA'S GROWTH

For most of the population of Florida, there is no stability. The ferment is immediate and close-in. Air, water, roads, and many other conditions affect the quality of life and are themselves affected by the numbers of people who cluster together and seek to use the same resource.

Between the years 1970 and 1980, the population of the state of Florida grew from 6.7 million to 9.7 million. By the time of the 2000 Census, the population stood at 15,982,824, making Florida the third largest state in the union. Census estimates in 2005 showed the population had increased another 11%, or by nearly two million people. Increasingly, the growth is in coastal areas. More than half the State's total population increase in 2000–2005 occurred in the 11 *Maximum* counties and Jacksonville-Duval, of which 11 are coastal.

The long-term implications of this growth are legion. The problems they pose and the actions they trigger are likely to occur at a dizzying pace. Historically, public value judgements have been made by local elected officials. The result has been a system which has not been "pretty" from a standpoint of either organizational nicety or consistency. There exist jurisdictional boundaries which are totally irregular and bizarre; pockets of poverty; and numerous elements of the infrastructure system (streets, utilities, etc.) which are either over or under-developed. The inevitable response to the chaos accompanying Florida's growth has been a call for better planning, in the assumption that greater anticipation can eliminate or at least reduce the number of mistakes and inadequacies of the past.

But planning alone is not likely to solve the profound problems faced by the State. Growth will occur in coastal areas, producing a significant limitation on available natural resources, particularly water. Land is finite. With large scale dredge and fill activity virtually terminated, all growth occurs on existing property, creating a zero-sum situation. There are only so many acres of land; and the competition for them becomes intense. Second, while the pressure for development is generated by "newcomers," the land is owned by current residents for the most part. Where it might be politically possible to place stringent controls on unknown persons, it is far less easy to do so on neighbors.

Several additional factors compound this growth problem. First, the public has been unwilling to pay the economic costs of rational and even incremental development. Second, the courts have historically supported the rights of the property owners versus the rights of those affected by the use of property. Third, in many ways the state's economy is driven more by national and international factors than by decisions of local government officials. Such forces make it very difficult to develop strategies that provide even a modest capacity to cope with existing and future problems.

Given the context of Florida's "open government" commitments that are embedded in the law, virtually all government decisions regarding land use are fully available to public scrutiny, debate, and contest. It is safe to assume, therefore, that there will be no more Reedy Creek [the site of Disneyworld] district developments. The success of that venture occurred in great part because the public was largely unaware of it. Property was purchased, planned, and construction accomplished by a single corporation, allowing virtually no public input. Since it functioned essentially as a city, the Disney property was exempt from all city and county regulations. Yet no single project has had a more dramatic effect on a community in the history of the state.

There is no doubt that the counties will play a major part in efforts to rationalize the growth process in Florida.

Further, the push to develop answers will put the counties on a collision course with the cities, who have had control over land use within their jurisdictions. As the municipalities have expanded and taken over land previously under county control, issues of rezoning have appeared. Will the county plan continue to prevail or will it be superseded by a new municipal dictate? These issues are emerging, and their resolution may profoundly affect the physical character of Florida in the future.

IV. SUMMARY

The purpose of this chapter has been to describe the tasks of the county and thereby to come to terms with its place in local government. In Florida it must be conceded that the counties are the dominant unit of local government; and the scope and dimension of their responsibilities are likely to increase in the years ahead. The basic explanation for the growing importance of the county is simple and straightforward: the territorial scale and coherence of the county provides a more effective foundation from which to launch public services whose impact is not limited by legal-formal boundaries. In essence, the bigger the unit of local government the better its chances of dealing with the complex problems of growth in Florida.

As is true in many other parts of the nation where recognition of the county's importance is on the ascendance, Florida's counties do not in fact fit into a single niche or role. Indeed, it is being increasingly recognized that counties are principal actors on three quite different stages: (a) as subdivisions of the state performing a widening array of traditional and non-traditional functions that have been identified as involving rights of all citizens, irrespective of the settlement pattern of which they are a part; (b) as quasi-municipal governments performing essentially all the direct urban services that incorporated cities, classically responsible for such undertakings, do: and (c) as area-wide organizations seeking to bring together all the community resources in geographic areas varying in size from 240 to 2,000 square miles on common problems of growth.

Overall, counties are engaged in activities that affect all their citizens. Increasingly, the major energies of counties are directed toward activities of an area-wide nature. While urban, municipal services are not a large part of the total work of the counties, they have major consequences for the quality of life in such highly urbanized, metropolitan counties in Florida as Dade, Orange, Hillsborough, and Pinellas. The Jacksonville-Duval consolidation, of course, creates a somewhat different institutional situation.

Although there has been increasing policy recognition of the interdependence among many governments and programs, little has yet been done to match their responsibilities with funds to support performance. As has already been emphasized and will be repeated elsewhere, the State government has been quick to recognize needs of citizens in the state and to place burdens on the counties. It has been far less swift in accepting the reality that decentralization is not a one-way street. The central agency has its obligation to support its local units in the performance of required tasks. The failure to build such a collaborative reciprocity has resulted in a great variety of economic and political dilemmas for Florida's county governments.

On balance it is likely that the prime role of the county will be that of leader and manager of efforts to deal with region-wide problems. In effect, the traditional responsibility for public health has already undergone the transition to regional responsibility. It is no longer terribly important that the county is a subdivision of the state. Public health in the counties is a major function because it is the most efficacious level at which to deal with a problem that skips over legal-formal boundaries easily.

In any consideration of the roles and purposes of the county, it is of course important to recognize that environment and circumstance do shape institutions. Florida's 67 counties differ dramatically because of these forces. In order to emphasize the extent of these differences, we separated the counties into four categories in relationship to the roles they either play or are likely to play in traditional county services, in the provision of urban services, and in regional leadership. We placed 11 counties (excluding Jacksonville-Duval) in the first, *Maximum,* category reflective of their already broad range of activities; 17 in the *Significantly Expanding* category, counties that are likely to play increasingly broad roles; 21 in the *Expanding* category, counties where we do not expect the growth in responsibility to be as rapid as in the second; and 17 in the *Continuing* category, composed of counties that are likely to concentrate on traditional services.

Regardless of the nature of the county, however, everyone will be affected by the dramatic growth of Florida, which has almost tripled in size in 35 years, from 1970 to 2005. If the state is to achieve success in managing such awesome growth, much will depend on the performance of the counties.

CHAPTER THREE

THE COUNTY GOVERNMENT AS A FLORIDA INSTITUTION

Counties in Florida pre-date the establishment of the State government. They go back more than 150 years to the time when Florida became a part of the United States. They are so central to the political culture of the State that their abolition would be unthinkable. Yet it has already been emphasized that their tasks and responsibilities over the last century and a half have both changed and increased dramatically. They are not the same governments they were even 50 years ago.

The fact that counties endure, regardless of the tasks they perform, endows them with a unique status as institutions. They constitute a special asset for their membership, in ways totally unavailable to the corner grocery, the cable television agent, and even the local manufacturing enterprise. The distinction between the status of the county as an institution and other organizations as utilitarian conveyers of goods and services is critical to the contemplation of their place and future in Florida. About 50 years ago, a sociologist, Philip Selznick, explained these differences in the following manner:

> ... "to institutionalize" is to infuse with value beyond the technical requirements of a task at hand. The prizing of social machinery beyond its technical role is largely a reflection of the unique way in which it fulfills personal or group needs. Whenever individuals become attached to an organization or a way of doing things as persons rather than as technicians, the result is prizing of the device for its own sake.[14]

---

14 Philip Selznick, *Leadership in Administration* (Evanston, Ill., and White Plains, N.Y.: Row, Peterson, 1957), pp. 17-19.

The test of infusion with value is expendability. If an organization is merely an instrument, it will be readily altered or cast aside when a more efficient tool becomes available. Most organizations are thus expendable. When value infusion takes place, however, there is a resistance to change. People feel a sense of personal loss when things are uprooted. The "identity" of the group or community seems somehow to be violated; and they bow to economic or technological consider-ations only reluctantly and with regret.

There are at least three elements of the quotation above that deserve further consideration:

a. *Prizing of an organization arises from the unique way in which it fulfills personal or group needs.*

The county is not just an economic unit, as are most business enterprises. It plays a major part in the social and political life of the community; and that is why it is very difficult to conceive of life without a county government. American Motors has gone out of business; but Jeep owners are little affected by the event. They can buy the parts and a replacement vehicle from the Chrysler Corporation.

b. *A test of institutionalization is the degree of ease with which the organization can be abolished.*

The more difficult it is to conceive of a Florida without counties, the more we may assume that they have achieved status as institutions.

c. *Institutions are harder to change than organizations precisely because they are valued for themselves, not necessarily for what they do.*

As will be discussed at many points in this book, one of the great prob-lems is achieving change in the ways that counties undertake their tasks. Despite monumental shifts in responsibilities, the underlying character of the counties has undergone relatively little transformation. Similarly, the political environment within which they must function also is much the same. It follows, then, that the reform of the counties is more challenging and more difficult than is the case in most other organizations.

There are, inevitably, varying degrees of institutionalization. While the coun-ties have a tradition of importance in public affairs, it must be assumed they have an obligation to serve their constituents. The valuing of an organization by its membership involves continuing relationships, in which tests are constantly being made of the degree to which personal and/or group needs are being met. Importantly, the relationship is between the organization and its members. There can be no intermediaries. Thus, the continued institutionalization of the counties depends heavily on their freedom to engage effectively in activities that are valued by their citizens. To the extent that inside or outside forces operate to inhibit a full response to public needs, the counties' future is jeopardized. In this sense an institution must have a high degree of autonomy; it must be free to do what is necessary to insure a continued valuing by its constituents.

In these terms, the institutional status of the counties has been consistently imperiled by an absence of autonomy, which requires the freedom both to mobilize resources and to allocate them. Certainly, the counties are jeopardized by the many fiscal constraints placed on them; but resources should not be perceived only in monetary terms. An organization able to deal with its environment and thus to be valued by its constituents must have a structure that is adaptable and able to cope with change. It is in the capacity to anticipate shifts in needs, to plan the appropriate responses, to secure needed resources, and to carry out such an agenda that the institutional purpose is served.

The structure therefore becomes critical to the building of organizations that are valued by their constituents.

I. ROW OFFICES IN THE COUNTIES

Very likely because of their history as subdivisions of state governments, counties generally possess a remarkably similar organizational structure across the country. While Florida counties have made some dramatic changes in the last half century that attracted nationwide recognition, the overall picture is much the same as elsewhere. Nearly all Florida counties are carbon copies of others in the United States. It is important to examine the county government system, then, in terms of its basic character, not the unique aspects that prevail in Florida. Several features of this broader system are significant:

a. High diffusion of power within the structure, essentially through the election of a number of administrative officers, in almost all cases. In the literature, the positions involved are known as "row officers," arising from their presence in a row on the ballot.

b. A system of formal representation through a small elected group, traditionally chosen at large, and functioning collectively on a part-time basis as a supervising body.

c. The absence of individualized political leadership. There is only now emerging a county office equivalent to president at the national level, governor in the states, and mayor in the cities.

Diffusion of Power through the Row Office System

There are many concepts of governmental accountability in a democracy, but certainly one of the most basic is that the relationship between the citizen and the government must be straightforward and simple. As one British political philosopher put it, the citizen should be able to function in a "shoe pinching" mode. If the shoe is too tight, there must be no confusion about who has responsibility for making things more comfortable. Thus there has been much preoccupation, and much reform effort, in terms of a "short ballot," such as exists at the national level. The citizen elects only a President, a Vice president, a Representative, and two Senators.

Even the short ballot of the national government does not handle all the accountability problems. The President and the Congress blame each other; and, if all else fails, the President places the guilt on the bureaucracy. Brief reflection on experiences in Presidential elections, however, leaves little doubt that most voters expect that their choice of a candidate will make a substantial difference in the handling of the nation's affairs. The President is assumed to be in charge. If he is not, that is his problem.

The arrangements in most counties, and certainly those in Florida, provide a sharp contrast to the national process for securing governmental accountability. Ballots are typically long and complicated. Thus, a vote involves not simply an expression of feeling that things are not going well but must pinpoint specifically who is responsible. Take the case of police protection, important to all but particularly crucial in the urban areas, and assume that an individual resident is highly dissatisfied with the time it takes a law enforcement officer to respond to an emergency call. Who is responsible for the inadequacy? Depending on where one lives, it might be the city police or county sheriff. A person has to be well aware of jurisdictional boundaries. If the elected sheriff is responsible, there is the question of resources available. The county commission basically provides the sheriff with the necessary money. Although a county commission may not, in fact, provide a sheriff enough money to reach acceptable levels of response time, it does not have to live with its decision. The sheriff does. Conversely, the money may be sufficient but is mismanaged by the sheriff. In such a case the commission can do little to secure greater accountability for the resources allocated to the elected official.

Such issues have been confronted at the state and municipal levels over a very long time, with the Short Ballot movement having begun over 100 years ago. With limited exceptions, the cities have moved to structures assuring much greater levels of accountability. In the large cities the mayors function like the President; and the Council-Manager form of government in the cities, also dating back to the early years of the 20th century, provided for a highly integrated system of responsibility under the authority of an elected city commission. While the reforms have not been as far-reaching in the states, a drive to integrate authority under the Governor has achieved considerable progress since its launching in the 1920s.

In addition to the candidates for the county commission, the long ballot in the Florida counties governed by the state's general laws require the voter to select a sheriff, a clerk of the court, a property appraiser, a tax collector, and supervisor of elections. These five positions are usually identified as the Constitutional offices. In addition, the ballot is likely to include the names of candidates for county superintendent of schools, judges, the state's attorney as the principal legal officer in the county, and the public defender. While these latter positions are not a formal part of the county hierarchy, most citizens do not draw fine organizational distinctions. In short, the average citizen is expected to evaluate a substantial group of people and come to some conclusions about the quality of their individual performance.

Considering only the five who are formal officers of the county, it is important to understand that the problems with the row officers only begin with the election. Though their jobs are essentially administrative, their accountability to the electorate and their legal status endow them with a high degree of formal independence. Further, the original concepts of decentralization, involving the administration of state laws by local people, have tended to emphasize the discretionary features of these positions. They have each developed a relatively unique political dimension, in which special constituencies tend to attach to each of the positions.

Row Office Ramifications

The Sheriff: Political Clout. The sheriff, as the chief law enforcement officer of the county, has many opportunities to affect the nature of community life. The sheriff's resulting agenda differs appreciably from that of a police chief in a municipality of equivalent size. The chief, appointed either by the manager or by the city commission, must meet the expectations of the appointing authority and does not have to stand for election. To be sure, performance must be of a sufficient level to secure community support and acceptance. Performance, then, is fundamental. The sheriff, on the other hand, must always recognize that an election is in the offing. Performance may also have high priority as good politics; but the maintenance of a powerful political support system must be regarded as critical to re-election. In a number of cases, elected sheriffs have performed with great distinction, very likely because of personal qualities and professional experience.

On the other hand, less adequate performers have retained office over long periods of time because they have taken full advantage of their political possibilities.

The Superintendent of Elections: Ideally Pure Administration. Particularly since the 2000 Presidential election, there has been an acute national awareness that a fairly lowly figure in a local government hierarchy can make a big difference in the way in which our democracy works. There were "hanging chads" and ballot design problems in several Florida counties that may have affected the 2000 election results. Then, in 2004, there was the matter of an under-vote of many thousands in Sarasota County, which was thought to have altered the vote outcome.

While getting voting procedures right would seem to be matters entirely of administration, the people in charge in all these cases were elected on a partisan ballot. The citizen could not even have assurance that neutrality ruled, much less that competence was present.

A case in Leon County, also involving the Supervisor of Elections, reveals how even the most routine of administrative responsibilities can assume a sharply political dimension.

For the first time in memory, a Republican was elected Supervisor of Elections in Leon County in the mid-80's. The victory, in large part, was achieved because the long-time Supervisor, a Democrat, was perceived as manipulating the system so as to have her son appointed her successor. The Republican campaigned on a platform of integrity and proven administrative capability. Yet his management of the primary election in 1986 was generally regarded as a disaster. The most frequently identified problems were purely administrative: lack of planning, too little training for elections staff, and inadequate testing and maintenance of voting machines.

Expert consultants were brought in to "advise" the Supervisor but essentially to run the general elections in 1986. Led by these technical people, performance returned to its old levels. After an investigation, Governor Bob Graham suspended the Supervisor in the waning days of his term of office. The County Commission, having had its own difficulties and concerns about the management of elections, appeared to support the Governor; but the Republicans blasted his action, defended their local officer, and vowed to turn things around in the Legislature. They did. The Supervisor was reinstated to his job by the Legislature, which concluded that poor performance is not a sufficient reason for removing a Constitutional officer. Such an attitude suggests the difficulties counties face in securing an organization structure sufficiently integrated and collaborative to meet the performance demands of Florida's highly urbanized society.

When Leon County adopted a charter in 2003, the only row office made non-partisan was the Supervisor of Elections. Such a status continues to be rare among Florida's 67 counties.

Clerk of the Court. The elected clerk of the court occupies another special niche in the system, as the incumbent also serves as *ex officio* clerk to the board of county commissioners. This latter role gives the clerk significant audit and fiscal responsibilities, which are specified rather loosely in statute. Generally, these obligations are viewed by the clerks as involving fiscal control, with an emphasis on what cannot be done, rather than as a dimension of the policy process. Since a balance is required between the processes of control and policy support, it is no surprise that a high degree of personal and structural tension has often been generated between the board of county commissioners, charged with providing direction to the overall government, and the independent clerk, with the task of assuring the fiscal integrity of the system.

To summarize, the row officers are independent actors in the county, each with a personal legitimacy, constituency, and sources of political support. The board of county commissioners, charged with directing the affairs of the entire government, is left with limited capacity to influence these Constitutional officers. It is an arrangement that goes against generally accepted organization theory because it provides insufficient support for integrating functions, i.e. bringing the entire enterprise together and causing it to work as a unit. The current arrangement is heavy on the differentiation side, in some cases reaching the point where there are really several organizations operating within a county government, rather than one. Obviously, a balance must be achieved between integration and differentiation; and the continuing question for Florida counties is how to move that balance toward integration.

II. THE BOARD OF COUNTY COMMISSIONERS AND THE SYSTEM OF REPRESENTATION

The counties, as elements in the oldest constitutional democracy in the world, must be subordinate to the will of their citizens. While the present system of row officers complicates the accountability process, there can be no doubt that the board of county commissioners is at the hierarchical center of the structure. It is assumed that individual commissioners will be responsive to the citizenry as a necessary condition for re-election, will work collegially to shape the directions of the county, and will have sufficient influence to see that the county performs its tasks.

With a few exceptions (notably Jacksonville-Duval with 16 and Miami-Dade with 9), the boards are composed of 5–7 people, elected for four year terms. Indeed, most of the 67 counties still operate with the classic five members. Typically, commissioners were elected at-large, but that was changed by a Constitutional amendment in 1984. They now represent districts. The job is considered part-time, though involvements in administration have made it far more demanding than is the case for councilors in most cities. Salaries, set by state law, are substantial, much better than the compensation in municipalities, but still modest in terms of the time commitments involved.

Before proceeding further with the specific problems of Florida counties, it is worth noting that a somewhat similar system of representation existed in municipalities during the first half of the twentieth century. It was called the Commission form of government and was similar to classic county arrangements in three respects: (a) a small governing body, usually three to five people; (b) no separation of powers, with commissioners functioning in both legislative and executive roles; and (c) elections were at large because executive responsibilities had to comprehend the whole of the government.

A principal and major difference from the traditional county system was that the commissioners were elected to perform certain functions, such as commissioner of public safety, commissioner of public works, and commissioner of finance. Thus, there was a high degree of differentiation in the Commission governments, with each of the commissioners functioning much like row officers do in the counties. While the legislative function was performed collectively, the problem of securing integrated administration of policies was little different from that encountered by county boards of commissioners.

The Commission form of municipal government received considerable notoriety and approval at the time of a major flood in Galveston early in the 20th century. The Commission of that city was regarded as having performed with high effectiveness, at a time when most local governments were under severe attack for their corruption and inefficiency. The Galveston experience, however, was not replicated elsewhere. The problems of integrating effort among numerous power centers appeared in many communities, and the response was to strengthen the executive hand of the mayor. Also, a new approach, the Council-Manager plan, with a commitment both to the separation of the legislative and executive functions and to organizational integration was recommended in the Model Charter published by the National Municipal [later Civic] League and today is utilized in thousands of municipalities. Most City Commission governments had been abandoned by World War II, and few exist today.

Certainly, there seem to be lessons in the municipal experience. One is that legislation should be distinguished from execution. The development of policies for a community should reflect the full range of affected interests; and a collegial body is very likely the best way of assuring that all points of view have been properly represented. Once policies have been made, however, all the horses need to be harnessed and moved in the same direction.

Interestingly, the issues specifically concerning the county boards tend to be associated with their legislative responsibilities: (a) the form of representation, i.e. whether it should be district [ward] organized or based on election at large; and (b) the size of the body. The minority community was particularly concerned about its extreme under-representation in the policy decisions of the counties and was therefore worried about the composition of the commissions. The argument over size has, in many ways, reflected the tension that exists between the discharge of legislative and executive responsibilities. The traditional view has been to keep the boards small, thereby easing the time required to make decisions and hopefully providing more coherence in the management process. But a small legislative group provides few people to process the many interests and demands that appear in a community of even modest size.

Form of Representation

With the U.S. Supreme Court decision in *Baker vs. Carr* in 1954, the stage was set for immense change in the legislative institutions of the nation. The idea that each individual had a right to expect that his/her vote would have equal strength played havoc with institutions that had been created in large degree to make sure that each vote was not equal. In effect, the one person-one vote doctrine required that electoral districts be of similar size in order that votes not be "wasted" on a candidate who represented a very large district and therefore had to poll many more votes than his colleague. Also, there was an intra-district dimension to the situation. If an electoral unit were quite large, a substantial minority interest could be overshadowed by the majority. Thus it was argued that persistent majority-minority divisions meant that the minority vote had no real weight.

The courts declared that there were three ways in which the form of representation could have discriminatory effects: (a) multi-member districts in which a minority's voting strength is submerged in a much larger group; (b) fracturing of the minority among districts; and (c) packing of minority voters into one or more districts in excess of the level needed to allow them to elect representatives, thus wasting votes.

The Florida Constitution of 1968 required that a commissioner live in the district he/she represented but that formal election depended on a vote of the entire county (Article VIII, Section 1 (e). Thus it was hoped that a commissioner would be the representative of a certain area but would also understand that the authority came from all the people of the county.

It was this at-large provision that ran afoul of emerging civil rights law. A landmark case was filed in Escambia County alleging that the "at-large" system for electing the five members of the Board of County Commissioners violated the civil rights of minority residents.

The Federal District Court agreed with the minorities' position in 1984, declaring that the at-large system in use discriminated against black voters and had been retained at least in part for discriminatory purposes. It ordered that the five commissioners be elected from single-member districts, and the Court of Appeals affirmed that decision.[15]

The courts were involved in several other counties, treating each case individually. The passage of a State Constitutional amendment in 1984, resulting from court-ordered changes for which there was no legal provision, deleted the at-large requirement for election and thus enabled non-charter counties to negotiate arrangements for representation on a district basis. Currently, there exist two possibilities for constructing the board of county commissioners in the non-charter jurisdictions: (a) the standard five-person arrangement set forth in the 1968 constitution and (b) the seven-person arrangement, where five are elected from individual districts and two at large.

The question can be raised whether the court cases and the constitutional amendment really changed things. There was an assumption by the court that Escambia County was electing its commissioners at-large. In fact, it was required under the 1968 Constitution to create districts (five or seven as it chose) and elect a member from each of them. The at large election that followed was more a matter of tradition than of law. Twenty years later all the non-charter counties were headed by five commissioners elected by district. In some a follow-up confirming election (sometimes referred to as a "referendum") is held. In others not. In practice the 48 non-charter counties appear to be operating in conformity with the 1968 Constitution mandate that, "One commissioner residing in each district shall be elected as required by law." (Article VIII, Section 6(e)

There has been a certain amount of interest in increasing the size of the boards, but that has occurred largely as counties have debated charter status. The proposal of the Escambia County charter commission in 2003, for example, was to increase the board to 11.

Today we can acquire some sense of the racial composition of boards across the state because web sites often post pictures of the commissioners. Our review of the

---

15 *Escambia County v. McMillan* 466 US48 (1984)

non-charter county Home pages with pictures revealed only a few racial minority members. There was evidence, on the other hand, of far greater gender equity.

Overall, the pressures to expand board membership tend to be weak, perhaps because of concerns for costs. There is little interest in the rural counties to increase further the overhead of their organizations. It is less easy to understand the absence of pressure for expanded governing boards in the larger counties. In effect, the boards continue to function much as they have in the past: a small group of citizens working on a part-time basis both to set the policies for the county and to see that they are implemented.

III. PROBLEMS WITH CURRENT ARRANGEMENTS

Since there is no such thing as a perfect organization structure, the present system may be regarded as desirable in certain situations. In others, the imperatives may differ greatly, calling for discrepant institutional arrangements. Certainly, the counties of Florida vary tremendously, and one must assume such differences should be reflected in their institutional structures. The fact that they are organized so similarly suggests not only that change and experimentation are difficult but also that there is a lack of appreciation for the importance of structure in engineering the most effective mechanisms for coping with rapidly escalating responsibilities.

Because the counties already have major obligations at the local level that will certainly increase, the capacity to deal flexibly and creatively with shifting problems becomes critical. Inevitably, such ferment requires that more risks be taken, as the search for new responses occurs. Yet there is much in the county structure and in its environment that is "steady state" in its orientation. The adherence to a virtually uniform organization structure is perhaps only a manifestation of deeper problems in responding to change. While it is true that the State has imposed many constraints on counties, charter status does provide the opportunity for many organizational options. Still, charters have been adopted in only 19 counties; and those adopting charters have shifted only modestly from traditional structures. It is apparent that there is much in the county that makes the engineering of change hard.

Certainly much of the difficulty rests with the kinds of problems addressed in this chapter. The row officers constitute a source of independent power which must be confronted. Further, they are strongest when their existence is threatened. The Constitutional offices in the counties have achieved high political presence over a long period of time; and it is difficult to remove them from politics.

The row offices create a condition of high differentiation within the county organization, in which the bias is toward uniqueness and separation from others. Up to a point, such differentiation is highly desirable; but it must be countered by forces of integration that enable the county to function as a total unit. It is on the integration side of the equation that difficulties tend to appear.

Even at the highest political level, there is essentially no voice of the county. At best, there are several county officials who speak for its interests. They include the county commissioners and the elected constitutional officers. The symbol of the mayor or the governor, as the stimulator of vision and commitment, is generally lacking.

At the same time that much of the required legitimacy needed to perform crucial integrating functions in the county has been lacking, steps have been taken to bring the system together in less obtrusive ways. These chosen strategies have tended to concentrate on process controls in such areas as budgeting, accounting, personnel, and purchasing. The position of administrative officer has been created in the counties to perform a number of mediating functions and to bring about greater integration of the total effort.

It is important to recognize that management controls become more onerous and compelling under diffused power conditions. When the budget is one of the few ways to gain influence over an elected sheriff, it is inevitable that its use will be greatly expanded. In contrast, the integrated structure, requiring that the different parts function as a collaborative whole, need rely less on indirect processes of integration and can deal more openly with difficulties of collaboration. It is becoming increasingly evident that the elaborated control processes which now characterize most of our large organizations have sometimes led to a stifling of creativity, flexibility, and innovative response. Indeed, some have argued that the worship of process controls has been so thoroughly ingrained in U.S. organizations as to seriously sap their managerial capacity, damaging our competitive position in international trade.

A structure with a bias toward differentiation and a resulting reliance on process controls is not one likely to appeal to people with high energy, motivation, and capacity. The outlets for expression are simply too limited. Creative responses to the major problems of the county can be stalled because of turf issues. Even modest initiatives cannot be mounted because of resistance from the budget staff; and recruiting and adequately paying the highly talented is often stymied by personnel procedures designed to keep agencies in line, rather than to reach out for the best people.

Such generalizations should not be construed as predicting the realities of behavior in a given situation. They are designed to indicate the panorama of possibilities that counties are likely to face in putting together the best people and the best teams to discharge their obligations as the predominant local governments in Florida.

V. SUMMARY

Counties are highly important institutions in Florida. They are more than instrumental organizations. They possess a special character and occupy an important niche in the political, social, and economic life of the state. They are valued for themselves, not just for what they do; and it would be hard to conceive of a Florida political system without counties. However, it is noteworthy that Connecticut did abolish its counties, which were involved only in the judicial system, in the early 1960s. While Connecticut's counties did not have the traditional significance of those in Florida, institutional status does require a continuing, beneficial transaction between the institution and its members. Put another way, counties do have to perform for their citizens. A failure to do so will result in a decline in the intrinsic worth that is attached to the county.

In order to maintain its institutional quality, the county must be relevant to its constituency. In the rapidly changing and urbanizing Florida context, that means responding effectively to an ever-widening range of citizen needs. Obviously, the county must be sufficiently free and flexible to deal with the elements of a turbulent environment. Importantly, it must develop an institutional structure that will foster creative response to emerging community needs.

County governments in Florida are largely characterized by the forces of differentiation operating within them. The elected Constitutional officers symbolize this differentiation. In many respects, they tend to make the parts greater than the whole.

Increasingly, it becomes important that the county function as a total unit. This is particularly evident in its increasing assumption of complex regional responsibilities that typically cut across traditional functions and require high collaboration among the many parts of the county system. The need for a greater integration of effort is manifested in problems of setting common goals and directions, in mobilizing community resources, and in achieving managerial cohesion.

Boards of commissioners are key leadership components in Florida's county governments. They have a wide range of legislative and executive powers; but their influence is limited by their own collegial form of leadership and also by the organizational differentiation of the counties which they head.

In Florida there has been a rather remarkable consensus on this type of leadership structure. All the 48 counties operating under the general law of the state, as well as most of the charter units, have the same structure: a very small governing body; with members having a special responsibility to a particular part of the county; an obligation not only to set policy for the system but to see that it is carried out, and to do all this on a part-time basis.

While at times there has been some restiveness with these arrangements, there appears to be little incentive to change. Even efforts through the courts to increase minority representation on the governing boards appears to have had little consequence. The arrangements for constituting the boards are essentially the same as when the new Florida Constitution was promulgated in 1968. Only a relatively limited movement to introduce the strong executive into the governance structure, currently limited to a very few large charter counties, suggests real change.

CHAPTER FOUR

THE NON-CHARTER COUNTIES: WHERE CHANGE AND TRADITION MIX

Although there were two specially granted charters to counties before 1968, the passage of the new state Constitution in that year provided the first real opportunity for the counties to deal more flexibly with their growing problems.

Up to that time the counties had been the inheritors of *Dillon's Rule,* a judicial decision concerning the powers of the municipality handed down in 1868. It declared that the municipality was a creature of the state and therefore had no inherent power. Its freedom was limited to the authority the state expressly granted. While the municipalities have struggled with *Dillon's Rule* since it became settled law at the end of the 19th century, the counties have always been in an even tighter vice. They clearly have been regarded as a subdivision of the state and have operated under the precept that the state decided what they could and could not do.

Florida's counties have been regarded as so much a part of the State that *Dillon's Rule* might be considered just an after-thought. The tight control meant that the State Legislature spent much of its time deciding how local issues were to be resolved. There was little time for major policy-making. In this respect the 1968 Constitution was a true ground-breaker in providing a home rule option, whereby Florida's counties could secure an institutional status with freedom to do anything not specifically prohibited or pre-empted by the State.[16] Further, the

---

16 "Counties operating under county charters shall have all powers of self-government not inconsistent with general law, or with special law approved by vote of the electors. The governing body of a county operating under a charter may enact county ordinances not inconsistent with general law. The charter shall provide which shall prevail in the event of a conflict between county and municipal ordinances." *Florida Constitution,* Article VIII, Section 6 (g).

placement of the home rule provision in the Constitution provided a regularized means by which a county could pursue greater flexibility. A special act and other arrangements were no longer necessary.

While the promulgators of the new Constitution certainly recognized that Florida was urbanizing and changing, thus needing a more responsive local government structure, it is interesting that only 17 counties adopted the more flexible charter arrangements in the nearly 40 years since the Constitution was approved.[17] In early 2007, the great bulk of Florida's counties, 48, were still dominated by the *Dillon's Rule* mentality. They have been content to follow the general laws of the State, with very few exceptions.

While only a minority of the State's counties enjoy charter status, most Floridians, about 75%, live under charter county governments. Their character and arrangements will be considered in a later chapter.

I. THE CHARACTERISTICS OF NON-CHARTER COUNTIES

In a state as big as Florida, the number of people in the non-chartered counties is still very large, nearly five millions. In this group there are five counties each with a population of more than 300,000 people. One, Pasco, ranks 12th in the state, and the other four, Collier, Manatee, Marion, and Escambia, are 15 through 18 in size. They also spend great amounts of money, with 2004 data showing Collier at $711 millions, Manatee at $525 millions, Pasco at $457 millions, and Escambia above $300 millions.

Table 2 provides an indication of the varied characteristics of the non-chartered counties, with Liberty and Lafayette the smallest in terms of population. Collier is second to Palm Beach County (and that only by a few square miles) in its territorial size. It is obvious that all the counties, even the smallest and most rural, are significant local governments.

Perhaps the most important statistic in Table 2 is the high percentage of unincorporated territory in the non-chartered counties, ranging from 40% to 97%. The average percentage of the population living in unincorporated areas for the 48 non-chartered counties is 76%, with only about a quarter of the population in cities. The circumstance is almost reversed in the charter counties, where about 60% of the population resides in cities.

Table 2 also indicates that the population densities in the non-chartered counties are substantially below those in the chartered. The population densities in the

---

17   Miami-Dade and Jacksonville-Duval adopted charters before 1968.

non-chartered jurisdictions range from 8.7 persons per square mile to 711, with an average density per square mile of 116. The average density in the chartered counties is almost four times as high, 808, and the range is from 3291 persons per square mile in Pinellas to 70 in Columbia.

Table 2
PROFILE OF THE 49 NON-CHARTER COUNTIES

Name	Population 2005 est.	Area in Square Miles	% Unincorporated 2005	Pop. Density (per sq. mile)	Expenditures (in $millions) 2004	Administration
Baker	23,953	585	78%	249.4	22.67	Administrator
Bay	161,721	764	40%	194.	132.15	Manager
Bradford	28,118	293	71%	89.	27.83	Manager
Calhoun	13,945	567	77%	23.	13.37	**
Citrus	132,635	584	92%	202.2	139.46	Administrator
Collier	317,788	2026	88%	124.1	711.12	Manager
DeSoto	32,606	637	78%	50.6	63.15	Administrator
Dixie	15,377	704	87%	19.6	20.08	**
Escambia	303,623	664	82%	444.7	337.84	Administrator
Flagler	78,617	485	74%	102.7	56.18	Administrator
Franklin	10,545	534	70%	20.3	21.60	**
Gadsden	47,713	516	64%	87.4	41.61	Manager
Gilchrist	16,221	349	81%	41.4	16.41	Coordinator
Glades	10,729	774	90%	13.7	17.99	Manager
Gulf	16,479	565	69%	24.	20.44	**
Hamilton	14,315	515	71%	25.9	20.79	Coordinator
Hardee	27,333	637	78%	42.3	44.06	Manager
Hendry	38,376	1153	71%	31.4	*	Administrator
Hernando	150,784	478	95%	273.6	210.06	Administrator
Highlands	93,456	1028	77%	86.	85.20	Administrator
Holmes	19,157	482	79%	38.5	12.88	Manager/clerk
Indian River	130,043	503	64%	224.5	214.38	Administrator

Name	Population 2005 est.	Area in Square Miles	% Unincorporated 2005	Pop. Density (per sq. mile)	Expenditures (in $millions) 2004	Administration
Jackson	49,691	916	65%	51.	46.23	Administrator
Jefferson	14,233	598	79%	21.6	13.61	**
Lafayette	7,971	543	87%	12.9	8.7	**
Lake	263,017	953	56%	220.9	208.74	Manager
Levy	37,985	1118	76%	30.8	49.89	**
Liberty	7,581	836	88%	8.4	11.20	**
Madison	19,696	692	79%	27.1	23.33	Coordinator
Manatee	304,364	741	74%	355.3	525.43	Administrator
Marion	304,926	1579	82%	164.	318.39	Administrator
Martin	141,059	556	86%	227.9	266.10	Administrator
Monroe	82,413	997	45%	79.8	255.85	Administrator
Nassau	65,759	652	75%	88.4	115.20	Administrator
Okaloosa	188,939	936	60%	182.2	197.61	Administrator
Okeechobee	37,765	774	86%	46.4	73.27	Administrator
Pasco	406,898	745	90%	462.8	459.43	Administrator
Putnam	73,764	722	78%	97.5	82.88	Administrator
St. Johns	157,278	609	87%	202.2	229.64	Administrator
St. Lucie	240,039	571	29%	336.8	280.09	Administrator
Santa Rosa	136,443	1016	90%	115.8	131.96	Administrator
Sumter	74,052	546	88%	97.7	100.25	Administrator
Suwanee	38,174	688	79%	50.6	40.16	Coordinator
Taylor	21,310	1042	67%	56.	31.58	**
Union	15,046	240	80%	56,	11.04	**
Wakulla	26,867	607	97%	37.7	37.50	**
Washington	23,097	580	74%	36.2	30.32	Administrator

* There was no report for Hendry County in the 2004 expenditure data compiled by the State of Florida.
** No information was available whether a chief administrative officer position existed in 11 counties, which are all small.

The overall profile of the non-chartered counties is of smaller populations, fewer cities with which to share governing obligations, large geographic areas of responsibility, and relatively fewer people to serve.

The absence of municipalities in the non-chartered counties is noteworthy. It means that the county becomes a far more significant local government. Whether the need is for traditional county services, urban services, or regional activities, the default government is the county for most people.

In Collier County, there are three cities, only two of which are large enough to be expected to perform urban services; and 88% of the citizenry lives outside the boundaries of all three. Collier has major urban service obligations. Its burdens are really no different than those of the chartered counties.

On the other hand, Levy County (2005 population about 37,000) boasts eight incorporated communities but none of them large enough to be considered a "full service" city. Further, about 75% of its area is unincorporated. Again, the County must be considered the dominant unit of local government. But there is a real question how much of its unincorporated area requires urban service. That is because it is rural. On its Home page Levy County describes itself:

> Levy County remains rural with vast, open wooded areas, springs and rivers, and more than 50 miles of coastline on the Gulf of Mexico. Its northern border is formed by the fabled Suwanee River. Commercial fishing in the Yankeetown-Inglis and Cedar Key areas is an industry grossing over $2.5 million yearly. Timber and other forest resources comprise approximately 500,000 acres, and forestry is an industry of more than $7 million a year in the county. There are over 40,000 head of beef cattle and calves, and three commercial dairies are located in the county. Agriculture is diversified, with the principal crops being corn, peanuts, grain and sorghum. Principal truck crops include watermelon, cucumbers, squash and peppers.

As might be anticipated, Levy County has a low population density, about 30 people per square mile, with the result that needs for urban services are low. Farmers generally take care of themselves. Thus, even though it possesses a major share of unincorporated area, the Levy County activity is likely concentrated in traditional areas, those managed by the Constitutional officers.

Without significant on-site study, it is difficult to state precisely how much the larger non-charter counties differ in their operations from the smaller ones. A cursory expenditure analysis, reported in Table 3, does not provide a great deal of help. The data, derived from expenditure reports made to the State by the counties in 2004, do not reveal marked differences. That is in part because all data are grouped in 10 categories, two of which are quite general themselves.

Table 3 has another limitation. Its data cover only six counties, selected because of their varying size. Three are among the largest, two the smallest, and one in the middle. As might be expected in this small sample, there are occasions where one jurisdiction may spend well beyond the norm.

It appears that the six counties devote about the same percentage of their monies to court-related expenses, to transportation, and to human services. The result in the case of human service seems somewhat surprising because the larger urban units might be assumed to spend more proportionately on health and welfare than the small, rural counties. It is interesting that the courts did not make a major draw on the money of any of the counties, with the largest outlay that of Citrus county at 4% of expenditures.

There are four areas in which the large non-charter counties appear to spend a greater share: general government, public safety, physical environment, and cultural/recreation activities. These outlays conform with expectations. A review of organization charts suggests that the larger counties have a considerably greater overhead structure, thus more money needs to be spent on general government. Crime and other law enforcement issues are far more prevalent in larger, urban areas. Planning and zoning have become highly significant components of the urban landscape and thus are likely to make greater claims on funds in the larger counties. The need for culture and recreation outlets become more important as communities increase in density.

TABLE 3
A COMPARISON OF EXPENDITURE PATTERNS IN PERCENTAGES
IN SIX NON-CHARTER COUNTIES OF VARIOUS SIZES*

	Pasco Population 406,898	Collier Population 317.788	Marion Population 304,926	Citrus Population 132,635	Lafayette Population 7,971	Liberty Population 7,581
General government	18.7%	18.3%	17%	26%	14.8%	13.6%
Public Safety	25%	26%	17%	26%	21%	19%
Physical Environment	15%	14.8%	8%	8%	6.4%	7%
Transportation	11.5%	14.5%	10%	10.9%	8.9%	20%
Economic Environment	1.8%	1%	.5%	.6%	5%	4%
Human Services	2.4%	1.7%	3.7%	4.3%	1%	3%
Cultural/Recreation	3.5%	5%	3.4%	2.6%	6.7%	1.3%
Debt Service	3.9%	4.5%	3.1%	7.5%	6%	4%
Other uses/inter-funds	13.9%	12.5%	23%	9.6%	28%	27%
Court-related expense	3%	1.4%	3%	4%	1.2%	2%

* The data in this table come from the Summarized County Data 2004 file maintained by the State of Florida Department of Financial Services.

The small counties placed a far greater percentage of their expenditures in the category, "Other uses," which provides little specificity. Over a quarter of the small county expenditures were located there, whereas the others, with the exception of Marion county, were far below that.

The unsurprising conclusion is that Florida's non-charter counties, large and small, are active on many fronts. The Home Page of Okaloosa county stated: "Counties are mandated by the State of Florida to provide county-wide service such as law enforcement, operation of county jail, appraisal of property, tax collection, election supervision, judicial services, construction and maintenance of the countywide road system, public health, job training, cooperative extension, veteran services, emergency management, mosquito and animal control, social and medical welfare services, and solid waste disposal." This is a list of functions which every county is obligated to perform. It is a good point of departure for considering management in the non-charter counties. Clearly, all counties in the state must see that these traditional responsibilities are met.

II. THE CHIEF ADMINISTRATIVE OFFICER PLAN IN 37 COUNTIES

For many years, the row officers performed a major share of the administrative tasks of the counties. That is still the case in the smaller counties. As Florida has grown, however, most counties have taken on new tasks and expanded many of the old ones, and they have been the direct responsibilities of the boards of commissioners. These plural boards have become the managers of significant government enterprises. Further, the Constitution requires they play this role in the non-chartered counties. It cannot be assigned to others.

This administrative burden has grown immensely, as is indicated in the statement of the Facilities Division in Collier county. The unit reports it has responsibility for 660 buildings containing three million square feet, performs daily janitor service on 845,000 square feet, and receives 75–150 work requests daily. It is apparent that this level of administrative activity needs extensive supervision that cannot be exercised by the board of commissioners.

The result has been that Florida counties, charter and non-charter, have delegated their responsibilities for supervising extensive public programs with large bureaucracies to public service professionals. As will be considered in greater detail later, the non-charter counties have had to work within the Constitutional constraint that the board of commissioners must ultimately be responsible. It is not legally possible to establish a system where there is a formal assignment of authority to a professional manager.

What has evolved in Florida over the last several decades is the Chief Administrative Officer Plan, which appears to be operating in at least 37 of the 48 non-charter counties. (We did not find a reference to such a position in the other 11 counties.) The CAO system has the advantage of providing for professional management without questioning the ultimate control of the commissioners. The powers of the CAO are thus contingent on the willingness of a board to delegate authority; but there is never a question where the final power rests.

While various efforts have been made around the nation to build county organizations with greater cohesion, the experience in Los Angeles County, California, provided a viable approach, the Chief Administrative Officer plan. Since Los Angeles County has been a major governmental unit for a very long time, its pursuit of organizational integration was lengthy and continuing. A Bureau of Efficiency, charged with studying systems and procedures, was established almost 100 years ago and provided the County with a cadre of highly competent analysts whose role and responsibility could easily be expanded. A second dimension was the reliance on the purchasing process to force a greater integration within the system. A particularly competent official, Wayne Allen, made purchasing a highly effective integrating vehicle, and the County board chose to expand his responsibilities and label him Chief Administrative Officer. The analysts in the Bureau of Efficiency became a part of his operation and made the budget another important source of power for him.

Managers in the Council-Manager plan and CAOs do, of course, share a common aspiration: to centralize the management activities of the organization. The manager is accorded power in his/her own right to engage in such integrating activity. In contrast, the classic CAO does not have such formal authority and functions as an agent of the elected board. As a result, many of the suspicions and concerns about the Council-Manager plan never arise. While the reality today is that many CAOs are more powerful in their communities than are many managers because of personal and situational factors, the fundamental distinction remains. CAOs do not have a legal "right to manage." They serve as agents of their boards

There have been many other cases in California where the CAO Plan has been adopted, both in counties and in cities. In many of these instances, there has been no formal restraint to setting up the chief executive as officially separate from the governing board. But, as in Florida, there have been many reservations about such a grant of authority. The fear has been that the appointed manager will become too powerful, free to pursue his or her own bureaucratic interests. The CAO has become a reasonable alternative. In many cases, CAOs have developed such close, trusting relationships with their governing boards that their real powers are greater than many managers with formal authority. Much depends, of course, on personal relationships.

Names for the executive position in Florida's non-charter counties provide some indication how these board-administration relationships are seen. Twenty-six counties employ the title county administrator, suggesting a general adherence to the idea of leadership and authority, but within terms established by the board of commissioners. The name administrator suggests a general commitment to the chief administrative officer idea.

Calling its particular approach "Commission-Administrator", and noting that it has been operating since 1980, Citrus County declares: "The Commissioners, serving as the board of directors, are responsible for establishing policies and procedures. The County Administrator serves as the chief executive and is responsible for implementing the policies set by the Board and for the day-to-day operations of the County Government. Departments and Divisions reporting to the County Administrator."

The Citrus county statement comes very close to one that would characterize a Council-Manager government. But the Florida Constitution's specification that the board is the "governing body" does not provide for a separation of these responsibilities. The Citrus Board may provide broad delegations to the County Administrator; but, in the last analysis, he/she is required to respond to any demand it may place on him/her.

There are four counties which label the executive position, county coordinator, suggesting that the administrative officer is more directly subordinate to the board. The implication is that lesser authority is delegated to the position, making it quite different from the Citrus County approach.

Then there are six counties which label their chief executive county manager. It appears that these counties want to do what they can, symbolically, to follow the Citrus philosophy. They likely want their chief executive to manage the enterprise. The name, however, cannot be considered to reflect a structure different from the CAO plan.

Collier County is by far the largest county to use the label, county manager. With annual expenditures over $700 millions in 2004, it is obviously one of the biggest governments in the state. The bureaucracy performing its numerous services is massive; and 37 operating units report to the County Manager through five divisions. There are also seven staff units under his direct supervision. One is the Office of Management and Budget. Thus the leader of this hierarchy has very major managerial responsibilities. On that ground alone, it may seem appropriate to label him County Manager. But the Constitution still requires that he be in a subordinate relationship to the five Commissioners on the governing board.

III. THE CONSTITUTIONAL OFFICERS AS ADMINISTRATORS

While professional administrators have assumed many important roles in the non-charter counties, the five elected administrators—the sheriff, the property assessor, the tax collector, the supervisor of elections, and the clerk of the court—continue to play significant roles. They are the elements that endow county governments with a significant degree of differentiation, as their elective status puts them generally beyond the reach of even the governing board, the commissioners.

In the smaller counties, the five Constitutional officers are almost the entire county government. They generally emphasize their unique circumstance within the structure, and they frequently have their own web sites. As the counties increase in size and activities expand, the emphasis on the Constitutional officers declines. On the organization charts of some of the larger non-charter governments, the

Constitutional officers do not even appear. In others they are plotted at the very top, adjacent to the board of commissioners, with the bulk of the chart given over to a detailed picture of the units reporting to the board through the administrator.

While the Constitutional officers occupy a less important place in the larger counties, they continue to be highly relevant. They are responsible for the performance of tasks that touch virtually every citizen in the county. There is the continued need to integrate these activities as fully as possible with others in the government.

Clerk of the Court

Among the row officers, the clerk of the court is one of the least visible. Yet it is perhaps the most important because it is involved in two different roles. One is the obvious one, that of managing the courts and thus insuring the judiciary is able to perform its work.

The second role, not nearly as well known, comes because of a provision in the Florida Constitution that the clerk shall function *ex officio* as clerk to the board of commissioners and will be the "auditor, recorder, and custodian of all county funds."[18] The result of this requirement is that the clerk has become a highly important figure in the internal management of the non-charter counties. Such influence derives from a simple fact. The clerk has a lot to say about how the money is spent and accounted for.

In effect, the clerk is the chief financial officer and is assigned the task of making sure expenditures are legal before they are made and also checking their legality after the transaction has occurred.

In two respects, however, the primacy of the clerk in county financial management has been receding. The post-audit role has diminished in all counties because of statutory requirements that each county must now secure an outside, independent audit on an annual basis. Some indication of perceived power attributes is provided in the prescribed arrangements for contracting the audit. The board and all the Constitutional officers except the supervisor of elections must agree on the person or firm to do the audit. By this test the supervisor of elections is clearly less powerful than his/her colleagues.

The emergence of administrative officers in the counties has also occasioned a declining presence of the clerks in county financial management. The reason is that money has increasingly been perceived as the arbiter of policy, rather than as simply something for which to be accountable. As the policy emphasis has emerged, the boards of county commissioners have tended to assign budget

---

18   Florida Constitution, Article VIII, Section 1 (d)

responsibility to administrative officers. Such assignments have generally encountered little resistance from the clerks, who have not been particularly interested in moving from their traditional accounting roles. The result has been, however, that there is no longer a monopoly on financial information. Indeed, some county boards, with the agreement of the clerk, have delegated the entire financial management responsibility to the administrative officer. The lessened role of the clerk in financial management has undoubtedly had implications for the power of the office, both politically and administratively.

At the same time that fiscal administration has become more complex, the clerk's role with the courts has expanded tremendously. With the abolition of municipal courts, the county judicial system has assumed enlarged responsibilities, inevitably increasing the burdens of the clerk as the chief administrative officer for each court.

Sheriff

Of the five Constitutional officers, the sheriff is generally recognized as the most significant and powerful. Such a status derives from the Constitutionally defined role as chief law enforcement officer for a large geographic area. In Florida, where there are no truly large cities and nearly half the population lives in unincorporated areas, the sheriff is in reality the police chief. And the fact that there is no reporting requirement to a higher elected official endows an already significant position with even greater power.

There is, of course, even more to the sheriff's role. The counties are important parts of the national corrections system; and the critical figure at the county level is the sheriff, who runs the jails. Finally, the sheriff plays a major part in the maintenance of discipline and security in the courts. In effect, the sheriff's obligations for the administration of justice lie at the heart of the traditional purposes of the county. It is no wonder that the office has had high visibility and has typically accorded its incumbents substantial amounts of autonomy and discretion.

Sheriffs are, understandably, the "most equal" of the Constitutional officers.

The independence of the sheriff is, however, slowly eroding. As professionalization develops in county management, an increasing number of well-trained people are being elected to office. Instead of resisting intrusion into their independent operations, there is an increased tendency to collaborate with county administrators and budget staffs in setting performance goals and necessary expenditures. There is an understanding that resources are limited; and the best strategy for capturing needed monies is through the widespread sharing of information on present performance levels and requirements for the future.

Also, the State has effectively removed itself as an element in protecting the independence and power of the sheriff. Traditionally, the sheriff had a court of appeal when the board of county commissioners failed to appropriate a requested level of funds. The sheriff could take the problem to the Governor and the Cabinet of the State government, surprising as that may sound. Equally astounding, the Governor and the Cabinet regularly sided with the sheriff, not the county board. When doing so, they awarded county money to the sheriff. Such a power arrangement came rather abruptly to an end in the early eighties, largely as a result of a collaboration between the Governor's budget office and the Florida Association of Counties. In 1981 there were 15 sheriffs who appealed funding decisions, and all lost. In 1982 the number dropped to five, and all lost. Since that time, the appeals have disappeared. It is now quite clear that the negotiation over funds ends with the board of commissioners. It should be pointed out, however, that statutes still provide for the budget appeal mechanism.

Property Appraiser

A third Constitutional officer, the property appraiser, also is more equal than others, in substantial degree because of a special relationship with the State government. Although the property tax is a source of revenue reserved to the local governments, the State has retained a continuing interest in its administration for two reasons: (a) A major portion of public school funding is derived from the property tax but is distributed by a legislative formula and (b) the Constitution requires that the Governor certify that the property appraisal rolls are meeting the 100% of value test. The appraisal of property, on the basis of which the tax rate is set and taxes levied, provides opportunities for manipulation, the substitution of private for public interests, and outright corruption through tax avoidance. If the property tax is to be a major source of revenue for local governments and thereby reduce the need for support from State revenues, it must be administered fairly and honestly. Indeed, the stakes for the State government are quite high.

Business organizations which operate in various parts of the state also have an interest in a system that is consistent and equitable. Through the process of property assessment, an organization's facilities in one county might incur a tax bill significantly higher (or lower) than in another. Such discrepancies can distort many economic decisions within the state and operate to an overall disadvantage.

As a result of these kinds of considerations, the budget of the property appraiser has effectively been taken out of the hands of the boards of county commissioners. Instead, the budget is developed in concert with the State Department of Revenue, which has broad responsibility for monitoring the administration of the property tax. When agreement has been reached between the appraiser and the

Department of Revenue, the budget goes to the board for funding. If the board fails to approve the request for funds, an appeal can be made to the Governor and the Cabinet, much as has occurred with the sheriff. In recent times, however, this has never happened. There is general acceptance that the involvement of the State Department of Revenue is a professional one that restrains any exuberance or excess. The boards have approved requests largely because they accept the process and also because they have little expectation that they will triumph in an appeal.

Tax Collector

The situation of the tax collector is much like that of the appraiser. Here, too, the budget proposal is developed in association with the Department of Revenue. Yet the power implications are not quite the same. Since all parties are agreed that taxes ought to be collected as fully, efficiently, and fairly as possible, the function of the tax collector excites little political interest. Indeed, the prime issue concerns the quality of performance.

As a result, the tax collector has a lesser imperative to call upon the State as a source of power. The need to maintain an effective administrative operation is typically sufficient to give the tax collector high independence and financial support from the board of county commissioners. The State is an interested supporter; and there is rarely a problem in the relationships among the three. The tax collector always has a valid argument that the better job he/she does in increasing revenues more than offsets the costs of collection. The arrangement tends to make the tax collector dominant in his/her sphere of activity but of modest influence in respect to the wider range of county policies and programs.

Supervisor of Elections

While the supervisor of elections is the least powerful of the Constitutional officers and has relatively little policy significance, we know from recent experience that the position is highly important in a democracy. The counties across the nation, as the governmental unit running our elections, have a particular obligation for making them accurate, honest, and credible. In 2000, 2004, and 2006, there have been serious failures; and Florida counties have been the sites of some of the greatest of them.

The inadequacies have all been administrative, including poor design of ballots, faulty processing equipment, unsatisfactory training, and generally slovenly procedures.

Supervisors of elections are monitored by the Florida Department of State, theoretically to provide integrity and consistency to state-wide elections. But the problems that arose in 2000 portrayed a Department more interested in securing a political result than in the integrity of the process.

Because the elections position is typically a partisan, elective one, change has been difficult to secure. A major step forward is found in the 2003 charter approved in Leon County. There the position was made non-partisan. Under Supervisor Ion Sancho the County had a substantial experience with an official who was committed to administering elections in a fair and honest way. Though a Democrat, he behaved as an administrative professional of high integrity. It was therefore easy for Leon County voters to accept the change to non-partisan status. Such a move, of course, would not have been possible in a non-charter county, where the Constitution rules. It was only when Leon adopted a charter that the reform could be achieved.

IV. MANAGEMENT TASKS IN THE NON-CHARTER COUNTIES

The growth of the non-charter counties has meant that increasing numbers of tasks have fallen to the administrative hierarchy over which their board of county commissioners presides.

Yet there remain substantial differences in the functions performed by the municipalities, the other major local government, and by the counties. The cities, whose roots are in the idea of a government established to meet the needs of an urban community, continue to have a preoccupation with police, fire, public works, planning and zoning, recreation and parks, and public utilities, all of which are typically found in municipal territory.

The counties began from a different base, as has already been emphasized. Starting with the Constitutional officers' responsibilities in law enforcement, the courts, jails, property assessment, tax collection, and elections, their duties have expanded to other areas where there is a need to provide a service throughout the county. The Okaloosa county statement, cited earlier, reveals further required tasks that include: construction and maintenance of the countywide road system, public health, cooperative extension, veterans services, emergency management, mosquito and animal control, social and medical welfare services, and solid waste disposal.

The reality that the non-charter counties are the only local government in a huge part of their jurisdictions demands that they also do much of what municipalities would do were they present. Thus counties fill a second role, purveyor of urban services. The sheriff, for example, becomes the local police department in the unincorporated area; and various government elements of the county perform fire/rescue services, building regulation and control, planning and zoning, public works that include urban streets, emergency medical services, recreation and parks, and various types of utilities including water, sewers, wastewater, and recycling.

The non-charter counties typically provide library services throughout their jurisdictions, though they are often regarded as an urban function. Typically in Florida, the library seems to have no urban-rural limits.

The third role for the counties, regional services and leadership, tends to be more ambiguous. That is because counties seldom venture beyond their own boundaries, but some of their activities have little regard for those limits. Thus, when an undertaking has involvements beyond the county, it is reasonable to consider it regional. A number of counties, for example, have airports. They are considered regional because their traffic is at least inter-county and more likely inter-state. Solid waste has become a county responsibility largely because the failure to provide for proper disposal within a county can have consequences far beyond its territorial limits. It has become clear that the problem has to be attacked at the highest possible level.

Growth management and environmental regulation have become major responsibilities for roughly the same reasons. As populations have increased and densities have grown, settlement patterns have become more significant. How the land is used has great environmental implications which, in turn, affect water supply and distribution, drainage patterns and flooding, air quality, traffic and transportation, and the general enjoyment of life. Obviously, the environment is affected by similar events; and so the counties list the environment as an area of increasing attention.

V. SUMMARY

The counties, more than the municipalities, have been regarded as creatures of state governments and therefore subject to controls from the higher level. There has been no doubt that *Dillon's Rule,* though originally directed to the municipalities, also applied to them.

That is why the Florida Constitution of 1968 must be considered such an important landmark in the history of county government in this state. For the first time counties were provided a means by which they could escape the heavy shackles of the State powers in Tallahassee. They could embrace a home rule option whereby they might secure an institutional status with freedom to do all that was not prohibited or pre-empted by the state.

The Constitution makers were already witnessing tremendous growth in Florida, and it seemed clear that the counties were facing increasing burdens of governance. The idea, then, was to give them a means to respond in their own way to the new challenges they faced. Such freedom seemed imperative because the counties functioned under strict controls, and any relief from these strictures required a special exemption from a Legislature already over-burdened with pica-yune local matters.

Further, two of the counties had already taken matters into their own hands and engineered legislative approval of new and radically different forms of government for their communities. One was Dade County, which made major changes in 1957; and the other was Duval, which merged with Jacksonville City in 1968.

Thus the stage was set in 1968 for significant transformations in the other 65 counties in Florida. But that has not happened. Forty-eight of the 67 counties still operated under the strict rules set forth in the 1968 Constitution in 2007; and only 17 had taken advantage of the Constitution's home rule provisions over a period of 38 years. Of these 17, most made very limited changes in the governing format set forth in the Constitution. Except for a very few innovations in the leadership structure, Florida's county governments operate very much as they have over the decades.

The 48 non-charter counties therefore provide a benchmark. They constitute the "pure" forms of county government in Florida, with the charter governments providing modest variations. Still, the non-charter counties provide the best and most representative means of ascertaining how this level of government is generally structured and operated in Florida.

Although the overwhelming numbers of Floridians live in the chartered counties, nearly five million people reside outside these large units. The non-charter counties vary greatly in their populations, the amount of their expenditures, the areas they cover, and the density of their settlements. The largest of these 48 counties is Pasco, which has a population over 400,000 and spent nearly $500 millions in 2004. Table 2 in the chapter provided a detailed profile on each of the non-charter counties.

A particularly important feature of these counties is the high percentage of unincorporated area they possess. Over three-quarters of the people in these counties lived outside cities. Further, even the cities in which about a quarter of them lived were quite small. Relatively few were large enough to be considered "full service" municipalities, with the result that the counties had even larger service obligations. To a marked extent the counties were the only real government in many of these communities.

The overall profile of the non-chartered counties is of smaller populations, fewer cities with which to share governing obligations, large geographic areas of responsibility, and relatively few people to serve for the areas they cover.

A continuing issue for all counties is to develop a leadership system capable of developing policies that reflect the interests and needs of the entire community and also one that will insure the execution of such policies. In counties governed by the State Constitution, both these leadership tasks are lodged in a plural executive, the board of county commissioners.

Issues of policy leadership have primarily focused on the composition of the board. There has been little demand that the size of these boards, which are currently five in all the non-charter counties, be increased. It is possible to raise the number to seven, but none of the present 48 non-charter counties have taken this step. What has been more of an issue is the character of representation. The courts settled that matter in the late 80's, declaring for a district arrangement. An at-large election was considered to be incompatible with one-man, one-vote standards. A few counties hold at-large referenda to give county-wide approval to district candidates. In effect, however, the boards of commissioners are composed of a representative from each of five districts.

In the execution of policies there has been more movement. However, elected Constitutional officers continue to play important administrative roles. Outside these traditional areas, there has been a significant trend toward integrating other administrative functions and bringing them under the control of a chief administrative officer, who reports to the board of commissioners.

We found such a role, variously named, in at least 37 of the 48 non-charter counties. In 11 we did not discover such a designated position, at least in the materials we reviewed. There is a substantial consensus in the 37 on what this top administrative person should be called. In 26 counties the label is county administrator. It is county manager in six, and county coordinator in four. The differences in title may reflect small differences in delegation intentions, but they all operate in roughly the same way.

That is because the Constitution places legislative and executive responsibilities in the boards of commissioners. Powers may be delegated to administrative officers by the boards; but the final responsibility cannot be passed on. As a result, we have labeled this approach the Chief Administrative Officer Plan, first established in Los Angeles County in the 1940s. The key idea is that the county administrator is the agent of the board and acts with its authority. Depending on the relationship between the board and the administrator, this arrangement can result in significant delegation and give the administrator the power to bring a high degree of integration to the bureaucracy over which he/she presides.

It is important to remain aware that the elected Constitutional officers continue to control highly significant parts of the administrative apparatus, largely outside the purview of the chief administrative officer. While the sheriff is the most visible as the chief law enforcement officer, the clerk of the court plays a highly consequential role internally. The Constitution makes the clerk *ex officio* "auditor, recorder, and custodian of all county funds." In effect, the clerk is the finance officer in the non-charter counties; and that takes a powerful administrative tool away from the chief administrative officer.

A review of the activities in which the non-charter counties engage reveals that the larger ones are performing in a wide variety of areas that span the three roles we have previously identified: (a) traditional county functions, (b) urban services; and (c) regional regulatory and leadership activities.

CHAPTER FIVE

REVOLUTIONARY REFORM: MIAMI-DADE

As America has urbanized over the last century, there have been increasing questions how to organize the large population centers that have emerged.

The first major effort to reconfigure the cities that were beginning to dominate American life occurred in New York in 1897 when the counties around Manhattan took the dramatic step of merging into the City of New York, with each of the counties becoming a borough of the largest municipality in the United States. In effect this was a mammoth consolidation in which a single city materialized as the dominant institution in America's largest metropolis.

But New York's was the one and only case where the growing confusion of governments in our metropolitan communities was resolved through consolidation for a very long time, indeed until 1968, when Duval county and the city of Jacksonville merged.

Not many years after New York, in the early part of the 20th century, a different reform strategy was undertaken in several metropolitan communities. It was labeled city-county separation and essentially divided the core municipality, which then held most of the urban population, from its rural county roots. The key idea was to reduce all overlapping, with each of the jurisdictions providing the entire range of services and controls required by their citizens. Baltimore, Denver, Boston, New Orleans, St. Louis, and San Francisco were metropolitan communities where such a reform package was adopted. In terms of bringing governmental integration to these areas, the approach was short-sighted and counter-productive. In a relatively few years, as populations increased and dispersed, the central cities became only a small piece of the whole. San Francisco, for example, rests on only 39 square miles of the huge amount of territory that is the San Francisco bay area. In effect these reforms did not bring more integration and greater accountability; instead, they produced more fragmentation and lessened accountability.

The experience was disheartening. At the half way mark in the 20th century, America's metropolitan communities were in a rut of overlapping, irresponsible governments, with a few fairly major annexations by cities providing the only band-aids. Indeed, the struggle to bring about a greater integration of urban services in the metropolitan areas never ends, and it will be a constant theme in these pages.

As Florida's urbanization increased its pace in the 1950's, metropolitan communities like Miami and Jacksonville began to experience the stresses that had been long present in many other parts of the country. But there was a difference. Two major reforms did occur in Florida. The first was the introduction of a two-tier government in Miami-Dade in 1957; and the second great change was the Jacksonville-Duval County consolidation in 1968. The two major reforms have given Florida a special place in the literature on metropolitan government in North America. A 1977 book by Horan and Taylor, for example, treats five cases of major structural change in the nation, two of which (Miami and Jacksonville) were in Florida.[19]

This chapter will be concerned with the first of these two undertakings with significant implications for county government in Florida, the Miami-Dade reform.

The Miami area experienced a high degree of urbanization early. The drainage of wet lands and generous Federal lending fueled a housing boom, particularly in the unincorporated areas of Dade County. The City of Miami had been incorporated in1896, Homestead in 1913, Miami Beach in 1915, and Coral Gables in 1925. But the land was cheaper outside the cities and the population in unincorporated areas zoomed from about 110,000 in 1950 to over 350,000 in 1960. By 1954 there were 26 cities in Dade County, and the State Legislature said it would approve no more. Many communities were incorporated to serve diverse and special needs, resulting in increased fragmentation and consequent difficulty in meeting area-wide needs. By 2007, when the most recent reform occurred, the population had swelled to 2,422,075 (2005 estimate) in Miami-Dade county, making it the eighth most populous jurisdiction in the nation. The unincorporated area accounted for nearly half of that, 1,134, 686. The number of municipalities was 35.

In the mid-fifties, Dade County had a conglomeration of officials elected under a commission form of government. There were 39 different public officers on whom citizens voted, including five commissioners, 10 heads of independent departments, and an assortment of judges. Uniquely, the Governor appointed a

---

19   James F.Horan and G.Thomas Taylor, Jr., *Experiments in Metropolitan Government* (New York: Praeger Publishers, 1977), p. vi

commission which set the budget for the County. Elections turned on individual personalities and past political experience. As early as 1945 a proposal to consolidate the cities and the County was brought before the Florida Legislature and defeated; other attempts were made in 1948 and 1953.[20]

I. CRITICISM AND PROPOSALS FOR BIG CHANGE

In 1954 the Public Administration Service (PAS), a nationally prominent public interest consulting organization, produced a study with sharp criticisms of current arrangements and proposals for major reform. The Service had significant credibility because it was part of a large public administration center in Chicago that housed the Public Administration Clearing House, the International City Managers Association, the American Society for Public Administration, the Municipal Finance Officers Association, and others. Its organizations produced most of the publications in the field. They were regarded as the best informed of anyone in the United States.

PAS was biting in its criticism of the situation. Services were pronounced totally inadequate in such areas as county-wide planning, law enforcement, fire protection (outside the city of Miami), traffic engineering, sewerage, and library services.[21]

Further, it declared that the multiplicity of governments produced varying forms of inequity: divergent and uneven levels of service, extremely varied tax assessments, and the payment by city residents for services in the unincorporated areas. Finally, there were serious administrative problems in a County where the commissioners had no direct control over their own budgets and were dependent on a host of separately elected department heads.

Toronto Two-Tier Model Proposed

In 1953, shortly before PAS was preparing the report on Miami, major reform was under way in the Canadian metropolitan area of Toronto, culminating in the establishment of a two-tier government on January 1, 1954. There a metropolitan government, Metro Toronto, was created by the province to perform region-wide services. Retained as a lower tier was the city of Toronto, four towns, and eight

---

20 David Bendel Hertz, *Governing Dade County: A Study of Alternative Structures* (Coral Gables: University of Miami, 1984), p. 10

21 Public Administration Service, *The Government of Metropolitan Miami* (Chicago: Public Administration Service, 1954), p. 194.

villages as purveyors of local services. It was an entirely new level of government, with a regional mandate. At the time the Canadian solution seemed very clean, highly rational, and received a great deal of attention throughout the world. The fact that the solution was imposed by the provincial government and allowed no vote by the citizens affected was reported but not emphasized.[22]

The PAS report sought to transfer the Toronto plan to Dade County, failing to appreciate the differences that existed. Perhaps not surprisingly, Miami-Dade still stands as the only U.S. metropolitan area where the two-tier model has been formally established. There are various types of metropolitan authorities throughout the nation but none was conceived as the comprehensive reform measure found in Miami-Dade.

In point of fact, the proposal was not as daring as much of the publicity suggested at the time. It was formulated to fit a political circumstance in which the municipalities had already shown their prowess in defeating consolidation; and, while the State was a major actor, there was little likelihood of a reform imposed from Tallahassee. Thus the Miami-Dade two-tier version retained the traditional county unit and a patchwork group of municipalities, with the unincorporated area having only the County to provide local urban services.

Incorporating the Los Angeles County Experience

This reality apparently caused PAS to look elsewhere for a model that would address these problems. It turned to Los Angeles County, even larger than Dade, with big unincorporated areas, and with an aggressive, activist county government. The immediate inspiration was the Lakewood Plan, which appeared in 1954 as the Miami-Dade reforms were being formulated. A large unincorporated area with a population of about 70,000 had determined to incorporate and to keep its costs low by buying its services from the County. At the end of its first year it had a total of 10 municipal employees. It appeared that Los Angeles had found a way to reduce duplication and enable communities to incorporate on the cheap. While it is not likely that Lakewood did more than produce a germ of an idea for Miami-Dade, it may certainly have stimulated the PAS proposal that Miami-Dade become a major purveyor of municipal/urban services to the unincorporated area. Where the Lakewood Plan led to an explosion of contract cities in Los Angeles, that has not occurred in Miami-Dade. There are only nine more than in 1954.

The result is that Miami-Dade remains the local government for more than a million people, with all the issues that suggests. As Hertz, writing in 1984,

---

22   Hertz, *op. cit.*, p. 10

observed, "What looked entirely workable in 1957, today has led to major overlap of services, jurisdictional conflicts, and citizen bewilderment over who is responsible and accountable for which services."

The record suggests that Professor Hertz may have been optimistic in writing that there was a favorable outlook in 1957. In fact, substantial controversy emerged over the proposal; and the path to adoption was not an easy one. First, the people of Dade County had to be granted the freedom to decide how they wanted to be governed. Such autonomy was not in the Florida tradition. The first required step was legislation that would place a Dade County home rule provision on the ballot. The statute provided the general framework for a charter, permitted the abolition of certain elective offices, and specified that the school system could not be changed. It secured grudging approval, according to Lotz, who commented further:

> [It was a] dramatic departure from the tradition of state government in Florida. At the time roughly half the states had some form of constitutional or statutory home rule provision and 3,000 cities operated under home rule powers. So it was not a new concept; it was just new to Florida.[23]

II. A NEW GOVERNMENT IN 1957

The Constitutional amendment providing home rule to Dade County was approved statewide in November, 1956, 322,839 to 138,430. The following year, on May 21, 1957, a new charter was barely adopted by a small turnout of local voters, 44,404 to 42,620. Lotz described the vote of Dade County in the following terms:

> Essentially the Dade County government had been transformed from a limited purpose county government into one capable of performing more municipal type services and enacting regulations on a county-wide basis. In short, Dade County now served as the upper tier (or level) of government.[24]

The cities were the lower tier within a charter framework that did result in some diminution of their powers. They managed to survive but they had lost ground. The charter declares, "Planning Director shall study municipal boundaries with

---

23 Aileen Lotz, *Metropolitan Dade County: Two Tier Government in Action* (Boston: Allyn and Bacon, 1984), p. 46.

24 *Loc. cit.,* p. 53

a view to recommending their orderly adjustment, improvement and establishment." A Planning Advisory Board was created that plays a role in these issues and also recommends on new incorporations, with the County Commission making the decision whether to put the question to a local vote. Subsequently, the County has imposed other constraints on incorporation and also on annexation. The effect has been to limit the growth of municipalities and to leave much of the County unincorporated. It does not appear that the Lakewood Plan has aroused a great deal of interest in Miami-Dade.

The two-tier approach brought many changes to the governance of the Miami metropolitan area. But it did little to reduce tensions. Regularly, there have been efforts to create new reforms.

Demographics Promote Continuing Dissatisfactions

Part of the reason for this continued dissatisfaction was the changing demographic composition of the area. It has been pointed out consistently that the Public Administration Service recommendations were designed for a homogeneous, relatively small population (about 80% non-Hispanic white), serving about 350,000 people in the unincorporated area, with a predominantly tourist-driven economy. By the 1980s these conditions were dramatically changed. The total population of nearly 2,000,000 was predominantly non-Anglo (35% Hispanic and 20% African-American) and by 2005 the percentage of Hispanics had soared to 57.3%. The African-Americans remained about 20%, and the non-Hispanic Whites had dropped to about 20%. Further, 50% of the residents in the 2000 Census were born outside the U.S., and two-thirds spoke a language other than English at home.

Interest orientations were far more complex even than the racial statistics suggested. The unincorporated area had grown to a population that roughly equaled the numbers living in the cities. Its population of 1,134,000 would have made it by far the largest city in Florida and one of the biggest in the nation. It was no simple job to construct a system that provided adequate representation for these numbers with such ethnic diversity.

In its effort to reconstitute Miami-Dade as a viable, vital metropolitan government, PAS placed major stress on its internal organization. There it also reflected the orientations of its counterparts in Chicago and opted for a highly integrated structure with all the features of the Council-Manager plan that had proved highly successful in many cities of the nation.

Great Change in Miami-Dade Internal Organization

Even today, Miami-Dade stands out for the extent to which its charter abandoned the "row office" traditions of county governments. A current organization chart shows how dramatic the reconstruction was. All the traditional elected officers' functions were folded into the County's appointed administrative structure. At the time the charter became operative, the following offices were eliminated: assessor, tax collector, surveyor, purchasing agent, and supervisor of regulation. In 1966, the office of sheriff was abolished.

As was indicated earlier, the essential idea of the Council-Manager plan is the separation of policy and administration. A small legislative body makes policy, appoints a manager, and assigns him/her responsibility for its execution. The only point of intersection between policy and administration is the manager's serving at the pleasure of the legislative body. There is a particularly strict observance of the separation with respect to administrative operations. Legislators are required to communicate only through the manager. It is a system built on the idea of accountability: legislators to the public, manager to the legislators, and operations to the manager.

The introduction of such an approach to Florida county government constituted revolutionary change. There was nothing like it in any other county. Further, it was not window dressing. Miami-Dade was the first in Florida to have a manager, not just in title but in real executive power.

A very senior, highly respected city manager was recruited. O.W. Campbell had served in other cities, including San Diego, and brought a very considerable reputation as a top-notch, outside professional to the new government. Miami-Dade took precedence among Florida's governments for the quality of its professional leadership, a status it held not only among counties but also among municipalities for a considerable length of time.

Aside from the difficulties of imposing such a radically different system on a culture, there were certain conceptual flaws with the Council-Manager plan that have emerged over time. They are not unique to Miami-Dade. The basic one is that the system was conceived as one where there would be accountability to a fairly homogeneous electorate. Hence a small group of part-timers could discharge the legislative responsibilities of the government. That view has become less realistic as our governments have grown, our populations have diversified, and expectations of representation have increased. The small legislative body elected at large has become less viable over time.

It has also become apparent that local governments are significant parts of the leadership structure of a community. The responsibility is not a passive one. Increasingly, there is recognition that governments must provide much of the foresight for their communities and must mobilize support and resources for the things that are important to do. Roles must therefore be constructed in governments that provide for this kind of leadership; and the part-time, collective body elected at large seldom has the capability or the credibility to handle these tasks.

It has also been increasingly recognized that policy and administration do not separate as easily as theory would have it. Managers, in fulfilling their executive responsibilities, are involved in much that is conceived as policy. As unelected professionals, they often find it difficult to navigate among many claimants in ways that are perceived as neutral. Their roles have evolved greatly from the early days when an engineer was hired "to get the street paved."

As a result of these considerations, there has been less enthusiasm about the applicability of the Council-Manager plan in large jurisdictions, like Miami-Dade. That worry arises particularly because of problems experienced in making sure that all interests are fully represented and also in mobilizing support and resources for the priorities of the community.

These kinds of internal issues have appeared over the last 50 years in Miami-Dade, as well as ones having to do with its role in the metropolitan complex. It has been frequently argued, for example, that the Council-Manager plan does not fit the present circumstance and that an elective mayor with full executive powers should replace the City Manager. The size and composition of the County Commission have also come under considerable attack. Proposals have been made both to expand the size of the Commission and also to provide for election by districts, in accord with a nationwide trend.

III. REFORM EFFORTS PERSIST

In May 1990 the Dade County electorate handed a 3-1 shellacking to two major proposals for internal change. One would have increased the number of Commission members to 11, with seven elected from districts and four from the County at large. The other would have expanded the powers of the Mayor by allowing the executive to hire and fire the City Manager, who was appointed by, and served at the pleasure of, the Commission.

It was not an election that settled these issues. The turnout was very small, only 17%, and the propositions were phrased in ways which raised reservations even among those who favored change.

Court Intervenes and Makes Changes

Meanwhile, minority interests in Miami had been pursuing reform through the Federal courts, pursuing the argument that the structure of representation on the Miami-Dade Commission, which typically resulted in the election of seven whites to the nine-member commission, did not accord with the one person, one vote principle. After six years of judicial activity, the Federal court ruled in December, 1992, that the structure had to be changed. Indeed, it went further and established a new pattern for the Commission, providing for 13 members elected by district. The Court abolished the position of Mayor but provided for its reinstatement in 1996.

Elections were held in March,1993, with 91 candidates, half of them Hispanic, running for office. As expected, the minority became the majority, with African-Americans and Hispanics dominating. While turnouts were relatively small, it was significant that 29% of the eligible Hispanic voters appeared at the polls, compared to 17% of the whites and 21% of African-Americans. In an editorial, the *Miami Herald* commented, "This special election was hard-won by minority interests, who sued for fairer commission representation. The new election was challenged but affirmed on appeal. The delay has kept Commission incumbents in office long past their terms."[25]

In the same election, voters rejected a proposal to create eight zoning boards, with seven members each, to operate in the unincorporated areas of the county. The margin was 2-1 against and meant that the County Commission would continue to rule on local zoning in the unincorporated neighborhoods. With the new Commissioners elected from districts and yet making judgements on local matters outside their districts, much apprehension about the future was expressed by the neighborhood groups.[26]

A New Crowd Appears in 1993

On April 22, 1993, the 13 new Commission members met and elected their new officers. A conservative African-American, a former member of the Reagan administration, was elected chairman after much maneuvering. His principal rival, an Hispanic, got no votes from Hispanic colleagues, indicating that ethnic interests played only a limited part in the political dynamics of Metro Dade.[27]

---

25 *Miami Herald,* March 12,1993, p. 26a

26 Joseph Tampani, "New commission: zoning friend or foe?" *Miami Herald,* April 23, 1993, p. 1B

27 Dexter Filkins, "Metro: New faces, new feuds," *Miami Herald,* April 23, 1993, p. 1A

It was apparent to all that the political machinations were a prelude for the later mayoral election

While the Federal court resolved the immediate problem of more equitable representation on the Dade County Commission, the broader issues of metropolitan two-tier government remained. On the one hand, there was the question whether the new structure provided for the political leadership necessary to deal with metropolitan regional problems. Perversely, at the other end of the range of problems, it was not at all clear that anything had been done to enable communities in the vast unincorporated area to deal with purely local problems.

In June 2001 a Charter Review task force proposed suggestions for updating the charter, none of them of major consequence. The task force considered the idea of a strong mayor for Miami-Dade but did not recommend it. At the time Commissioner Dennis Moss said the task force did "... not support a strong-mayor form of government of any kind." That turned out to be one man's opinion, however. The idea was far from dead and was increasingly seen as an important path out of many of Miami-Dade's problems.

IV. ALVAREZ ELECTED MAYOR IN 2004; PRESSES FOR STRONG MAYOR

In November, 2004, Carlos Alvarez, with nearly 30 years of service in the Miami-Dade government, was elected Mayor. He had been Police Chief for seven years and had a reputation for integrity and ability. Further, he had the right credentials. He was born in Cuba and came with his parents as a child on one of the last boatloads of immigrants in the late 1950s.

Alvarez had a strong conviction that Miami-Dade should depart its weak mayor system and move to the strong mayor. Basically, he believed the system was chaotic and unworkable. He observed that, as Police Chief, he had worked under four different Managers in seven years. At one point he was offered the Manager's job. He said,"I turned it down. It is a no-win situation.... We have a system of government laced with bureaucracy. Our government must be structured in a way that leaves no doubt as to who is accountable for decisions that affect the lives of our residents."[28]

Pros and Cons in 2007 Referendum Debate

The comment above was made in the course of a debate with Bruno Barreiro, chairman of the Board of Commissioners, a few days before the vote for a strong mayor on Tuesday, January 23, 2007.

Here are some of the points Mayor Alvarez made:

- The strong-mayor proposal is simply a transfer of authority from the County Manager to the Mayor.

- I philosophically believe that the Mayor—a countywide elected official—should be responsible and held accountable for the day-to-day operations of County government.

- The strong mayor proposal would return power to the people by transferring the authority to run day-to-day operations of the County from an appointed County Manager to a countywide elected official.

- The strong-mayor system will cut through bureaucracy.

- Under our current system, decisions that could take days, take months. Decisions that should take months, take years. Why? Because the County Manager serves 14 bosses and must build consensus before taking action. It is a constant juggling act to please the Mayor and 13 individual County Commissioners—all with different constituencies, priorities, and agendas. The County Manager's job is an unfair position for anyone.

Chairman Barreiro did not have as much to say but was no less adamant in his view that the strong-mayor was a bad idea. He commented:

- The Mayor would be able to issue regulations touching every program and service that the County delivers, all without oversight by the Commission. Presently, the Manager can issue regulations, which have the force of law, but they must be approved by the County Commission.

- With so much power concentrated in the hands of one person, the people who live in districts that are represented by Commissioners who dare to hold the Mayor accountable will find themselves with a government that ignores their needs.

- Miami-Dade government would be less responsive, less professional, and less diverse than it is today.

- All links to State government would be under the Mayor's control, as would all local groups that oversee everything from arts to transportation.

- The charter amendment would turn every County position into a patronage position.

- Because this proposal was hatched by a secret group, there hasn't been an open and transparent review.[29]

Those who favored the strong-mayor also expressed the belief that too much power rested with the Miami-Dade Commission and that a separation of powers between the legislative and executive would provide more balance. They particularly objected to the fact that the Manager, an appointed official, was in charge of the $7 billion budget. Further, the absence of balance in the present system was seen as leading to cronyism, influence-peddling, and corruption.

Those opposed to the strong-mayor also concentrated on the power aspects of the situation. In their view it was the Mayor who would have too much; and they expressed the belief that cronyism was more likely to flourish under a strong mayor. A University of Miami professor also entered the debate, declaring that the strong mayor plan suggested for Miami-Dade was undemocratic because it required a two-thirds majority of the Commission to overrule the Mayor in hiring decisions. That was a violation, he said, of majority rule.

Alvarez Wins and Becomes a Strong Mayor

The proponents of the strong mayor won the election January 23, 2007. But it was not a great victory that reflected an overwhelming mandate for change. The turnout was slightly over 14%, with about 150,000 votes cast by a registered electorate of over a million. Within this limited turnout, however, the victory was clear-cut, 56.5% to 43.5%. Council-Manager government was definitely out in Miami-Dade. It was a new day with a strong Mayor, Carlos Alvarez, who said he would assume direct supervision of "… most of the County's 66 department heads …"

The Mayor's Sources of Power

The key change, of course, was the insertion of the Mayor at the top of the administrative hierarchy. He has four sources of power that make him a very strong executive.

First, he has hiring and firing authority not only over the Manager, whose position was maintained, but all the department heads as well. The Commission's only recourse is to reject any appointments by a two-thirds majority no later than the next scheduled meeting. The firing power appears absolute. The charter says, "The Mayor shall have the authority to dismiss the County Manager."

---

29 Ibid.

Second, the Mayor has freedom to veto virtually all the Commission's decisions within 10 days of their adoption. It takes a two-thirds vote to override a veto. The Mayor also has the right "to attend and be heard" at any Commission meeting.

Third, the Mayor is virtually untouchable by the Commission. His term is four years, with the limit two terms. This is unlike the Manager's position which Mayor Alvarez described as "untenable" because of service at the pleasure of the Commission and hence the need to negotiate with 14 different people. It was clear that the Commission was quite prepared to fire managers, as indicated by Alvarez's statement that he served under four different managers in his seven years as police chief.

Fourth, the Mayor was placed in full charge of a highly integrated administrative structure. The charter is clear on the extent of his power, "The Mayor shall be responsible for the management of all administrative departments of the County government ..." He has no "row officers"with whom to deal.

Despite the major reform dictated by the January 23 election, the position of County Manager was retained in the charter. It now specifies that the Manager will "assist" the Mayor and serve under his direction. The budget arrangements specified by the charter suggest, however, a seminal role for the Manager. He is responsible for budget preparation and recommendations, which are then sent to the Mayor, whose written response accompanies the transmittal of the budget document to the Commissioners. It is clear, though, that the Mayor holds the power. Relations with the Manager, as well as other subordinates, will evolve. The Mayor had retained the Manager in the first two months of his new administration.

Where the powers of the Mayor defined in the charter are largely of an internal nature, the broad assignment of responsibilities to the Commissioners was much as it had been. A review reveals how extensive is the mandate of Miami-Dade as a metropolitan government. There is the statement that the Board of Commissioners "... shall be the legislative and governing body [and] ... shall have the power to carry on a central metropolitan government." What it means to be the "governing body" is not entirely clear and could bring conflict with the strong Mayor.

However, "governing" does not mean interference in administrative operations. The charter is clear about that, retaining restrictions from the Council-Manager era. "No commissioner shall direct or request the appointment of any person to, or his or her removal from, office by the manager, any administrative department director, or any of their subordinates ..."

"Except for transmitting and routing constituent inquiries, commissioners shall deal with the administrative service through Mayor or Manager, and no

Commissioner shall give orders to any subordinates of the Manager, either publicly or privately."

Calls for Change in Structure of Board of Commissioners

With the arrival of the strong Mayor, there have also been calls for change in the Board of Commissioners, particularly now that its role must be more clearly legislative. There is the demand, for example, that the Commissioners "… stop interfering with administrative functions." The handling of zoning matters in the unincorporated areas continues to be an issue, and it has been suggested that a system of administrative judges be instituted, much as has been done in Orange County.

Most of the criticism, however, is directed to the size and makeup of the Board and also to levels of pay. There seems to be substantial feeling that the Board, which now comprises 13 members, all from districts, could perform its policy-making functions better with more at-large members, presumably less subject to parochial local interests. As significant as the Commissioner's job is, it still is regarded as part-time employment and carries a compensation of $6000 per year. There seems to be substantial opinion that the positions should be recognized as full time and paid accordingly. Full time pay proposals vary from $84,000 to $114,000 (half of the mayor's salary), and one individual has suggested that an expanded at-large group be full-time but that district representatives opt for full or part-time, with consequent differences in pay.

Finally, the idea has been expressed that there be a new name for the Board of County Commissioners, one that conveys the sense of a legislative body. The name, Assembly, used by the lower houses in some state legislatures, has been suggested as one possibility.

Mayor Alvarez' preoccupations, however, will not be only with the Board of County Commissioners and the administrative hierarchy. As the highly visible leader of the County, he will have a particular role in charting Miami-Dade's future in a complex metropolitan system of government.

V. WHERE THE TWO-TIER SYSTEM STANDS

To this point it appears that he will be working with the same standard scenario that has been operative for about 50 years, two-tier government. Official materials on the Miami-Dade web site continue to emphasize the theme of two-tiers:

Miami-Dade County has operated under a unique metropolitan system of government, a 'two-tier' federation, since 1957 ...

Unlike a consolidated city-county, where the city and county government merge into a single entity, these two entities remain separate. Instead, there are two 'tiers', or levels, of government: city and county. There are 35 municipalities in the county, the city of Miami being the largest.

Cities are the 'lower tier' of local government, providing police and fire protection, zoning and code enforcement, and other typical city services within their jurisdictions. These services are paid for by city taxes. The county is 'upper tier', and it provides services of a metropolitan nature, such as emergency management, airport and seaport operations, public housing, health care services, transportation, environmental services, solid waste disposal, etc. These are funded by county taxes, which are assessed on all incorporated and unincorporated areas.

It is then reported that about half the residents of the county live in unincorporated areas, "the majority of which are heavily urbanized. These residents are part of the Unincorporated Municipal Services Area (UMSA). For these residents, the County fills the role of both lower- and upper-tier government, the County Commission acting as their lower-tier municipal representative body. Residents within UMSA pay an UMSA tax. equivalent to a city tax, which is used to provide county residents with equivalent city services (police, fire, zoning, water and sewer, etc.)"

In effect, nearly half the County's residents currently live under a single tier government. That percentage has not changed significantly over time. Since the 2000 Census, the decline of the unincorporated areas is about 70,000, or about 5%. With the exception of Homestead, whose population increased about 18% in five years, Miami-Dade's cities experienced relatively little increase in population between 2000 and 2005. There is little to indicate that more Miami-Dade residents will soon be experiencing two-tier government.

Any answer to this problem obviously requires an expansion of the "lesser tier," i.e., more municipal government. A change in the scale of municipal activity, either through more cities or annexation, is very much a matter determined by the County. Through its Municipal Advisory Committees and ultimately the County Commission, it sets the rules and procedures for annexation, decides when and where cities can be created, and determines when they should be dissolved. It has also been reported that Miami-Dade has imposed other constraints on incorporation. If an area seeking to incorporate is affluent and pays more in taxes than it receives in services, it is identified as a "donor community" and must pay a negotiated "mitigation fee" annually, in order to limit tax increases in unincorporated areas. Also a new city has to contract with the county police for its first three years, remain within the fire-rescue and the library districts, and continue Miami-Dade water and sewer and solid waste management services.

It is also the case that the County sometimes retains zoning control over specific areas within city limits. It is reported that Doral and Miami Gardens have had this experience.

Apparently, there have been some suggestions that Miami-Dade move toward the Lakewood Plan, establishing new local governments so that communities can gain control over local zoning. Most services would be provided under contract with the County. It has been suggested that townships, a type of government that does not exist in Florida, be the structure adopted to enable such a community takeover.

In the last analysis Miami-Dade is half two-tier and half consolidated, a bi-polar arrangement that has existed for a very long time. Even with its contradictions, there seems little incentive to confront the many institutions, interests, and prejudices that would have to be cajoled into making basic change.

The irony is that Toronto, the icon of the two-tier system, abolished it in 1998. Change is somewhat easier in Canada. Just as the provincial legislature decided in 1953 that the Toronto metropolitan area needed an "upper tier", it determined in 1997 that it was no longer necessary. Toronto Metro became an issue in the 1995 provincial elections; and the victors, who advocated its abolition, won. The claim was that the upper tier was expensive, duplicative, and bureaucratic. The new metropolitan government is the unified City of Toronto, composed of all the municipalities that formed the "lower tier." The shorthand name for it is "unicity." It is, in effect, a consolidation that has been reported to have saved some money. While there was vigorous opposition before the provincial legislature acted, it soon disappeared. "… Virtually all the residents have since accepted the decision on unification and have committed themselves to building the new city."[30]

VI. SUMMARY

Fifty years ago the metropolitan reform in Miami-Dade commanded the attention of the entire nation. It was a time when there was major awareness of a significant disarray in the governmental arrangements in our largest urban areas. The proposal for revolutionary reform in Miami-Dade struck a responsive chord.

---

30   P.S. Reddy, "The Greater Toronto area revisited: from metropolitan government to unicty," *International Journal of Public Sector Management*. 15: 69-86. (No. 1, 2002) This quotation was taken from an abstract that appeared on the Internet.

It was not just a Florida event. The whole country was intrigued and interested to see how things worked out.

No doubt the two-tier model installed in Toronto, which involved the placing of an entirely new level of metropolitan government on the existing cities and towns of the area, served to heighten the interest. Toronto commanded the attention of the world, and its clear adaptation to the Miami situation suggested we might have expected to see a lot more Toronto-like reforms.

Things have not worked out as anticipated, however. That's true both in Miami and in Toronto. Almost from its inception, there has been friction in Miami, and many changes have been proposed and others imposed over the 50 years. In Toronto the two-tier plan was summarily dropped in the late 1990's, and a one-tier strategy, a unicity, has been the replacement.

It has long been suggested that a dramatic shift in the size and composition of the population in Miami-Dade accounted for many of the problems of the reforms. From one perspective, i.e., issues having to do with the structure of the new government, that is certainly a reality.

In the degree to which the essence of the reform was the borrowing of the two-tier model from Toronto, however, such an explanation seems less than satisfactory. The problem begins with the initial assumption of the consultants that the Canadian experience was directly transferable to Miami. Dade County simply did not have the power granted to the new Toronto regional government. Its municipalities were well established and had their own independent bases of power. It was not entirely clear how the two-tier system would work with them; and there was also the vast unincorporated area, where Dade County was the only government. It was a complex of jurisdictions where many of the relationships had not been resolved.

In the ensuing years these issues have remained. The unincorporated area still houses nearly half the population in Miami-Dade, which functions as a municipal government for this huge number of people. Though it may not be quite as large today, it was said in the past that Miami-Dade was directly responsible for the ninth largest city in the United States, far larger, of course, than the city of Miami. That has meant that the Board of County Commissioners has been perennially involved in all kinds of highly local issues, notably in zoning. Instead of concentrating on the major regional questions, the Board has spent time dealing with the most immediate of neighborhood issues.

Little has been done over the years to handle these intractable matters. The unincorporated area, in which many of the problems exist, continues very large. The two-tier vision for Miami-Dade remains about as distant in 2007 as it was in 1957.

This situation is in marked contrast to Los Angeles County, California, whose basic circumstance has in many ways paralleled Miami-Dade. It will be recalled that it launched its Lakewood Plan (later generally known as the Contract Cities program) in 1954, just about the same time that Toronto and Miami-Dade came into being. The purpose of that program was to "decentralize policy and centralize administration." Communities like Lakewood were encouraged to incorporate and to minimize costs by contracting with the County for services. At the time of its establishment, Lakewood had about 70,000 inhabitants and 10 employees.

In the roughly 50 years since, 37 cities, each with its own local council, have contracted with Los Angeles County for virtually all their services. There are 88 municipalities in the County, and all, "in varying degrees" contract for services. It is clear that virtually all the new cities established in the last half-century have done so within the framework of the Lakewood Plan.

A striking aspect of these developments is that less than 10% of the Los Angeles County population (about 1 million) now lives in an unincorporated area. That means that more than 90% of the population lives under a two-tier government, thus realizing an aspiration for Miami-Dade many years ago. Miami-Dade has about a fourth the population of Los Angeles but more people living in the unincorporated area; and it has 34 cities, most of which were operating at the time of the 1957 reform. Clearly, it has not followed the Los Angeles County path toward two-tier government.

The change prescriptions of the 1950s were based on the continuation of a white-centered local government. Proposed was a classic Council-Manager plan, itself fairly alien to Florida traditions, that had particular success in communities with a reasonably homogeneous population and a high consensus on values. Under those circumstances it was possible for a small, part-time legislative body to process claims and articulate policies, delegating to a professional manager their execution. What had not been taken into account was the degree to which population growth and heightened diversity would make the negotiation of interests a far larger part of the action, both at the legislative and administrative levels, in Miami-Dade.

It is questionable whether the Council-Manager form was right for Miami-Dade even in the 1950s. As demographics dramatically changed the Miami landscape, it certainly became less so. The Board of Commissioners was revamped, largely as a result of court action, and a weak Mayor was installed. The Manager remained but his credibility as a professional declined over time. A former Police Chief, Carlos Alvarez, was elected Mayor in 2004 and immediately began the campaign for a strong mayor system. He had little good to say about the Council-Manager plan and noted that he had served under four Managers in his seven years as Police Chief.

In 2007 Mayor Alvarez succeeded in his campaign to expand his powers. He is now one of three strong mayors in Florida's counties.

CHAPTER SIX

REVOLUTIONARY REFORM: CITY-COUNTY CONSOLIDATION. SUCCESS IN JACKSONVILLE-DUVAL BUT FAILURE IN TALLAHASSEE-LEON

The most major surgery the governments in a metropolitan community can undergo is consolidation. In principle, that makes all of them one. And usually it is the largest municipality that survives as the operating unit. There is only one tier; and the city as the residual government takes control of everything.

Again, the Toronto experience is instructive. Its involvement with two-tier government lasted about 50 years, after which time the political leaders came to believe there was too much government, excessive overlap, and glaring inefficiencies. The provincial government, which has the power to impose reform, decreed there would be consolidation, with the greater city of Toronto as the remaining government.

Though things were not that simple in Jacksonville, the effect was very much the same. The consolidation of the city and the county there gained nationwide attention. For more than 40 years, Jacksonville has been regarded as one of the greatest cities in the country, with a jurisdiction that covers more than 700 square miles.[31] If the County had been the residual government, there would have been little thought of a "big city," Jacksonville.

Inevitably, the structure of local governments in a county will influence whether consolidation is even remotely feasible. The more local governments, the more likely that consolidation will be perceived as a threat. And, since the State

---

31   The official land area of Duval County is stated as 774 square miles.

government in Tallahassee does not have the commanding power of a province in Canada, any real change will depend on the local population. Where there is a dominant city government, the county is in the shadows and typically does not find it interesting to sponsor its abolition.

As a result, consolidations are rare in the United States. They may promise a lot in terms of clean, accountable government but the barriers to adoption are monumental. Jacksonville deserves special attention in this book because such major reform was achieved.

I. THE JACKSONVILLE-DUVAL CONSOLIDATION

In October 1956 a four-person delegation from Dade County visited Jacksonville. In many states the purpose of their visit would have seemed bizarre. They were seeking Jacksonville's support for the constitutional amendment that would allow home rule and permit the creation of Metro Dade. As Richard Martin put it, the amendment "… would make it possible for Miami-Dade to regulate local governmental affairs without having to petition a legislative delegation or wait on biennial legislative sessions to conduct routine county business.[32]

Duval County voted 2-1 in support of the Miami-Dade constitutional amendment, at least in part because of its own frustrations with an arcane, highly politicized process of reform. As one newspaper editor wrote:

> Duval Countians may well watch the Dade experiment in home rule with more than passing interest because Florida's major urban areas have many problems in common. The handling of these through local bills in the Legislature has presented legal, political, and other difficulties which proponents of the Dade amendment hope it will reduce if not cure.[33]

The history of the Jacksonville-Duval consolidation, like that of Metro Dade, reveals the barriers imposed by the State government to major metropolitan reform. These hurdles remain for the most part; and it appears that only metropolitan communities facing total disaster are likely to mobilize sufficient support to secure major change.

---

32 Richard Martin, *Consolidation: Jacksonville Duval County: The Dynamics of Urban Political Reform.* (Jacksonville, FL: Crawford Publishing Co., 1968), p. 50.

33 *Florida Times-Union,* October 16, 1956, p. 51.

Serious Government Problems and Needs for Change

Certainly the City of Jacksonville had a history of very bad government since its incorporation in 1832. Duval County served a large rural, sparsely populated area surrounding Jacksonville.

A burst of reform in 1917 brought the city one of the strangest structures of government ever concocted in the United States. It was called a commission-council form, in which a nine-member elected council set policy and a five-member elected commission executed it. The office of Mayor was abolished and one of the Commissioners served *ex-officio* in that role. The driving force for the reform was elimination of corruption through a system of checks and balances. As Martin observed, the system was termed, "... unique by political scientists and no wonder."[34]

Furthermore, it was corrupt. In 1931 the grand jury returned indictments against 75 public officials, primarily in the schools and in the courts.

In these circumstances, consolidation has typically been a popular reform theme. When checks and balances seem to produce neither honesty nor effective performance, the solution is thought to lie in clear, unambiguous lines of accountability. David Hertz summarized the persistent, recurring appeal of consolidation in these terms:

> ... Consolidation has a number of features that speak favorably of it. If all services, except those of a purely local nature, were provided through one central government, coordination and economies of scale would be noted benefits. At the same time, one county government would take much of the confusion out ... Consolidation would also eliminate the duplication of services at the municipal and county levels.[35]

Not surprisingly, movements in favor of consolidation are recorded in Jacksonville as far back as 1918. In 1924 an amendment to the Florida Constitution would have permitted Jacksonville "... to establish, change, and abolish a local government extending territorially throughout Duval County."[36]

That proposal was defeated both in the state at large and in Duval. In 1934 a similar amendment was placed on the ballot and passed by a slimmer margin in the county than in the state as a whole. But it passed and it appeared that consolidation

---

34   Richard Martin, *Florida Times-Union*, October 16, 1956, p. 15

35   David Bendel Hertz, *Governing Dade County: A Study of Alternative Structures*. (Coral Gables: University of Miami, 1984), p. 40

36   *Loc. Cit.*

was on its way. However, it was more than 30 years before an amendment provided the authority for consolidation.

What happened in the 1930s revealed again how critical the State Legislature has been to local government change. A citizens' charter group was formed at the time and proposed the substantial merging of city and county functions. The legislative delegation then intervened and ordered drastic changes, sufficient to gut the plan. The shell of consolidation was approved by the Legislature and put on the ballot. But it was a bad scene. Many who had been for consolidation came out against the weakened proposal. Old-time politicos took advantage of the situation to launch a campaign against the gutted consolidation plan. There were many accusations of unfair campaign tactics by those in office. Not surprisingly, the referendum was defeated, 9,499 against and 7,175 for. Outside Jacksonville the vote was 3-1 against. The experience was so bad that the notion of consolidation was buried for three decades.

Despite heavy spending on new building projects in the city after World War II, Jacksonville experienced changes that were occurring nationwide. The minority population was increasing in the City and resulting in white flight to the suburbs. That left the City with a poorer population and lessened ability to cope with its growing problems.

By 1965 Jacksonville was in a state of rapid deterioration. The City was still unique in its confused authority structure. Duval County was virtually a caricature of the problems of county government in the United States, with 74 elective offices and no one in a position of overall leadership responsibility. The municipality of Jacksonville was suffering from the typical central city problems. In 1962 leaders described it as having to provide services to half a million people with a tax base resting on fewer than 200,000.

Demographic changes were continuing to exacerbate the situation. In the period 1950–65, the City lost population; but the County had jumped from about 100,000 people to over 325,000. Where the City had twice as many inhabitants as the County in 1950, it had only about 60% as many in 1965. Further, its racial composition was changing; it was 41% African-American in 1960. Its costs were going up with a population less able to pay. Municipal government spent $116 per person in 1950; in 1965 the per capita cost had risen to $479, a growth of 300%. Increased expenditures did not halt declining service levels, and 80% of the city's industrial and residential waste was being dumped raw into the St. Johns river.

In the suburbs the County government was unable to cope. It had a poor tax base because of traditionally low assessments and because a major share of property was not on the tax rolls. There was no sewer system. More than 180 private

utilities, most of them in poor condition, were operating; and police and fire protection was inadequate for urban communities. The most blatant problem, however, was in the school system, which served all Duval County. An independent
school district, it was crowded with elected officials and starved for funds.

The schools were dependent on the County for the administration of their
main source of revenue, the property tax. In 1964 it was estimated that property
was being assessed at only about 30% of actual value, which deprived the schools
as well as the general County government of very large amounts of revenue. Yet
the elected tax assessor would not change the assessments and was returned to
office in 1964. Following that election, the southern association dis-accredited all
15 high schools in Duval.

Martin summarized the problems facing the metropolitan area:

> Public education, pollution of air and water, sewers, lack of adequate police
> and fire protection in county areas outside the city, high costs of government
> and soaring taxes were among the problems which prepared the county for
> consolidation. There was also a rising crime rate, widespread and deteriorating
> slums in the city, population shifts tending to increase the Negro-to-white ratio
> in Jacksonville thereby threatening the political imbalance favoring whites, and
> then an economic slowdown.[37]

In appraising the possibility of transferring the Jacksonville experience to other
metropolitan areas, analysts have been in consensus that the situation there was
particularly desperate. They express doubt that a similar level of breakdown was
to be found elsewhere.

Annexation Efforts Fail

Before the move to consolidation, an effort was made to strengthen the City
of Jacksonville through annexation of unincorporated territory in the county.
Municipal growth had not, however, been favored in Duval County. Only nine
annexations had been approved in Jacksonville history, the last in 1931. In the
period 1960–65 the voters outside the City limits, who had to agree, rejected
annexation proposals on six different occasions. An ambitious plan to annex 66
square miles and 130,000 people was voted on in 1963. As usual, it was approved
by City voters and defeated by those in the affected areas. A similar plan was again
defeated in 1964. Thus, annexation as a means of strengthening the central City
and bringing needed services to the suburbs was not a viable alternative.

---

37   Martin, *Consolidation ...*, p. 39.

In 1965 new consolidation proposals were being made at about the same time fresh scandals were emerging. An investigative report by a TV station in 1966 revealed that the City was spending $1.3 million per year on insurance, more than the combined costs for the cities of Miami, Tampa, and St. Petersburg. Also, in 1966, a series of grand jury investigations resulted in the indictment of four of nine councilmen, two of five commissioners, and two department heads. In a four-year period the city bought 168 automobiles from one dealer, paying the maximum price. No other dealers received orders, and the grand jury concluded, "Political patronage controlled the purchase of those automobiles."[38]

A final report said there were people on the payroll who did no work and other employees who were used for private purposes, including political campaigns.

But there was good news with the bad news. People were appearing on the scene with a zeal for reform, and they were strong backers of consolidation. A 15-year veteran of City government became Mayor in 1965. Lew Ritter was pro-reform, pro-consolidation. Though he had substantial popular approval, the insistence on change was so great in Jacksonville that he was narrowly upset by a newcomer, Hans Tanzler, a 40-year-old criminal court judge, in 1967. As James B. Crooks wrote, "… Ritter was popular and had a substantial record of achievement as Mayor. But 1967 was different, and Tanzler epitomized the non-partisan reformer advocating open and honest government without spoils or patronage.[39]

There was also an elected Sheriff in Duval, Dale Carson, who pronounced himself in favor of consolidation. He had significant credibility because he had brought about visible improvements in the Duval policing operations. *Wikipedia*, the online encyclopedia, noted that he had support "… from both inner city blacks (who wanted more involvement in government) and whites in the suburbs (who wanted more services and more control over the central City.)"[40]

Other Jacksonville leaders also took strong stands in favor of consolidation. It enabled compromise on key points in the charter that could have resulted in defeat. Two key problems were negotiated. The four existing municipalities, originally slated for extinction, were untouched, and Dale Carson, the Duval Sheriff, was accepted as the head of law enforcement for the new government. Personalities made a difference in securing success in Jacksonville.

---

38 Martin, *op. cit.*, p. 83.

39 James B. Crooks, *Jacksonville: The Consolidation Story, from Civil Rights to the Jaguars* (Gainesville, FL: University Press of Florida, 2004), Florida History and Culture Series, p. 51

40 "Jacksonville," *Wikipedia*, posted on line, March 21, 2007.

Consolidated Government Established in 1968

The scandals were said to have been a major factor in a nearly 2-1 victory for consolidation in the referendum election of August 2, 1967. More than 86,000 people voted, with more than 56,000 favoring the move and slightly less than 30,000 against.

The densely populated urban fringe areas weighed in with a 6-1 margin of support. Even though the African-Americans would have less clout in the larger government, they also were strong supporters. Lower income groups in the rural areas of the county were more negative, supporting the referendum by only a small majority. The unions were officially opposed because it was feared that more competitive bidding would bring in outside, non-union firms. Overall, the consolidation was regarded as a great victory, and enthusiasts declared it the biggest reform event of the 20th century. The over 700 square miles involved did make it the largest territorial consolidation on record in the U.S.[41]

The new government took office on October 1, 1968, and rapidly proceeded to make major changes. The consolidation was not total, of course. Four cities outside Jacksonville remained.

Subsequently, the three beach municipalities have grown. Jacksonville Beach is the largest, with a 2005 estimated population of 21,531; Atlantic Beach numbers 14,079, and Neptune Beach has 7,256 inhabitants. Baldwin remains small, with 1,634 people. Thus a little more than 5% of the county population lives outside the City of Jacksonville. In a very limited degree Jacksonville-Duval is a two-tier government. Generally, these cities maintain their own services. In 2006, however, the city of Baldwin abolished its police department and contracted for service with the Jacksonville-Duval Sheriff.

Uniquely, residents of the four municipalities enjoy full citizenship status in the consolidated government. They are, after all, residents of Duval County. Not only can they vote for Jacksonville offices, but they can be candidates as well. John Delaney, the fifth Mayor in the consolidated era, was a resident of Neptune Beach when elected in 1995. He served until 2003.

The renovation of the Jacksonville administrative structure that serves the entire community was profound. Of the changes, perhaps the most significant in the long run was the separation of the legislative and executive powers and the

---

41   "When consolidation took effect on October 1, 1968, Jacksonville was suddenly transformed from a City of 39 square miles to an astounding 840 square miles [sic]— the largest metropolitan city in land area in the world. Overnight the city's population catapulted to 27th in the nation from a 75th ranking a day earlier." Jacksonville Historical Society web site, observing the 35th anniversary of consolidated government in Jacksonville, 2002.

institution of the strong mayor. Since then, there has been much discussion of creating a strong mayor in other communities; and, as has been reported in the last chapter, it was established in Miami-Dade county in January, 2007.

The Jacksonville organization was the one that made the Mayor a dominant figure. All the traditional county positions were brought within the hierarchy and made appointive. The exception was the Sheriff, who was no longer a Constitutional officer but retained his elective status. That arrangement resulted from the immense popularity of Sheriff Carson, who stayed in office for a number of years after the consolidation. His tenure was regarded as a highly successful one, and his legacy continues. The Sheriff elected in 2003 was a 32-year veteran of the department.

In addition to his hierarchical position at the top of the organization, the Mayor also enjoys the powers that often accompany his role. He has the freedom to hire and fire his department heads, and he also has veto power over all resolutions and ordinances of the City Council.

The City Council was reformed. It was expanded to 19 members, 14 from districts and five at-large. However, the at-large representatives became an issue because they typically were elected from the same area of the consolidated community. In the early 1990s voters approved a change that created five at-large districts, from each of which a representative must be chosen. In effect, the council now has two types of district representation, 14 from the conventional districts and five from the "mega" districts. Councilmen were paid and accorded significant policy-making responsibilities.

Structural integration went only so far in Jacksonville, however. A substantial number of local government functions are operated through independent units, which are subject only to indirect controls by the city. The official Jacksonville city web page lists the following independent boards and agencies: Airport Authority, Children's Commission, Housing Authority, Housing Finance Authority, Port Authority, Electricity Authority, Transportation Authority, Public Library, Police and Fire Pension Fund, and Water and Sewer Expansion Authority.

As is customary, the school board remained independent, but with only seven members.

Appraisals of Consolidation

There is a high consensus among observers that the consolidated government has made a substantial difference in the governance of the Jacksonville metropolitan area. The new institution has strong political leadership through the office of Mayor; and the larger number of Council members, with district election, are felt to have made the system more representative and more accessible. The tax structure was significantly reformed, removing some of the confusion over responsibility and payment for services. Levies are made in support of a General Services District, which is obligated to provide services to the entire County; and other funds are collected in support of an Urban Services District. A more integrated hierarchical system, with an infusion of professional staff, brought improved fiscal and management policies. Total property taxes increased 50% in three years, for example, as property was placed on the rolls and reassessed. Major infra-structure investments were made, and about 200 private utilities were acquired. Sewerage systems in both the city and the county were developed or rebuilt. The amount and quality of various services were particularly expanded outside the old city.[42]

In October, 1978, the *Jacksonville Times-Union* published a special supplement, entitled "Consolidation," in which an attempt was made to evaluate a decade of experience.[43]

The newspaper commissioned a poll which revealed a continuing, strong support for consolidation. Unfortunately, details of the poll procedure were not reported. Seventy-seven percent of respondents felt that services had improved with consolidation, rating fire protection the most improved; and 73% believed that the Jacksonville area was a better place in which to live because of consolidation.

There was no agreement on whether taxes had gone up or down. People who had lived in Jacksonville before consolidation were less enthusiastic but conceded that there was less corruption and more services. Although some African-American leaders were critical of the consolidation results, the poll showed 70% of them still supportive.

The consolidated police service, led by an elected Sheriff, was seen as a major benefit of consolidation. It was agreed that people in the former county areas were getting better service, with no decline in the old city. Jurisdictional disputes, which had been a big problem, were obviously eliminated. On the other hand, there was significant dissatisfaction with the new government's performance in planning and zoning, labeled the "worst failure." While new purchasing processes had eliminated the insurance and automobile excesses of the old system, central services management was a major problem 10 years later.

The least satisfaction with consolidation seemed to center in the four small municipalities. Their leaders were reported as saying they had gotten nothing from consolidation, had been neglected, and were taxed for services they did not get. The problem conceptually was more difficult than in Miami-Dade. There a

---

42   James F. Horan and G. Thomas Taylor, Jr., *Experiments in Metropolitan Government* (New York: Praeger Publishers, 1977), pgs. 46*ff.*

43   *Jacksonville Times-Union,* October 1, 1978.

two-tier system legitimated such local units; Jacksonville was a one-tier system in which there was presumably no place for other cities.

Questions were also raised about the continued existence of the special authorities. While consolidation had tied them more closely to the City through both appointive and budget controls, they were still seen as having a high degree of independence. It was observed that the question whether elected officials should have more control was "continually debated." The chairman of the Jacksonville Electric Authority at that time declared that elected officials would (a) have difficulty making unpopular political decisions, (b) be unlikely to respond quickly to enterprise needs, and (c) not have the experience in technical matters. In an interview about two decades after consolidation, a highly placed city official reaffirmed these views, noting that such enterprises must be run like businesses. The conclusion was that they were. "Thank God," he said, "they are free from politics to set rates."

Benton and Gamble sought to test the hypothesis that a consolidated government will have lower property taxes and expenditures by examining data for Jacksonville-Duval during the period 1955–1981. They evaluated the impact of consolidation in three areas: property tax revenues, total expenditures, and public safety expenditures. The findings proved to be discouraging for advocates of consolidation. Property tax revenues increased after consolidation; and the rate of growth of general expenditures over the long term went up, as did public safety expenditures. Commenting on their data, Benton and Gamble wrote:

> These findings demonstrate that city-county consolidation has produced no measurable impact on the taxing and spending policies of the consolidated government which was the focus of this study—Jacksonville, Florida. In fact, both taxes and expenditures increased as a result of consolidation, a finding completely opposite to the main reform hypothesis and other research.[44]

Given the chaotic state of Jacksonville-Duval public services prior to consolidation, increases in taxes and costs may have been inevitable. Indeed, Benton and Gamble observe that the outgoing City Council voted big salary increases for the fire service to take effect with consolidation. They called it an "obvious attempt" to embarrass the new government. There is the possibility, of course, that economy and efficiency arguments are simply sloganeering, employed to overturn the old political order.

---

44 J. Edwin Benton and Darwin F. Gamble, "A City/County Consolidation and Economies of Scale: Evidence from a Time-Series Analysis in Jacksonville, Florida," *Social Science Quarterly*, March, 1984, p. 196.

There can be little question that the consolidated government has enjoyed a high degree of stability. It has not experienced the turbulence found in Miami-Dade; and the structure remains very much as it was at the beginning in 1968. In nearly 40 years there have been only six mayors, with an average tenure of more than six years. Of the first five, three served two terms.

A recent article by Jeff Brumley in the *Jacksonville Times-Union*[45] suggests that the African-American community may be the least satisfied currently with consolidation. He reported that the Jacksonville Leadership Coalition had been established with the intent to abolish the consolidated government. The organization sought to reverse "decades of disparities" and thus to "balance the economic playing field." The Sheriff was a particular object of criticism, and the group went so far as to propose a Federal takeover of the Jacksonville police activities.

> Prior to consolidation in 1968, blacks in Jacksonville made up a higher percentage of the city's population and enjoyed corresponding political and economic influence, said Juan Gray, chairman of the Jacksonville chapter of the Southern Christian Leadership Conference.
>
> Returning to separate governments for Jacksonville and Duval County would make city government and police more responsive to minorities' concerns and needs, he said, and would ultimately reduce the homicide rate.[46]

Others, however, have had a different view. In 2002 the Jacksonville Historical Society marked the 35th anniversary of consolidation by proclaiming it one of the two most important events in the city's history. The other was a disastrous fire in 1901.

In his 2004 book, James B. Crooks concurred in a general consensus that African-Americans had gained the least. He reported one study that showed that the African-American economic condition, as compared to whites, had changed little in the 1970–1990 period. On the other hand, he observed that the election by district for the Jacksonville City Council had resulted in greater African-American representation than was the case in much of the southeast. He also quoted a Jacksonville University professor, writing in 1977, that the "... general thrust [of consolidation] had been favorable to the interests of blacks."[47]

---

45   Jeff Brumley, "Group calls for equality from city," *Jacksonville Times-Union*. February 20, 2007, posted on the Internet.

46   *Loc. cit.* University of Akron Professor Abel A. Bartley wrote a book on race relations in Jacksonville, *Keeping the Faith: Race, Politics, and Social Development in Jacksonville, Florida, 1940–1970* (Westport, Ct.: Greenwood Press, 2000)

47   Crooks., *op. cit.*, p. 208

"For Jacksonville," Crooks wrote, "consolidation proved to be the right move."[48] He explained his conclusion further:

> As the twentieth century ended, however, Jacksonville had distinct advantages over many American cities because of consolidation. In northeast Florida, with almost three-quarters of the region's population, it remained the dominant player in the metropolitan area along Florida's First Coast. While economic growth along with suburban sprawl had begun to expand beyond the consolidated city's boundaries into the surrounding counties, it had not and, for the foreseeable future, would not overshadow the central city. Clearly expanding growth required increasing regional cooperation to combat land, air, and water pollution to maintain a healthy environment. Transportation planning and growth management also required regional efforts. These were the frontier for twenty-first-century metropolitan governance.[49]

A reviewer of the Crooks book, Professor S. Willoughby Anderson of the University of North Carolina, generally agreed with his assessment, observing "Consolidation seems to have been, for Jacksonville, a generally positive solution to the problems facing the modern urban center."

Comprehensive consolidation, found very seldom in the United States, does involve radical change in local political institutions. Commenting on the Jacksonville case, Rosenbaum and Kammerer wrote that it "... did significantly hasten the transformation in the socio-economic base of the city's formal and informal political leadership."[50]

II. THE FAILURE OF CONSOLIDATION REFORM IN TALLAHASSEE-LEON COUNTY IN 1992

As time has passed, the Jacksonville consolidation becomes even more impressive. It was, of course, a rare event—the only one ever in Florida. Further, such drastic reform has seldom been attempted in Florida. In those few instances there has been nothing approaching the Jacksonville success.

---

48   Ibid., p. 222

49   Ibid., p. 225

50   Walter A. Rosenbaum and Gladys M. Kammerer, *Against Long Odds: The Theory and Practice of Successful Government Consolidation*, (Beverly Hills, CA: Sage Publications, 1974), p. 12.

The limited attempts at consolidation in Florida result from the way which the State's governmental institutions have evolved. Big cities have not been a part of the picture; and the presence of a large municipality seems a requisite to engineering a move toward one-tier government.

Tallahassee-Leon the Logical Candidate

Table 4, below, suggests how limited are the consolidation options in Florida. If one works from the assumption that possibilities for consolidation are greatest when there is a dominant city to occupy the one-tier role, only the City of Tallahassee seems to meet the test. It houses about 65% of Leon County's population. The next largest municipalities, as a percentage of total county population, are Tampa at 29%, St. Petersburg at 27%, and Cape Coral at 26%. Politically, that means roughly 75% of the citizens in these counties have relatively little institutional reason for supporting a proposition that leaves one of these three cities as the last government standing.

It is conceivable, of course, that the one remaining government could be the county. But such a reform would face profound resistance from residents of the cities. Though counties have evolved greatly in Florida and provide many municipal services, the culture of the United States embraces the cities as the "real" local governments. They established themselves long ago as the antagonists of the states. Thus, while it is possible to conceive of the county at the heart of the consolidation, that is likely to occur only where there is very limited experience with municipal government. Pasco County, whose largest city has only four percent of the population and the six cities in Pasco together boast only about 10% of the citizenry, is possibly the best candidate of the counties to serve as a vehicle for consolidation. About 90% of its population is already experiencing one-tier government, with Pasco the provider.

Orange, Hillsborough, and Sarasota would seem to be possibilities, but more remote. While they provide one-tier government to approximately two-thirds of their populations, the reality is that a third of their people live under a two-tier system. Engineering agreement from them for consolidation could be very difficult. Municipal residents may be in the minority but they typically have the organization and cohesion to represent their interests with great effectiveness.

TABLE 4
SUMMARY OF 15 COUNTIES AND THEIR POSSIBILITIES FOR CONSOLIDATION

County	County Population (in 1,000s) 2005 est.	Largest City pop. 2005est.	Largest City % of total county	No. cities in county	Pop. of cities not incl. biggest	Other Cities— % total county	Unincorp- orated Population 2005 est.	Unincorp- orated % of total county
Brevard	531	75	14%	15	210	40%	246	46%
Broward	1,748	171	10%	31	1,529	87%	44	3%
Escambia	303	55	18%	2	1.7	<1%	247	82%
Hills-borough	1,131	326	29%	3	55	5%	750	66%
Lee	549	140	26%	5	117	21%	292	53%
Leon	271	174	65%	1	0	0	96	35%
Miami-Dade	2,422	386	16%	34	902	37%	1,134	47%
Orange	1,043	217	21%	13	149	14%	677	65%
Palm Beach	1,265	101	8%	37	605	48%	559	44%
Pasco	406	16	4%	6	24	6%	366	90%
Pinellas	947	253	27%	24	411	43%	283	30%
Polk	541	90	17%	17	113	21%	338	62%
Sarasota	367	54	15%	4	67	18%	246	67%
Volusia	494	65	13%	17	315	64%	114	23%

The counties least vulnerable to consolidation reforms, in terms of the data provided in Table 4, are Broward and Volusia Counties. Broward has virtually no unincorporated area (about 3%); does not have a dominant city, Fort Lauderdale accounting for only about 10% of its population; and it has 31 cities, whose citizens generally live under two-tier government. Things are just a little less stacked against consolidation in Volusia, where the principal city, Daytona Beach, has about 13% of the total population, where there is a total of 17 cities administering to more than 75% of the population, and where less than a quarter of the population lives within a one-tier system of county services.

These situations may be interpreted variously by different analysts, but it is quite evident that institutional structures in Florida do not facilitate consolidated, one-tier governments. Tallahassee-Leon provides the one case in the state where structural circumstances would seem to give consolidation a chance.

As a result, the experience with consolidation reform in Tallahassee-Leon has relevance. It is a story of failure. The major effort in 1992 was rejected by voters by a 3-1 margin. Its contrast to Jacksonville's success has raised at least one basic question. How bad do things have to get before reform becomes viable? In Jacksonville-Duval things were really falling apart. The opposite was the case in Tallahassee-Leon. The City was regarded as one of the best run in the state, and the County as performing satisfactorily and improving. Hence there was no pressing imperative for reform. Consolidation in Tallahassee-Leon had to be sold on the ground that it made good, long-run sense.

It is fortunate that one of the outstanding city managers in Florida, Jack M. Schluckebier, determined that the consolidation experience in Tallahassee-Leon was of sufficient significance to make it the subject of his doctoral dissertation at Florida State University. He knew Tallahassee well. Between managerial stints in Michigan and then in Lake City, Florida, he served as deputy budget director for the city. From Lake City he moved to Casselberry, where he was city manager for several years. In 2007 he occupied that role in the City of Melbourne.

Concentrating on the 1992 consolidation reform effort in Tallahassee-Leon, Schluckebier provides a comprehensive history of the experience. The report that follows is based entirely on his work.[51] However, the analysis and conclusions are the author's.

Previous Consolidation Efforts

Like much of Florida, the Tallahassee-Leon County area had major population increases in the 50-year period between 1940 and 1990, growing from 31,646 people in 1940 to 192,493. Both units of government had experienced substantial growth, but it was nearly twice as great in the City, whose expansion had come largely through annexation. In the 10 years, 1980–90, Tallahassee had increased in size from about 26 square miles to over 75, nearly a 300 percent hike. That pattern also separated Tallahassee from Jacksonville, which had been singularly unsuccessful in annexation efforts. The difference was utilities—electricity, gas, water, and sewers. These services were highly attractive to developers faced with the problem of providing essential infrastructure in areas on which they were planning to build. Also, Tallahassee used revenue from its utilities to keep municipal

---

51   Jack M. Schluckebier, *A Study of the 1992 Consolidation Charter Proposal for Tallahassee and Leon County*. A Dissertation submitted to the Reubin O'D. Askew School of Public Administration and Policy, Florida State University, in partial fulfillment of the requirements for the degree of Doctor of Philosophy, 1995, typescript, 214 pages.

taxes low, thus reducing substantially the differences in tax bills between the City and the County.

Tallahassee was growing and providing a substantial number of urban services in Leon County, and the idea of consolidating the two governments appeared to gain increasing favor in the period after 1970. There were proposals in 1973, 1976, 1980, and 1986, all of which were unsuccessful. In 1980 things never got beyond a straw vote. The 1986 proposal, which seemed to hold much promise for passage, was aborted by the local legislative delegation. It considered the issue too divisive and refused to put the matter on the ballot. Such votes as were held were close enough, however, to provide encouragement to the advocates of consolidation.

These proposals had roughly similar features and generally followed the contours of the Tallahassee City government. Only one, that in 1973, deviated from the Council-Manager plan, which Tallahassee had embraced for many years. A strong mayor was proposed in 1973 but was dumped in succeeding efforts. While the City provided the basic model for a consolidated government, it is significant that all these proposals retained the County's traditional pattern of row officers. The Sheriff and all the other Constitutional positions were continued, which suggested how deep was the commitment to the election of local officials.

The Launch of the 1992 Campaign

It was the involvement of Representative Al Lawson in 1990 that moved things to a vote two years later. First, he wanted to be assured there was real community commitment to considering consolidation. He asked that he be presented with a petition holding 10,000 signatures before he would seek enabling legislation to establish a consolidation charter committee. Within a relatively short time 7,000 signatures were collected, and that convinced Lawson the community meant business. Lawson's concern was important because a major criticism of earlier efforts was that there had been insufficient community involvement.

It was a time when relations between the City and County were causing considerable concern. Issues producing tension involved growth management and relations between the City police and the County Sheriff.

Progress toward a decision on consolidation moved on schedule. The legislature approved the enabling legislation in early 1990, and the plan for a charter committee was laid before the electorate in November, 1990. This preliminary skirmish produced a highly positive vote, 33,240 in favor to 23,569 against, a 59%-41% margin. At the time there was considerable optimism that consolidation was in the offing.

The charter committee of 23 members was designed to reflect the many interests in the community. Nearly half the members, 10, were nominated by organizations deemed to have a special stake in the character of the local government, ranging from the Chamber of Commerce to the NAACP to the Sierra Club to the Police Benevolent Association (the union in the Tallahassee Police Department). The Presidents of the two universities, Florida State and FAMU, agreed to represent their institutions; and President Bernard Sliger of FSU was elected chairman. The other 13 members were nominated by the State legislative delegation (3), the City (5), and the County (5).

Between January and December, 1991, the charter committee met 35 times, usually discussing issues among themselves. There was very little outside attendance at the sessions, though the Tallahassee City Manager and the Leon County Administrator regularly attended. Other officials of the two governments, with big stakes in the outcome of the deliberations, also made regular appearances. A mainstay was the reporter for the *Tallahassee Democrat*, Margaret Leonard, who produced over 100 articles and news briefings about consolidation during the year. The publisher of *The Democrat*, Carrol Daddisman, was a strong supporter of consolidation and on occasion expressed his view in the pages of the newspaper.

The Proposed Charter

What emerged from the committee deliberations was a Tallahassee-style structure. The leadership role was assigned to a chairman of an enlarged legislative body, given the title of Mayor. He would chair the policy body, sit with two others on the budget committee, and have the power to line item veto the capital budget. The obvious intent was to make a small concession to the strong mayor idea.

Issues involving representation on the policy body received a great deal of attention. It had been a matter of importance in the earlier consolidation efforts. The conclusion was that the new Commission should be composed of eight members chosen by district, plus the Mayor elected at large. That was larger than the City Commission, which numbered five, and the County Commission, with seven members.

The drawing of districts from which the representatives would come posed real difficulties. Ultimately, it was decided to enlist the services of the Supervisor of Elections, who developed a proposal for four districts of roughly equal size from each of which two representatives would be elected. The plan was adopted without much debate, there being considerable relief that the tedious process of drawing district lines had been handled. The legislative jobs were to be part-time, with the salary set at $20,000 per year.

In previous consolidation proposals there had been a pronounced trend toward non-partisan election of these local officers. That seemed to be the predisposition of this charter committee as well, voting 11-7 in April for a non-partisan ballot. Surprisingly, that decision did not hold. At a turbulent meeting in December, the committee registered 11-9 in favor of partisan balloting. Seven of the committee members changed their votes.

Following the approach taken in Jacksonville and in the previous consolidation attempts in Tallahassee-Leon, the charter committee established two taxing districts. One, coterminous with the city, was designed to provide a full range of urban services and to secure the revenues to support them. All the utility income, which was a major part of city financing, was to be spent in this district. The other district, rural services, basically ratified the level of county activity in the unincorporated area. It carried a lower tax rate.

At the time the establishment of these two taxing districts aroused little discussion. Left unaddressed was the reality that the county was already experiencing difficulty in providing and financing needed services to its non-city population. A provision to deal with this problem in the longer run aroused bitter opposition in the rural area. It declared that the governing body could shift the boundaries between the urban and rural taxing districts on its own initiative after the consolidated government had operated for two years. What may not have been fully appreciated was that Tallahassee's highly active and successful annexations had largely come in uninhabited areas, arranged by developers anxious for its utilities. The referendum requirement in inhabited annexations was seen as an important safeguard by those who wanted no part of the city.

The administrative structure was classically Council-Manager. A Manager would be the operating head, with virtually all key people reporting to him/her. He/she would be accountable to the Commission and serve at its pleasure. And the traditional rules of Council-Manager government would apply, the Commissioners being required to work through the Manager on all matters pertaining to the bureaucracy.

With a couple of exceptions, the Manager would deal with a fully accountable staff. There would be no Constitutional officers. The Clerk of the Court would no longer have control over finances; and an elected Treasurer-Clerk would report to the commission, similar to the arrangement in the city. Two other Constitutional officers, the Property Appraiser and the Supervisor of Elections, would remain elective but serve under the charter, not the Constitution. The position of Tax Collector would be abolished, and its functions merged into the regular bureaucracy.

By far the most hotly contested issue was the future of the Constitutional Sheriff. The political battle lines were formidable. The police department had its own representative on the charter commission, appointed by its union. While the Sheriff had no official representative on the commission, he was one of the most powerful figures in town. His was an office accustomed to doing favors, and there were many chits that could be called in. Neither side was in any mood to compromise. The police officers said they would vigorously oppose the consolidation were a Constitutional Sheriff included in the plan. On the other hand, the powerful Sheriff said he would accept nothing but Constitutional status. He declared a charter-elected Sheriff, as was operating in Jacksonville, "wrong."

Of the two, the Tallahassee police department was far the larger and more professionalized. It handled two-thirds of the calls in the county for service; and it took care of three-fourths of the felony crime. There were charges that the two agencies duplicated services, and a Grand Jury investigation in 1991 declared that about $1.2 million a year was lost in waste and duplication.

The decision over policing also had significant union implications. The City police department was fully unionized, the Sheriff's department was not. Further, the Sheriff declared there was no way in which he would allow unions in his organization. Thus there was no room for accommodation. If a Constitutional Sheriff were included in the charter, union presence in policing was dead. The Police Benevolent Association was not likely to accept that.

With such truculence, the charter committee had to accept one bad alternative or the other. It decided to go with the City model and made the director of law enforcement appointive, at the same time separating policing from corrections, which was another responsibility of the Sheriff.

The decision seemed to satisfy no one. All those who wanted a Sheriff were obviously unhappy, but others who favored the City solution were also worried. They knew this was a big enough issue to bring down the whole consolidation effort. The Chamber of Commerce led a move to create a charter-elected Sheriff. Others felt the issue was so divisive that the present arrangement of two police departments ought to be included in the charter, with a provision for resolution at a later date.

At this point Representative Lawson entered the picture. Such waffling was unacceptable. He said the charter had to deal with the problem and resolve the matter of law enforcement duplication. At a meeting in December the charter committee returned to the issue and took up the Chamber of Commerce proposal for a charter-elected Sheriff. The Chamber idea was defeated 13-8, leaving the powerful Sheriff an implacable enemy of consolidation.

With the charter now in reasonably final form, four public hearings were held. Attendance was poor. The total time involved in the four meetings was about seven hours, with 56 people speaking and six appearing at more than one meeting. In the rural areas the concerns tended to focus on two issues: a perceived loss of representatives for the rural localities and the elimination of the Sheriff. In the urban areas the issues were more diverse.

After the hearings, the charter committee held a meeting that lasted eight hours. Much controversial ground was again traversed, but the charter remained unchanged. On December 12, 1991, the committee voted 18-3, with two absent, to propose the charter for the November ballot. There is only one well articulated statement of reasons for opposing the charter. It came from an African-American, the appointee of an African-American City Commissioner. He felt the charter was "... not good for blacks." At-large elections in the City and two Commissioner races in the County were bringing significant African-American victories. He thought the proposed district system would be a negative for minority interests. Finally, he concluded that the consolidation was wrong because it merged a progressive City and a conservative County.

The charter was then presented to the legislative delegation, which specified there should be another hearing. That meeting was held on January 13, 1992, and attracted a large crowd. Few spoke against consolidation. It appeared that things were in good shape.

Charter Goes on Ballot—and to a Crushing Defeat

After the January 13 meeting, approval was given to put the charter on the ballot, with only a few technical changes.

There had been limited polling of citizen attitudes toward consolidation, and the results had been mixed. The most authoritative involved 861 respondents and was completed in November, 1991, too late to have a great effect on the charter committee deliberations. The good news was that more than half the respondents said they were generally in favor of consolidation; but the bad side was that more than half declared they had not heard anything about the issues involved. As it turned out, it was even more disquieting that roughly 75% declared their preference for an elected law enforcement head; over two-thirds indicated their preference for a strong Mayor, rather than an appointed City Manager; and less than half supported the elimination of the Tax Collector position and the transfer of the Clerk of Court's financial duties. The poll certainly indicated where the trouble spots were.

More reassuring but not altogether satisfying were the findings of the annual City of Tallahassee poll of its citizens, held in March, 1992. Of the 815 citizens who responded, 45% declared themselves in support of consolidation and 29% opposed. Worrisome were the 26% who said they had no opinion on the issue. Informing and convincing them of the virtues of consolidation would certainly be an imperative in the forthcoming election.

There were two elections in 1992 that may have had an influence on the November outcome. The first was a referendum in March on shifting the District School Superintendent from elective to appointive status. The issue was tightly contested with the move to an appointed Superintendent defeated 51% to 49%. The African-American community did not support the change. The results provided further evidence that the citizens of Leon County liked to elect people.

The other event was the primary election of the Democratic party in September. It was a great victory for the minority community because an African-American won the nomination for one of the County's at-large seats. The significance was that he was able to garner support throughout the area, not just in the African-American community. It showed the power of the minority group to obtain leadership positions in a community that was still predominantly white. The incumbent Sheriff, who had established himself as opposed to consolidation except on his terms, came very close to being defeated. He won by 1,000 votes, with 40,000 cast. It should be noted that Leon County was overwhelmingly Democratic and victory in the primary meant success in November.

There was another aspect of the primary election in September that may have influenced the consolidation outcome. It was decided by the leaders that the campaign should be restricted to the time between the primary and general elections, leaving about eight weeks for an effort. The theory was that there was too much going on earlier, and voters would not be ready to think about consolidation.

Even so, the consolidation forces had a great advantage. They raised and spent about $50,000, with another $10,000 of in-kind contributions. The campaign against the charter was minimal, concentrated in the last 10 days, and involved expenditures of about $16,000.

But these formal figures were perhaps only the tip of the iceberg. While neither the City nor the County took an official position, there was a solid phalanx of County officers who were active and vociferous in their opposition, most notably the Sheriff. An African-American County commissioner, well known and respected in her community, announced herself strongly opposed. On the other hand, the City Commission appeared divided. Two were for consolidation, two took no position, and one, another African-American, was opposed.

The list of supporters for consolidation was long and generally composed of establishment groups. The opponents were few. Significantly, they included two African-American organizations, the NAACP and the Southern Christian Leadership Conference. The County officials, of course, formed a solid front.

The campaign for consolidation was at best low key and at worst listless. Only about a third of the charter committee members were active in it, and the general observation was that the perceived leaders of the community did not get involved. It was difficult to argue there would be any real savings from the merger; and, indeed, the Sheriff claimed that putting the two police forces together would require an expenditure of an extra $1.7 million a year.

The campaign themes were largely generalities, with few evidences provided that the fairly massive changes would have an effect on day-to-day operations. Where the pros argued that there would be greater accountability with one government rather than two, the antis countered that two good governments would be replaced by one big bureaucracy and that bigger government is not better government.

The pros fixed on a major issue between the two governments, growth management, and claimed that a single decision system would work better. They also declared that home rule would be advanced, noting that Leon County currently operated under the general laws of the State and had little discretion.

The antis made a Populist argument. They said that citizens would be allowed to vote for fewer people and that the reform required giving up the elected Sheriff.

In general it was a flat campaign, in which the pros' conception of change was not framed in commanding and compelling ways and the antis could rely on the citizen disposition to prefer no change over change.

Despite the lackluster campaign, the election results were a great shock. Consolidation lost by a huge amount, far beyond margins that had been recorded in earlier efforts. The proposal was coupled with the ballot for U.S. President, and so turnout was high, 83% of eligible voters. Further, about 95% voted on consolidation, recording 36,833 in favor and 55,814 opposed. It was clearly a great defeat.

The beating occurred throughout the area, with only eight precincts favoring consolidation. Five of these eight were in the city's affluent northeast. In 33 precincts, on the other hand, the opposition vote was greater than two to one. In two the margin of defeat was 10 to 1.

Further analysis showed that the African-Americans, the majority of whom lived in the City, recorded 7,496 votes against and 3,734 for, close to a 2-1 margin. Residents in the rural areas registered a vote of about 70% against, 8,484 opposed and 3,967 for. Even in the northeast and downtown, consolidation lost, though by small margins. In the south and northwest, the votes against were more than 60% of the total.

What Happened? Why Such a Defeat?

Although the circumstances prevailing in Tallahassee-Leon will not be duplicated elsewhere, it is important to generalize on what happened in this case.

There is the question whether the decision on consolidation was that of an informed electorate. A year earlier, a poll indicated that about 25% of the respondents had no opinion on consolidation and were generally uninformed about the issues. A month or so later, the charter committee completed its work, and nothing was done about consolidation for the next eight months. Then there was a campaign of about eight weeks to inform the voters and press for a favorable vote.

Whether voters had a substantial incentive to interest themselves in the issues of consolidation is debatable. Certainly the concepts offered in the campaign were not electrifying. Further, it is not clear that the need for change really entered the consciousness of voters. In Jacksonville there was governmental chaos, with a major consensus that something had to be done. In Tallahassee-Leon there was a highly successful City government and a County that was seen as improving in quality and openness. The "no change" predisposition was attractive because there were no significant complaints about the present system. It may have seemed to some that this was more a theoretical claim for improvement than an anxiety about a really pinching shoe.

Florida tends to be a Populist state. Its citizens like the idea of electing people, which may explain the general reluctance to dispense with the row officers in the counties. Elections, in the popular belief system, are more enforcing of accountability than bureaucracies.

The lightening rod for this Populism in Florida is the Sheriff. While the Tallahassee police department drew high marks for its performance as a law enforcement agency, it was seen in far more bureaucratic terms. The Sheriff personalized policing. People felt his accountability to them. To deprive people of a vote on this office, then, was seen as a real loss.

There can be little doubt that handling the Sheriff was one of the most basic strategic issues facing the charter committee. It was really between a rock and a hard place because there was no give on the part of a Sheriff, who had just been re-elected for another four years. The Sheriff's absolute insistence on his continued status as a Constitutional officer, with his freedom to retain a non-union organization, had to harden the position of the unionized Tallahassee police department. Acceptance of a Constitutional Sheriff would have essentially abolished the highly professionalized, unionized City agency. Thus, there was no give, and the charter committee was required to make a decision that was bound to have immense political consequences.

There was, of course, a way out: an elected Sheriff as a charter officer. It was a compromise proposed by the Chamber of Commerce and voted down, 13 to 9, by the charter committee. The consequence of that vote was foreordained. It left nothing resolved because the Sheriff insisted his office remain Constitutional.

A few turns of fate might have made the charter arrangement eminently viable. If Dale Carson of Jacksonville had been Sheriff, there would have been no problem. He believed in consolidation and was willing to compromise on elected charter status. There is no doubt that his immense credibility did much to tilt Jacksonville-Duval toward consolidation. Someone like him might have made a big difference in Tallahassee-Leon. And it would have taken only 501 votes to give Tallahassee a new Sheriff in 1992. The losing candidate had been an executive in the Tallahassee police department before his retirement. With his background, he likely would have been much more inclined toward merger and a change in his status to charter. The reality was, of course, that an uncompromising Sheriff was in office, and he fought savagely against consolidation.

Though it never gained great consideration in the charter committee deliberations, the strong mayor idea may have been a more significant factor in voter thinking than is generally thought. Bear in mind that the system in both City and County Commissions was one of rotating leadership. That held considerable appeal, particularly in the African-American community where recent election triumphs were putting minorities in line for leadership. The proposal to create a Mayor elected at large but with very little power seemed almost the worst of all worlds. Leadership status would be denied a number of key people, with virtually no gain in terms of a strong and powerful executive leader.

It is also possible that the Council-Manager plan of the City of Tallahassee did not inspire as much support as might have been thought. The Manager in office at that time, a highly regarded and thorough-going professional, was believed by virtually everyone to have played a significant leadership role in bringing the City its success. Yet, even with the accolades provided him for his accomplishments and capacities, he was an appointed leader. For some he was unaccountable because they saw the Commission doing his bidding. It should be emphasized these were perceptions, not necessarily the reality, but the presence of a strong Manager may have offended the Populist inclinations of the electorate. They may have been disappointed that the strong Mayor, who seems to have played such a major role in the Jacksonville experience, was not included in consolidation plans.

Minor though they may have seemed in the grand scheme of things, issues of representation seemed still to trouble voters with Populist orientations. The raw numbers were somewhat bothersome. The City voter was currently casting a ballot for eight different policy making positions. He/she made a choice for all five on the City Commission, which operated under an election at-large system; and he/she also elected three County Commissioners, one from a district and two at large. Under the consolidation proposal, the City voter's ballot involvement was cut by two-thirds to three people, the Mayor elected at large and two representatives from a district.

In the county, things were not nearly so dire. Under the existing system, one voted for three people (two commissioners at large and one from a district). There would be the same number of votes under the charter. However, the change meant that the individual would be voting for three people on a board of nine, rather than for three of seven.

If influence is measured by the number of people for whom you vote, reductions are bad. Some concluded that these reductions in perceived influence alienated a considerable number of voters.

Finally, the seemingly innocuous establishment of the taxing areas under a new consolidated government held a political booby trap. It was the provision that the commissioners could reset taxing district lines after two years of consolidated government. For some in the county this was a provision fraught with peril. They had felt secure in their resistance to City intrusion on their unincorporated land by the requirement of a referendum of property owners in the affected area. The history of annexation in Florida made it quite clear that the acquiescence of affected property owners was hard to get. They felt safe in their rural status. The ability of the consolidated Commission to reset the boundaries without their agreement would change all that. For some it was a highly important issue.

Overall, it is easy to see why the consolidation effort failed. It is always difficult to mobilize support for change; and it is apparent that people have to feel real imperatives to amend their accustomed ways of doing things. That has led to the theory that "triggering events" must provoke action by a typically lethargic body politic.

The incentives for change were not apparent in the Tallahassee-Leon situation, which may account for the relatively limited involvement of the leadership in the campaign for consolidation. It may also suggest that the citizenry felt little need to learn the details about consolidation because they had already made up their minds that consolidation was neither important nor necessary.

Another theme was Populism, seen in Florida as the primacy of the individual and his/her ability to influence the course of government events, largely through voting. A common belief is that elected officials are inherently more accountable than those in a bureaucracy. In Florida's counties, the Sheriff is the prime example of this belief in the elected official, and it is always politically difficult to tamper with him as a person or as an office. Even shifting his status from Constitutional officer to a charter officer seems difficult. The charter commission certainly experienced that problem, where it had to contend with the personal power of the Sheriff and also with the broader dimensions of Populist feelings among the electorate.

Though Leon was unique among Florida's counties because its single city, Tallahassee, boasted about two-thirds of its population, this institutional arrangement did not prove to be enough. The people spoke. They roundly rejected a change that worked in Jacksonville.

III. SUMMARY

Consolidation is a very attractive structural arrangement for a large urban community. It is simple. There is one government which is clearly accountable. If it is so attractive, why is it so seldom employed? The answer is equally simple, obvious. Other governments on the scene do not take kindly to their abolition. They are a formidable obstacle to the development of a one-tier government.

There are relatively few places where conditions are ripe for consolidation. Ideally, there should not be a large number of governments in the area, thus keeping the centers of resistance at a minimum. In Florida the optimum structural situation is found in Leon County, where the City of Tallahassee possesses about two-thirds of the population, and the remaining one-third is unincorporated.

Duval was almost as inviting. It had five municipalities, but Jacksonville was overwhelmingly dominant. It was the major actor; and the other four probably counted themselves lucky to survive the establishment of the consolidated government. Today two-tier government is provided to about five percent of the Jacksonville population, though the smallest recently contracted with the Sheriff for police services.

Jacksonville is a case where the governments, both of the City and of the County, had deteriorated to such a point that action was an imperative. It was a reform born of crisis. Strange organization concoctions in both jurisdictions were bound to leave things in chaos. The City arrangement was called a commission-council plan, in which a nine-member council made the policy and a five-member Commission executed it.

Consolidation was overwhelmingly approved in Jacksonville. The margin was 2-1, with more than 86,000 people voting. Not only did this ballot success bring dramatic reform to Jacksonville but also provided it with new status. Jacksonville immediately became the largest city in the world, in terms of the land area within its jurisdiction. And it rose to No. 27 from No. 75 among America's most populous cities.

While the fact of consolidation was the single most significant feature of this reform, the adoption of the strong mayor structure has also proved to be highly important. It was a dramatic departure for Jacksonville, which had contended with all kinds of commissions and other forms of plural leadership. Yet there seemed to be little difficulty adapting to this new system. While individual Mayors have come in for their share of criticism, the strong mayor structure itself has become deeply imbedded in the Jacksonville culture. The six Mayors who have served under the consolidated government have enjoyed substantial stability. Three of the five whose service has been completed have been re-elected, and the average length of service has been about six and one-half years. By 2007 two other large counties in Florida had moved to a form of the strong mayor plan. It is rather regularly suggested for others as well.

As has been regularly observed in these pages, the Sheriff is a highly important political figure in Florida's counties. It was certainly evident in the fight to secure change in Jacksonville. The Sheriff at the time, who held a Constitutional office, declared his support for consolidation and agreed to change his position to elective charter. Thus citizens still had the power to elect their Sheriff, undoubtedly a concern for many, but he worked successfully within the organizational framework of the consolidated government and was a campaign positive, not a negative.

In general, the consolidation has been regarded as a success. In a book published in 2004, James B. Crooks wrote, "For Jacksonville, consolidation proved to be the right move."

Most of the criticism in recent years appears to have come from the African-American community. It has not been happy with the economic situation of its people, who are not considered to have shared fully in the economic gains of the community. There has also been dissatisfaction with the Sheriff, whose policing practices are seen as discriminatory toward minorities.

Certainly Jacksonville's experience has been successful enough to argue for its replication elsewhere in the state. However, such a transfer is much easier said than done. There are, of course, many rural counties in the state where the issues raised in the urban setting of Jacksonville do not appear. Among the larger urban counties, the presence of a large central city and the absence of many satellite municipalities are rarely to be found. Only Tallahassee, with 65% of the population in the County and with no competing cities, seems fully to meet the conditions that make this major reform possible. Other cities like Tampa, St. Petersburg, and Cape Coral house within their borders barely more than 25% of the County's population. And all co-exist with many other municipalities.

As might be expected, there have been efforts in Tallahassee-Leon to secure consolidation. The most major undertaking was in 1992, when a consolidation charter was developed and put to a vote. Despite the many favorable conditions, that undertaking went down to a crushing defeat. It left many with the belief that Jacksonville was a highly unique event in Florida and that the possibilities of consolidation, of securing a one-tier government, were virtually nil.

Fortunately, a respected city manager, Jack M. Schluckebier, wrote a doctoral dissertation on the drive to consolidate the Tallahassee City and Leon County governments in 1992. His work has permitted a careful examination of this experience.

What emerges from his study is that situational factors were significant determinants of the outcome. Inherently, there was a favorable structural condition (One major city, no competitors) that may have prompted a positive first response on the part of the citizenry. As we have often heard, however, the devil is in the details. As a 23-person committee, reasonably reflective of the community, began to put together a charter, there were many dilemmas. One was whether there were such serious failures in governance that a merger was needed to correct them. This line of thinking was generally unproductive because the City was considered a highly successful government and the County an improving one. It wasn't at all clear that the one government would perform much better than the two.

The lack of a real imperative to drive change has significant implications. It gives the *status quo* great presence. Change is difficult for all of us, and we seek change only when there is a tension between where we are and where we want to be. Clearly there was very little tension in this situation. It seemed quite reasonable to hang with the *status quo*.

There is always the problem of citizen lethargy, and the absence of tension in this situation posed real problems for the change agents. Not only was it difficult to develop excitement about the consolidation campaign, but there was a real question where voters had sufficient motivation to learn about the issues involved. It is possible that a large number of voters reacted to a few simple ideas in making their decisions at the ballot. To understand the charter and the issues involved really required substantial time. Given a perception of low stakes, it is possible that relatively few had much understanding what the election was all about.

Personalities—and particularly one—were highly important in framing the negative response. The Sheriff, a popular and powerful person in the community, was in no mood to compromise. The consolidation had to leave his Constitutional office untouched. On that issue he was unwilling to bend. But the charter committee had to contend with a professional, unionized City police department that did the larger share of policing in the community. Accepting the Sheriff's demands, with its non-union dimension, would really have meant the end of the Tallahassee police department. That was unacceptable, and so there was no way to work things out between the two sides. It was very different from Jacksonville, where the Sheriff supported consolidation, accepted charter status, and became a positive factor in the campaign.

There were other personalities, essentially all of them opposed to consolidation, who let the populace know how they felt. The Constitutional officers in the county, except the Supervisor of Elections, were vociferous. But it was the African-American leadership group which was particularly active. Basically, its members were satisfied with the *status quo* and distrusted a merged government.

Tallahassee-Leon provides an interesting case example of the many variables that affect collective decisions. In theory, one-tier government had a lot of positives; but they were insufficient to override a common feeling that a change of this magnitude was risky and not particularly necessary.

CHAPTER SEVEN

CHARTERING WITH ANTICIPATIONS OF SIGNIFICANT CHANGE: EXPERIENCE IN THREE COUNTIES

While the 1968 Florida Constitution provided a major opportunity for the counties of the State to use the home rule provision to customize their organization and operations to suit their own needs, there has been relatively little interest in doing so. As has already been reported, 48 of the 67 counties have not even taken the first step. They continue to operate under the general laws of the State, rather than setting up their own organic statutes.

Of the 19 with charters, two (Miami-Dade and Jacksonville-Duval) did not wait for a new Constitution. They took a more difficult route for their major reforms, securing Legislative and Statewide approval. That leaves 17 counties with charters adopted under the provisions of the 1968 Constitution. It would be an error to assume, however, that these 17 exploited the freedoms available to them to change appreciably the way they did business.

Only three appear to have taken their flexibility seriously. Three of the large urban counties—Broward, Orange, and Volusia—have engaged in some substantial revamping or made an effort to do so. There has been a testing of new approaches, some of which have been modified, and others jettisoned, as these counties sought the best ways of serving their citizens.

Each of these counties has charted its own course; and it is the purpose of this chapter to identify the various ways they have approached things. They share a common, physical character—big, urban, complex jurisdictions.

While all three are major units of government, as revealed in Table 4, Broward County is by far the largest. A part of the greater Miami metropolitan area, it is a huge land unit, with a population moving close to two million. It has the highest population density of the three, over three times that of Volusia. The scale of its operations, as indicated by its expenditures, is also significantly greater.

Municipalities exist throughout Broward county. The size of its unincorporated area, which includes slightly less than 3% of its population, is the lowest of any county in the state and raises implications for the kind of role it is likely to play in the metropolitan community. Its circumstance contrasts dramatically with Orange county, where 65% of the population lives in unincorporated areas.

TABLE 5

Comparative Characteristics of Broward, Orange, and Volusia Counties

Date Chartered	Name	2005 (est.) Population	Land size (sq. miles)	No. cities/ no. under 7000	% County Unincorp- orated.	Population Density (sq. mile)	2004 Outlays in Millions
1975	Broward	1,740,987	1209	31/5	3%	1346	$3,121,08
1986	Orange	1,043,437	908	13/7	65%	988	$1,994,54
1971	Volusia	494,699	1106	17/6	23%	401	$500,761

Where Broward is a key part of Florida's largest metropolitan complex, Orange and Volusia lie further up the coast and anchor metropolitan communities of lesser scale. Orange county, with the Disney theme parks, is a destination for tourists from all over the world. It continues to grow. Its 2005 estimated population was slightly over a million. What is really different from Broward is its urban situation. Because so much of the county is unincorporated, it is not surprising that it boasts far fewer municipalities, 13 as contrasted with 31 in Broward. Further, seven of those cities have populations less than 7,000, suggesting they may more likely depend on the County for urban services. In contrast, only five of Broward's 31 cities have a population of 7,000 or less, with a population average of about 15,000. About 1,680,000 people are citizens of Broward municipalities that have the capacity to provide a full range of services. Full service cities are available to serve only about one-third of Orange County residents.

Volusia, located further up the Florida east coast and therefore more removed from the state's principal population centers, has statistics that are reflective of this position. Though its land area is almost as large as Broward's, its population is less than half a million, only about one-third as big. Its expenditures are proportionately even smaller, about one-sixth those of Broward and only about one-fourth those of Orange. Its urban service obligations lie somewhere between Broward and Orange. About two-thirds of its residents live in full-service cities; and the County is likely to have obligations to meet urban needs for only about 130,000 of its residents.

I. VOLUSIA

Volusia was the first county to take advantage of the home rule powers granted in the new Florida Constitution of 1968. By 1969 a 21-member committee had begun work on a charter proposal, which culminated in a successful referendum on June 30, 1970. It took effect January 1, 1971.

What was unique about the charter was that it constituted a clean sweep from the classic pattern of county government. Adopted was the Council-Manager form that had achieved popularity in municipalities and was seen as the best vehicle for securing good and clean government. So devoted were the charter writers to the precepts of the municipal reform movement that the legislative body was named the Council, rather than the Commission.

The organization adopted was in accord with classic Council-Manager principles. There was the formal separation of the policy and execution processes, with the Council the policy body and the Manager in charge of administration. As was characteristic, the Council had a special power, in that the Manager was appointed and served at its pleasure. To reinforce the separation between policy and administration, the charter included a strong prohibition against any legislative intrusion in administrative operations. Such a provision has always been a defining component of a "true" Council-Manager government and has been subsequently adopted by Florida's charter counties in substantial degree. Article IV, Section 404 in the Volusia charter stipulates:

> Except for the purposes of inquiry and information, the council and committees or members thereof are expressly prohibited from interfering with the performance of the duties of any employee of the county government who is under the direct or indirect supervision of the county manager. Such action shall be malfeasance within the meaning of Article IV, Section 7 (a) of the Florida Constitution.

The Council is the small policy body typically found in Council-Manager governments, with seven members. Five are elected from districts and two at large. Members serve staggered, four year terms, and leadership and decision-making are shared.

In the early 70s there were increasing questions across the country whether the classic Council-Manager plan adequately provided a community with needed political leadership. It was generally agreed that this was a role the manager could not play, and the issue was whether a collective leadership had the credibility and the energy to fill such a role. Many thought not, and a separately elected mayor was increasingly appearing in Council-Manager cities. This was not a strong mayor system, as the manager continued in charge of the administrative system. The mayor remained on the council, typically chairing it, and was expected to utilize his greater legitimacy as mayor elected by all the people to become the political leader.

After 30 years of operating under the traditional system, Volusia county moved in 2002 to establish a position of political leadership. In a referendum vote, citizens approved a charter change that provided for at-large election of the chairman of the Council. Interestingly, the title given this new position was County Chair, not Mayor. However, the duties assigned are characteristic of those of a mayor in a Council-Manager city. He/she chairs the council and has a full vote, is the formal representative of the County, and is the ceremonial leader. There was no mention of political leadership responsibilities.

A real test for the Volusia effort at reform through the home rule provisions of the Constitution was the handling of the Constitutional officers. Would they remain? Or would the charter makers seek seriously to create a new structure in accord with Council-Manager norms? Would the administrative structure be integrated, with the Manager given the capacity to manage the whole system?

The charter makers, and ultimately the citizenry, registered strongly on this. The county norms were jettisoned. There would be no Constitutional officers in the Volusia County government. Nine "initial departments" were established which comprehended the full range of activities of the County. Four Constitutional offices—Sheriff, Property Appraiser, Tax Collector, and Supervisor of Elections—were abolished, and the Clerk of Court was no longer to be the auditor and custodian of funds.

The Department of Finance was to pick up the work of the Tax Collector as well as that of the Clerk of the Court. Three new departments were established, Public Safety to assume the Sheriff's responsibility; the Department of Property Appraiser, to do the property appraising; and the Department of Elections, to handle the tasks of the Supervisor of Elections. The provisions were unambiguous, as is to be seen in those that applied to the Sheriff: "All functions and duties now prescribed by the Constitution and laws of the state of Florida for the office of sheriff are hereby transferred to the department of public safety, and the constitutional office shall thereupon be terminated, further providing that all functions relating to corrections and rehabilitation, the county prison farm, the Volusia county jail, and all other similar facilities shall be transferred to the department of corrections." (Volusia County charter, Article VI, Section 601.1.)

At the same time the Constitutional officers were abolished, three elective charter positions were established: a sheriff, to head the department of public safety; a supervisor of elections; and a property appraiser. Each of these charter officers stands for election every four years.

In 2007 the Volusia County government was described in the following terms on its web site (March 10, 2007):

> Under Volusia County"s Council/Manager form of government, voters elect a County Council which consists of seven members that serve four-year terms. Five are elected by district: the County Chair and the At-Large representative are elected countywide.
>
> The County Council makes broad policy decisions much like the board of directors of a major corporation. It also reviews and approves the annual budget and passes ordinances as necessary.
>
> The County Council appoints a County Manager who is the County's chief executive officer and oversees the County's day-to-day operations.

The Volusia county organization chart, posted on the Internet March 10, 2007, reveals an administrative structure very different from that set forth in the original charter. Only one of the "initial departments" remains, Public Works. Three—Public Safety, Property Appraisal, and Elections—are now individualized. There is a Property Appraiser, an Elections Supervisor, and the Sheriff.

In some degree Volusia has returned to its original county moorings. It has three elected officials operating three significant functions within its administrative system. The Property Appraiser and the Elections Supervisor perform roughly similar tasks to those found in other counties. The Sheriff's role is somewhat circumscribed, in that corrections lies outside his authority. The difference from the traditional counties is that these three elected officials hold offices created under the charter, not under the Constitution. Their roles can be amended or abolished at any time by the community.

Two Constitutional offices have not resurfaced in their old form. The functions of the Tax Collector continue to be handled in the revenue unit and the Clerk of the Court has not regained any financial functions. That role is strictly concerned with the courts.

Two deputy county managers have direct supervision of the various units. One covers these activities:

Finance and Administrative services, which includes management and budget, personnel, finance (accounting and revenue), facilities, information technology, purchasing, and fleet management.

Community services, which include community assistance, library services, veterans services, agriculture extension, and Votran.

Other reporting units are community outreach, community information, economic development, airport and ports, ocean center, and internal auditor.

A second deputy county manager supervises three major units:

Growth and resource management, which includes land acquisition and management, leisure services, environmental management, planning and development, and building and zoning.

Public Works, which includes water resources and utilities, engineering, solid waste, road and bridge, mosquito control, and traffic engineering.

Public Protection, which includes fire services, corrections, animal control, medical examiner, emergency medical services, emergency management, and beach safety.

II. BROWARD

When the possibility of a charter was under consideration in Broward in 1973, there were the same problems of an outmoded county structure that confronted Volusia leaders, as well as others. With the great migration from the northeast to the Miami metropolitan area, Broward had experienced tremendous growth. That resulted in the creation of many new municipalities that contended for space, recognition, and viability in the County. What was the role of Broward County in this large, complex system?

A dissertation by Ronald Kenneth Vogel has been very helpful in understanding the Broward situation. It was completed in 1986 and is titled, *Decision Making in Broward County: A Political Economy Approach.* Vogel was fundamentally concerned with the Broward power structure and its behavior. Because he recognized that the County government constituted an important piece of that larger system, he devoted a chapter to it. That is the part of the dissertation we have found useful.[52]

---

52 Robert Kenneth Vogel, *Decision Making in Broward County: A Political Economy Approach.* (A Dissertation presented to the Graduate School for the PhD, University of Florida, 1986), 198 pages

Vogel traces the problems of the County in substantial degree to the nature and processes of its development, which were largely driven by construction interests. He writes:

> In the past, as a developer built a large development, he would go to Tallahassee and incorporate the area. This served the developer's need to control development and put needed infrastructure in place by drawing on municipal taxing powers without an aggressive city council regulating the types of development permitted. Developers could also avoid the need to comply with the County's or City's (if it were annexed) planning and zoning requirements. As development occurred and sufficient population moved in, a council would be set up. These development cities were by and large completed before citizens had sufficient power to challenge or request changes in the types of development to occur. Many cities are still dominated by developers today.
>
> While this pattern of development served the developers' needs rather nicely, it resulted in Broward having a very fragmented structure of government—29 municipalities and a weak County government that has a rural mindset. The municipalities were very independent and competitive. Development regulations were often very lax …
>
> … There is a long history of government reorganization in Broward County, which is rooted in a desire to overcome the fragmented governmental structure produced by rapid development.[53]

Reform efforts were directed to three basic areas: (1) improving the administrative structure of the county; (2) consolidating and rationalizing the municipalities; and (3) enlarging the role of the County as a means of achieving functional consolidation. Later, Vogel declared that reforms focused on "developing a strong and effective leadership" by creating a strong mayor government instead of the plural executive typically employed by the counties.

A government efficiency study in 1969 concentrated on two areas, the consolidation of municipalities and the merging of services. After a year, there were two basic recommendations: (1) reduce the number of 29 municipalities then existing; and (2) consolidate such services as water, sewer, fire, police, and beaches, parks, and recreation. "The effect of both proposals would have been to centralize authority in the County government," Vogel wrote, "by reducing the number of independent municipalities and providing for uniform service delivery of certain basic services by one central government."[54]

---

53   Ibid., pp. 94-96
54   Ibid., p. 98

The Legislative delegation, however, failed to take action. Nothing was done.

Growth was continuing at a break-neck pace, and the cumbersome County government provided a ready site for corruption and graft. Allegations of money mismanagement were appearing regularly in the press. Even the County Commissioners were persuaded of the need for reform.

It was within this context that the County Commission voted unanimously to ask the legislative delegation to establish a charter commission, composed of 15 members. Nine months of work resulted in a charter proposal, which was approved by referendum on November 5, 1974, with a vote of 77,889 in favor to 59,898 against. The charter took effect on January 1, 1975, making Broward the third county in the State to take such a step. Volusia was the first and Sarasota the second, both having established charters in 1971.

Clearly the new Broward charter was constructed with a view to what was politically acceptable in a community with dominant municipalities. Charter change was said to have gone as far as "practicable," and the campaign for its adoption particularly emphasized Broward's differences from its neighbor, Miami-Dade. The idea was not to create a central metropolitan government with powers over the municipalities *ala* Dade but to "streamline" the County government. Vogel summarizes a campaign paper of the time, which made these points:

1. The Dade charter established a Metro government with power to redraw city boundaries and determine functions and powers of cities.

2. Dade provided for a much greater degree of functional consolidation.

3. Dade gave commissioners more power to act "in the common interest of the people of the County."

4. Instead, the Broward approach established a limited County government lacking authority over municipalities except in the area of land use.[55]

While the Broward charter did not provide for the sweeping change found in Miami-Dade, it did constitute a major shift of power with respect to land use planning. It declared that municipal land use plans had to conform with those of the County. In effect, steps were taken to provide County-wide control over growth. Article XI. Section 11.0 of the charter states:

> Any county ordinance in conflict with a municipal ordinance shall not be effective within the municipality to the extent that a conflict exists regardless of whether such municipal ordinance was adopted or enacted after the county ordinance. A county ordinance shall prevail over municipal ordinances whenever the county acts with respect to the following:

---

55 Ibid., p.105

a.   Sets minimum standards protecting the environment through the prohibition or regulation of air or water pollution, or the destruction of resources in the county belonging to the public.

b.   Land use planning.

Vogel observed that the County was now in a position to coordinate growth management policies "unilaterally," not only in the unincorporated areas, but in the cities themselves. He continued, "Indeed, the County government now has the power to override individual cities' growth policies ... There is little doubt that any differences of opinion between the cities and County will be decided in favor of the County." He cited a charter provision that "... the powers granted by this charter shall be construed liberally in favor of the County government."[56]

The streamlining of the County government came with the establishment of a County Administrator with the power to hire and fire employees, and to coordinate the work of 65 departments previously reporting to the County Commission. Two Constitutional authorities were eliminated. The Tax Collector position was abolished, and the financial functions were separated from the Clerk of the Court. Article III, Section 3.06 of the charter declared, "The fiscal functions and duties now prescribed by the Constitution and the laws of the State of Florida for the office of the Clerk of the Circuit Court and the County Comptroller, which relate to these duties as the custodian of all county funds, auditor, and recordation of public documents shall be the responsibility of the department of Finance and Administrative Services."

Three Constitutional officers remained, the Sheriff, the Property Appraiser, and the Supervisor of Elections.

The membership of the Board of County Commissioners was increased from five to seven, originally with five elected by district and two at large. Soon after, in 1977, the pattern was changed, with all seven elected by district. There was also a short flirtation with the non-partisan election of commissioners, from 1976 to1980. At that time elections were made partisan again.

As had been the custom, the leadership of the Board continued to be rotated on a yearly basis. Election to the post was by a majority of Commission members, with re-election permitted. The chair continued to operate in a way that was largely a carryover from the non-charter times.

A significant change occurred with the redefinition of the roles of the Commission and the County Administrator. There was a separation between the legislative and administrative functions. The charter language. though, is not entirely specific. It declares, "The County Commission comprises the legislative

---

56 Ibid., p.101

branch ... the Administrative Branch is hereby created." It was only in 2002 that specific "non-interference" language was instituted. At that time the charter was amended to require the County Commission to adopt an ordinance that would prohibit interference by Commissioners with County employees. This non-interference requirement is important because, along with the charter statement, it enforces a basic principle of Council-Manager government. Aside from the fact that its elective officers are Constitutional and not charter, Broward's government now functions on many of the same precepts as Volusia's.

Ken Jenne, who was serving his ninth year as Sheriff in 2007, provides an interesting bridge to the past. A crusading prosecutor, he became executive director of Broward's charter commission in 1974. Vogel has cited some of his writings in that role: "On the management side, County government is unevenly administered, and lacks the necessary structure for strong and coherent adherence to the policies of the governing body. Professional management was unknown to County government ... The County Commission had functioned since 1915 wearing two hats, those of policy-maker and the administrator of day-to-day affairs."[57]

Jenne later served as chairman of the County Commission, then was elected to the State Senate. He stayed there for nearly two decades and was appointed Broward sheriff in 1998. He presides over an organization with 6,300 people that essentially lies outside the hierarchy under the County Administrator.[58]

It is interesting that Jenne's office provides contract law enforcement services to 14 of the 31 municipalities in the County. The Sheriff's service to the 14 cities is to be noted because of its collision with recommendations made by another efficiency committee reporting about a decade after the charter came into effect. Its mission was to tackle service delivery and functional merger issues, presumably avoiding the tense question of the cities-County relationship. Its basic proposal was that the County get out of the business of providing municipal services, an activity in which Sheriff Jenne is obviously engaging.

The committee clearly sought to establish two-tier government in Broward. Vogel quotes the committee:

> The committee feels two-level government will improve accountability by making an easily identifiable unit responsible for each government service.

---

57 Ibid., p.100.

58 Sadly, Ken Jenne resigned as Broward County Sheriff in early September, 2007. It was reported that he had agreed to plead guilty to three counts of tax evasion and one count of conspiracy to commit mail fraud. He could serve up to two years in prison, and the plea deal spared him the possibility of indictment on a more serious charge of money laundering. *The New York Times*, August 10, 2007. p. 23.

Better service and public facility planning will also result from a clear definition of the role and function of local government. The Committee recommends that Broward local government move toward service delivery on a system of two levels, municipal and areawide.[59]

The problem was that the committee found few functions that were really local. Considered area-wide were water, wastewater, solid waste, regional parks, social services, building inspection codes, and detention. Left to the cities were fire protection, neighborhood parks, and police road patrol.

The committee also raised the issue of political leadership. It proposed that a position of mayor be established, with election at large and with a principal responsibility to chair the County Commission. A strong mayor was not suggested and the committee envisioned a position very similar to that established in Volusia in 2002.

Neither the two-tier plan nor the elected mayor proposal found approval. They died.

Writing in 1986, Vogel reached three conclusions from his research:

1. The County will wind up providing area-wide services because the costs associated with them are beyond the financial capability of most municipalities.

2. It was doubtful that the County could withdraw from providing municipal-type services. He felt there would have to be some fundamental realignment of municipal boundaries to make such a change feasible. He pointed out that Broward, unlike Miami-Dade, did not have the authority to alter municipal boundaries.

3. He thought the strong mayor idea was far from dead, particularly noting that it had support in the Chamber of Commerce. He also felt that the adoption of the strong mayor would lead to single member districts in legislative bodies, rather than at-large systems.

Though he was writing over two decades ago, Vogel seems to have sized up the future quite insightfully.

Broward still is in the business of administering municipal-type services, as is particularly to be seen in the case of the Sheriff, where nearly half the municipalities depend on the County for law enforcement.

A rather significant revision of the charter occurred in March 14, 2000, when the size of the County Commission was increased from seven to nine members, all

---

59 Vogel, *op.cit.,* p. 108

to be chosen from districts on a partisan basis. Also imposed were term limits. No Commissioner could serve more than three four-year terms.

That the strong mayor idea was not totally dead appeared in the November, 2002, elections when a major revision of the charter was put to vote. Most of the changes were minor, but the word Mayor now appeared in the charter. The chair of the Commission was provided a new title and a few extra duties. Essentially, though, this was a matter of labeling. Broward had not really moved toward the strong mayor, but its lexicon now included the term. The charter change also revamped the position of Commission Auditor. The name was changed to County Auditor, a blue ribbon panel was to make recommendations on appointments, and the term of service was put at five years. The Auditor had freedom to roam among all county agencies, including the Constitutional officers.

It has been reported that the County's charter review committee is considering another strong mayor proposal, and it may be on the ballot in 2008. By early 2007 the battle lines were already being formed. A Broward County Commissioner was quoted as saying a strong mayor would upset the system's checks and balances and that the review committee should not think of the position as "benign."[60]

On its home page, on March 10, 2007, the Broward county government described itself:

> The County Administrator is the chief executive officer of Broward County Government and directs the day-to-day functions of County government under the auspices of the Broward County Board of County Commissioners.
>
> The nine-member elected Board of County Commissioners is the legislative branch of Broward County Government. A separation between the legislative and administrative functions of County Government is provided for in the Broward County Charter, which was established in 1975.
>
> As a regional provider of programs and services to its residents and visitors, Broward County employs over 7,000 employees [*this figure apparently does not include the 6,300 in the Sheriff's department*] in nearly 100 different agencies in the areas of transportation, human services, planning and recreation. Broward County's regional services include one of the nation's fastest growing airports, a bustling international seaport, an award-winning library system, an ever-growing mass transit network, an expanding park system, and a variety of community services.
>
> While the diversity of Broward's population of 1.7 million creates unique challenges in delivering services and providing information to our citizens, that diversity also contributes to a dynamic cultural environment that makes

---

60   Madeline Baro Diaz, *Miami Herald on line,* January 23, 2007.

Broward County one of the interesting and robust places in the world to live and work.

The Broward administrative structure that falls under the policy dictates of the County Commissioners and the managerial direction of the County Administrator is large and complex.

There are two staff agencies reporting directly to the Commissioners: the County Attorney and the County Auditor.

The Administrator has a large staff, including a deputy and two assistant administrators. In addition there are six staff offices: management and budget, economic development, office of public and government relations, office of equal opportunity, emergency management agency, and the greater Ft. Lauderdale convention and visitor bureau.

Seven departments form the core of the structure:

Environmental Protection, which includes air quality, biological resources, environmental monitoring, pollution prevention and mediation, and water resources.

Human Services, which includes childrens' services, elderly and veterans services, family success, medical examiner trauma, program development and evaluation, and substance abuse and health care.

Urban Planning and Development, which includes building code services, development management, housing and community development, planning services, and transportation planning.

Aviation, which includes administration, business, finance, information systems, operations, and planning and development.

Community Services, which includes animal care and regulation, consumer affairs, cultural division, extension education, libraries, mass transit, and parks and recreation.

Port Everglades, which includes business administration, business development, finance, and operations.

Public Works and Transportation, which includes construction management, facilities maintenance, fleet services, highway and bridge maintenance, highway construction and engineering, seaport construction and planning, traffic engineering, waste and recycling services, water and wastewater services.[61]

---

61 From *Departmental Structure of Broward County,* posted on the Internet March 9, 2007.

III. ORANGE

Where both Volusia and Broward sought charters early, Orange was more leisurely. Including Miami-Dade and Jacksonville, nine counties had been chartered by 1986, when Orange and Charlotte counties achieved such status.

In many ways Orange has continued to operate like a traditional county government. There is, however, one big difference. It diverged greatly from the others in the way in which it handled the political leadership question.

In November, 2004, its strategic direction was fully legitimized when the leader of the Orange County government was recognized as Mayor. His situation does not leave him "weak," and yet he is to be differentiated from the occupants of "strong mayor" positions in other local governments. As other counties in Florida struggle with issues of leadership, Orange County will continue to deserve special observation.

We have little knowledge of the forces that propelled Orange's citizens to vote the adoption of a charter in November, 1986. It is likely, however, that it was not considered an earth-shattering event. It did not contain any of the bombshells that were present in Miami-Dade, Jacksonville, and Volusia. There appeared to be a greater commitment, however, to non-partisan local elections in Orange than was the case in other parts of the state. As a result, a significant feature of the new charter was the abolition of all the Constitutional officers. They continued to be elective, however, but in charter, non-partisan positions.

The charter provided that "… all Charter offices shall be nonpartisan. No candidate shall be required to pay any party assessment or be required to state the party of which the candidate is a member. All candidates' names shall be placed on the ballot without reference to party affiliation." (Article IV, Section 605)

The non-partisan stipulation lasted only about 10 years, however. The Sheriff, the Property Appraiser, and the Tax Collector were returned to Constitutional status (and partisan election) in January, 1997. Sub-section A of Section 703 of the charter was specific about the change. It said:

> The charter offices of property appraiser, tax collector and sheriff formerly created by this section 703 are abolished. The functions and duties of each of these respective charter offices are transferred to the property appraiser, tax collector, and sheriff as county officers under Article VIII, Section 1(d) of the Florida Constitution and each of these offices is hereby reestablished …
>
> This sub-section A shall take effect on January 8, 1997 …

In 2007 there was the customary array of row offices in Orange County. The three transferred to Constitutional status in 1997 continued, as well as the Supervisor of Elections. The Clerk of the Court, still elected, had no financial responsibilities. An elected Comptroller discharged those functions, and there was also an elected Medical Examiner. In this respect, then, Orange was structured very much in the traditional pattern, fairly similar to the non-charter counties.

The big difference, as already reported, was the major move toward individual political leadership. Not long after the charter had been adopted, in November, 1988, "a new form" of government was adopted by Orange County voters. It called for the chairman of the seven person governing board to be elected at large, the only one to go before the entire county. The other six came from districts.

Mel Martinez, in 2007 a U.S. Senator from Florida, was serving as chairman of the board when he was selected by incoming President George W. Bush to serve as Secretary of the U.S. Department of Housing and Urban Development in his new administration assuming office in 2001. Richard W. Crotty, a Republican long active in Florida politics and at the time the elected Property Assessor, was appointed by the Florida Governor to succeed Martinez. Crotty was overwhelmingly re-elected in 2002. Then, in November, 2004, voters approved a change in his position title from Chairman to Mayor. Orange county had put the preferred label on one of the most powerful leadership positions in Florida counties.

Crotty's position is very different from that of the typical strong mayor. The traditional separation of powers does not exist in Orange County. As chairman of the Board, the Mayor has a major hand in legislative affairs. But, once policies are established, he has the responsibility for seeing that they are carried out. There is no separation for him. He is a big actor in both realms of policy and execution.

It is interesting that the charter's Article I, Section 108, Division of powers, declares that there is a separation between the legislative and executive. It states: "This Charter hereby establishes the separation between the legislative and executive functions of the government; the establishment and adoption of policy shall be the responsibility of the legislative branch, and the execution of that policy shall be the responsibility of the executive branch."

What does not appear to have been contemplated, however, is that the same person will play a central role in both branches. In that sense the approach is very different from strong mayor governments elsewhere and raises the further question whether this can be conceived as a separation of powers in fact.

There is also a bit of an irony in that the charter contains a "non-interference" provision (Section 212) that prohibits Commissioners "… from interfering with employees, officers, or agents under the direct or indirect supervision of the County Mayor [who is, of course, himself the chairman of the Commission].

From another perspective, these provisions make it clear that the position of Mayor comprehends great power. Thirteen duties are assigned the Mayor in the charter (Article III, Section 302, D), revealing his pivotal presence in the system.

As might be expected, the list focuses on the two big parts of the Mayor's responsibilities.

In his *legislative* role, he calls the board into regular and special sessions; serves as chair; votes on all matters, prepares and publishes agendas for all meetings, and signs ordinances, resolutions, and documents for the Board.

In his *executive* role, he manages the operations of all elements of County government under the jurisdiction of the Board consistent with the policies, ordinances and resolutions enacted by the Board; appoints and dismisses heads of County departments, divisions and other agencies under the jurisdiction of the Board except that all appointments shall be made annually and shall be subject to confirmation by the Board; assures the faithful execution of all ordinances, resolutions and orders of the Board and all laws of the State which are subject to enforcement by the County Mayor or by officers who are subject under this charter to the Mayor's direction and supervision; is responsible for the execution of all contracts and legal matters; presents annually at a time designated by the Board, a "state of the County" message, setting forth programs and recommendations to the Board; supervises the daily activities of employees; and carries out other powers and duties as required by this charter or might be prescribed by the Board.

The thirteenth responsibility is ambassadorial: "serve as the official representative and ceremonial dignitary for the government of Orange County, with prerogative to issue proclamations."

Such a list is all-encompassing, and it argues that the Orange Mayor position deserves a careful review of its performance in carrying out its broad leadership obligations. It is important to keep in mind, of course, that significant parts of the County government lie outside the jurisdiction of the Mayor or the governing Board.

In providing leadership to his community, the Mayor does not face many of the inter-governmental problems of Broward county. Even in 2005 roughly two-thirds of the Orange population continued to reside in the unincorporated area; and the only large city in the County was Orlando, with a population of about 217,000, roughly 20% of the Orange total. Nevertheless, the charter did recognize the County's role as a regional agency. It declared that the County would set minimum standards for regulating adult entertainment and for protecting the environment.

The special place of the municipalities in the governmental system was specifically recognized. While the County was free to establish standards for the whole area, they operated in the municipalities only when the cities had not met such minimum levels. More generally it declared that "... No County ordinance shall be effective within a municipality if the municipality maintains an ordinance covering the same subject matter, activity or conduct as the County ordinance." (Article VII, Section 704)

Generally speaking, Orange charter makers chose to operate within roughly the same set of constraints as the non-charter counties.

An organization chart, which carries no title but has a date of January 9, 2007, covers only that portion of Orange county under the Mayor and the Board of County Commissioners, both of whom occupy a single box at the top of the chart. Omitted are the elective officers responsible for major functions, Sheriff, Property Appraiser, Tax Collector, Supervisor of Elections, and Comptroller. There are other elective officers but they are in the judiciary.

The County Administrator, who is appointed by the Mayor and confirmed by the Board but who serves at the pleasure of the Mayor, has three staff offices reporting directly to him, three deputy county administrators, and a director of public safety.

The three staff officers are county attorney, government relations, and professional standards.

One deputy county administrator supervises the following units: human resources, communications, information systems and services, purchasing and contracts, business development, economic trade and tourism development, management and budget, fiscal and business services, risk management, and the convention center.

A second deputy county administrator supervises community and environmental services, including parks and recreation, code enforcement, environmental protection, animal services, neighborhood service, fiscal and human resources; administrative services, including real estate management, facilities management, energy management, fiscal and human resources, fleet management; health and family services, including citizens' committee for children, cooperative extension, youth and family services, mosquito control, community action, head start, corrections, health services, fiscal and human resources, mental health and homeless issues, regional history center, medical directorate.

The third deputy county administrator supervises utilities, including fiscal and administrative support, solid waste, engineering, water reclamation, water, customer services, construction, public works, including traffic engineering, development engineering, storm water management, roads and drainage, fiscal and administrative, transportation planning, public works engineering, highway construction; and growth management, which includes building, planning, zoning, housing and community development, and fiscal and administrative services.

The director of public safety supervises fire rescue, including fire administration, fire operations, emergency management, logistics, fire communications, training and information technology; corrections, including in-custody support services, in-custody security management, professional services, inmate programming support, community corrections, human resources/fiscal; and public safety communications and drug free communications.

IV. SUMMARY

One of the first two counties to charter under the 1968 Constitution was Volusia. The year was 1971; Sarasota also chartered in that year.

It is possible that the action by the Volusia voters most conformed with the hopes and aspirations of the framers of the Florida Constitution. They sought to provide the counties with the freedoms that the municipalities had come to enjoy. It was likely anticipated that the counties would leap to their new opportunities. Nearly 40 years after the grant of these new discretions, however, there has hardly been a leap. Better to call it a tentative step.

Back in 1971 Volusia suggested a promising future. It essentially wiped the slate clean and adopted a governing style quite removed from county traditions. It borrowed extensively from municipal experience and adopted a form of government that enjoyed great popularity among mid-size cities in the United States, the Council-Manager system. This approach clearly separates the policy and administrative functions, with a small elected board setting the course and providing sufficient oversight to be certain that things are staying on track.

The responsibility for managing the affairs of government falls to an official who is appointed and is generally chosen for his professional credentials. He/she is identified as the manager and serves at the pleasure of the policy board.

That is an approach which has prevailed in Volusia county for approximately 35 years, very much in its original form. Its administrative structure is somewhat less cohesive because three of the original Constitutional officers were later reinstalled as charter officers, subject to popular election. The title, Mayor, is now assigned to the person selected annually to chair the board. However, it is a case where the political leadership rests with a plural body, the Volusia Council.

As is to be seen in Chart 6, the Volusia approach contrasts sharply with Orange County. There we find a very different strategy for providing executive leadership. Where Volusia followed a course that had been well tested in municipalities across the United States, Orange followed no models. It created its own. A very short time after it had secured chartered status, the Orange voters in 1988 declared that the Chairman of the County Commission should be elected at large and really take responsibility for the government. In 2004 a vote changed his title to Mayor. In 2007, Mayor Richard Crotty was very likely the most powerful single individual in Florida local government.

He really occupies two positions, and that is unprecedented. He is the chairman of the governing body and votes along with other members. At the same time he runs the operations of the government. He is, in effect, an elected manager. He is stronger than the leader in a strong mayor government because he is also the key figure on the legislative side. Thus far the system seems to be working. Crotty overwhelmingly won his race for re-election in 2006.

Table 6
A Comparison of the Institutional Characteristics of
Broward, Orange, and Volusia Counties

Name	General Style	Number on Board	How Elected	Partisan or Non*	Political Leader	Head of Administration	Constitutional Officers**
Broward	Commission-Manager	9	District	Partisan	Plural Board	Administrator	Sheriff Appraiser Elections
Orange	Strong Mayor	7 (6 plus mayor)	Mayor at large, 6 by district	Varies	Mayor	Mayor	Sheriff Appraiser Elections Collector
Volusia	Commission-Manager****	7	2 at large, 5 by district	Non	Plural Board	Manager	None***

* Covers only charter officers, not Constitutional.
** The clerk of the court is a Constitutional officer in all three counties but has no finance functions.
*** Volusia has three elective officers (Sheriff, Supervisor of Elections, Property Appraiser) but they are charter, not Constitutional.
**** Titling is for purposes of simplification. Volusia calls its system, Council-Manager.

As Florida counties struggle to discover how best to provide for political leadership, it seems that Orange offers one possibility.

When Broward county framed a charter, it took important steps toward operating as a Council-Manager system; and, in the subsequent years, it has essentially met the standards for recognition as that kind of government. But it seems not to have found ways to satisfy its quest for political leadership.

That problem seems much more major in Broward than in Volusia, which has only a little more than a fourth the population. And Volusia does not face the multitude of municipalities which occupies nearly all of Broward territory. The problem of establishing a regional presence in a world of competing organizations is more serious in Broward, where there is also the question of determining how and in what degree the County should stay in the business of providing munici-pal-type services when so many others are involved. It may also be that Volusia got its act together earlier, before massive growth occurred. Broward was one of the first hit by major migration, and at least 29 of its 31 cities were up and operating before chartering even occurred.

In both Broward and Orange, the Constitutional officers occupy a major role. In Orange the full set of row officers—Sheriff, Appraiser, Tax Collector, and Supervisor of Elections—continue to operate as if there had been no char-tering. Further, a major share of financial responsibilities rests with an elected Comptroller who does not appear on the organization chart as an integral part of the administration. While there can be no denying the power of the Orange Mayor, it is also true that major parts of the government lie outside his control. It is far different in Volusia, in Jacksonville, and even in Miami-Dade.

Much the same problem exists in Broward, though at least the financial func-tions have been absorbed into the general government. The Tax Collector has been eliminated and the Clerk of the Court has been freed of any financial responsibili-ties. That is true, incidentally, in all three counties.

The Broward Sheriff, in particular, operates a major government within a gov-ernment. On his web site he reports 6300 people on his payroll, whereas the general county government declares it has 7000. If the Broward charter revision committee should propose a strong mayor plan and it should be adopted by the electorate in 2008, the new chief executive would certainly have his problems in dealing with the county's Constitutional officers.

It seems fair to say that each of these counties has either accomplished or sought significant change. Early on, Volusia made its reform and has enjoyed compara-tive stability since. Without much fanfare, Orange made a grand, experimental move toward executive leadership, really by combining the legislative and execu-tive branches. Judging by election results, the system is working and therefore deserves greater scrutiny. Of the three, Broward's seems to have had the most troubled history. Its efforts at change have been numerous, and some reform has been accomplished. But its situation appears to demand a major dose of political leadership.

CHAPTER EIGHT

EVOLUTIONARY CHANGE: CHARTERING AND THE 14 OTHER CHARTER COUNTIES

Thus far in this book, the characteristics of five charter counties have been considered. That leaves 14 who have charter status but who have yet to command any real attention. In the heading above, they are identified as the "14 other charter counties."

This somewhat demeaning characterization of them is not because of their lack of importance in Florida government. As will be noted in Table 7, they are major units serving large parts of the State's population. They have been assigned less status in this book because their chartering has resulted in only minor changes in their traditional structures of government. The new grant of freedom they received to manage their own affairs did not result in any great change in arrangements for doing the public business.

A sense of the frustration many observers have felt is found among the materials presented for the successful charter adoption effort in Columbia County:

> When all is said and done, one is led to the inescapable conclusion that the county charter movement has not lived up to its expectations or potential. The Florida political landscape of the past 20 years is littered with failed charter attempts and weak charters ... While progress in (county government) structural reforms (the problem of constitutional officers notwithstanding) has been steady, the promise of charters as mechanisms to address the assignment of functional responsibilities at the local level has been largely unfilled.[62]

---

62 From Columbia County Website. There is no citation but only the statement, "one author concluded in 1989 ..."

Reference to a few statistics will reveal how important these 14 governments are, irrespective of their reform inclinations. With the exception of Columbia, which has a population of about 60,000, these counties serve a great many people. Two (Palm Beach and Hillsborough) have populations over a million, and six of the 14 are meeting the needs of more than half a million people. They spend a lot of money. Four laid out more than a billion dollars in 2004 and nine of the 14 had expenditures over half a billion dollars.

These are urban counties (with the possible exception of Columbia). One, Pinellas, has the highest population density in the state (3291 people per square mile), outstripping Miami-Dade and Broward counties. Two others, Charlotte and Seminole, have population densities over 1000, and half of the group has density levels of 500 people or more per square mile.

Table 7
A General Profile of the Other 14 Charter Counties

Date Chartered	County Name	Population (est.) 2005	Area in Square Miles	No. of cities/ no. under 7,000	% of Pop. Unincorp- orated	Pop. density per sq. mile	2004 Outlays in $millions
1971	Sarasota	358,867	572	4/1	68%	570	$719,659
1980	Pinellas	947,799	280	24/12	30%	3291	$1,452,482
1983	Hillsborough	1,131,541	1951	3/0	66%	951	$2,542,177
1985	Palm Beach	1,265,900	2034	37/20	45%	573	$2,412,149
1986	Charlotte	154,030	694	1/1	89%	1347	$401,694
1987	Alachua	240,764	874	9/7	42%	249	$273,004
1989	Seminole	411,744	308	7/0	49%	1186	$523,947
1991	Clay	169,624	601	4/3	90%	234	$202,910
1992	Osceola	235,156	1322	2/0	64%	131	$638,553
1994	Brevard	531.970	1018	15/5	40%	459	$519,695
1996	Lee	549,442	804	5/2	53%	548	$1,647,558
1998	Polk	541,840	1875	17/11	62%	258	$510,882
2002	Leon	271,111	667	1/0	36%	359	$272,476
2002	Columbia	60,453	797	2/1	82%	71	$67,298

Institutional arrangements are sometimes complex, with four of the counties dealing with 15 or more municipalities. Palm Beach has the most, with 37. But there is another factor to be noted. Twenty of those 37 have populations less than 7000, which makes them less likely to be full service cities. Indeed, there are 73 municipalities in the 14 counties with populations under 7000, making it likely they are calling on the counties for urban services.

This demand on the counties to engage in urban services is exacerbated greatly by the large percentage of people living in unincorporated areas, leaving them with the county as their only local government. Around 90% of Clay and Charlotte Counties is unincorporated. In the two there are only five municipalities, four of them with less than 7000 population. Twelve of the 14 charter counties have unincorporated areas where the population is at least 40% of the total. Only two, Pinellas with 24 cities, and Leon, where the city of Tallahassee dominates the county, provide urban services to a lesser percentage of the population.

Like all counties in the state, each of the 14 has a large territory for which it is responsible. Palm Beach County is the biggest, with over 2,000 square miles, and Hillsborough and Polk each come close to 2,000.

Given the size and complexity of these units, one can appreciate their interest in chartering. At the same time the relative disinclination to move away from traditional patterns is more perplexing.

I. CHARTERS AS VEHICLES FOR HOME RULE

The very fact that charters do provide governments with more freedoms, even though they are unused, should be appealing. Further, there are data that charter counties are less dependent on the State Legislature, and specifically on their local representatives, to shepherd specialized enactments for them. This argument dates back to pre-1968 days, when nearly any local policy change had to be submitted to the Legislature. One of the purposes of the home rule provisions of the 1968 Constitution was to eliminate that wasteful expenditure of time by State legislators. The charter study group in Columbia reported that in the 1965 session of the State Legislature 2,107 local bills were introduced. There is this further comment:

> Home rule has changed this cumbersome process. Cities and counties now routinely legislate on a wide variety of local issues, a fact that is so obvious to contemporary observers of local government that it is difficult to understand that it was not always so. Although no hard data are readily available

to document the extent to which special acts would be necessary if the old Constitution were still in place, even a cursory review of the numbers and breadth of city and county ordinances since 1968 strongly indicates that Florida governments have seized the opportunity to legislate on their own, with few if any complaints of abuse coming to the attention of the legislature. During the past quarter century, the number of local bills introduced before the Florida legislature has decreased substantially.[63]

While just having a charter may create some incentive, the fact is the 48 non-charter counties, some of them very large, have been content to operate under the general laws of the state. Home rule is an important idea, as we have empha-sized throughout this book, and it is crucial to maintaining successful and vital local governments. There is a reason for concern when essentially all counties in the state have either failed to avail themselves of home rule powers or have done so in the most minimal degree. Ideally, all counties in Florida should be enjoy-ing home rule and actively experimenting with different mechanisms for meeting their broad and complex obligations. Some of these challenges were recognized by the charter study group in Columbia county:

> Charter counties enjoy the strongest form of home rule. It is important to understand why the Constitution so provides. Aside from the state-local tensions evident in the historical home rule debates, there has been in more recent times an emerging tension between local governments. As the state has become increasingly urbanized, cities became contiguous with each other. County governments which once provided skeletal administrative functions have become full-service units of government for urban but unincorporated populations, often jostling with their constituent cities for jurisdiction over service and regional regulation. The 1885 Constitution, as it stood when it was superseded, had already recognized the potential for such tensions in the major urban centers of Dade, Duval and Hillsborough counties (as well as Monroe). The former Constitution provided the opportunity for these communities to redistribute local power by revising or consolidating their city and county gov-ernments. The 1968 Constitution afforded the same opportunity to all coun-ties, and many urban and urbanizing counties have seized that opportunity.
>
> Should the grant of home rule powers and the opportunity for their redis-tribution be used as an incentive to solve local tensions and rethink the way local governments, especially counties, are organized? The framers of the 1968 revision obviously thought so. But the constitutional promise has fallen short,

---

63 *Loc. cit.*

because the local governments however constituted must still operate within, and often compete for, a fixed and limited revenue base.[64]

It may be that home rule is so unappreciated that the lengthy process of developing a charter and submitting it to popular referendum seems hardly worth the effort. The 14 chartered counties have followed the procedures established in Chapter 125, Part II of the Florida statutes, which involved the establishment of a charter study committee, lengthy analysis to determine how the county operates and whether improvements might be achieved by chartering, and, where warranted, the preparation of a charter for citizen consideration and vote. Obviously, it tends to be a lengthy process.

Though it has not been utilized, there is an alternative, as the Escambia County charter commission observed.[65] Chapter 125, Part IV of the Florida statutes includes an "Optional County Charter Law," which allows a board of county commissioners to propose a charter by ordinance. However, it does have limitations with regard to the form of government that can be adopted.

II. THE CHARTERING PROCEDURE

The Columbia County charter review commission has helpfully included on the County's Web site the steps required in progressing to a charter. The text comes from relevant portions of state law.

125.61 Charter commission.

(1)   Following the adoption of a resolution by the board of county commissioners or upon the submission of a petition to the county commission signed by at least 15 percent of the qualified electors of the county requesting that a charter commission be established, a charter commission shall be appointed pursuant to subsection (2) within 30 days of the adoption of said resolution or of the filing of said petition.

(2)   The charter commission shall be composed of an odd number of not less than 11 or more than 15 members. The members of the commission shall be appointed by the board of county commissioners of said county or, if so directed in the initiative petition, by the legislative delegation.

---

64   *Loc. cit.*

65   Escambia County charter commission, "Structure of Form of County Government," available on the Escambia county Web site, no date.

No member of the Legislature or board of county commissioners shall be a member of the charter commission. Vacancies shall be filled within 30 days in the same manner as the original appointments.

125.62 Charter commission; organization.

(1)   A charter commission appointed pursuant to s. 125.61 shall meet for the purpose of organization within 30 days after the appointments have been made. The charter commission shall elect a chair and vice chair from among its membership. Further meetings of the commission shall be held upon the call of the chair or a majority of the members of the commission. All meetings shall be open to the public. A majority of the members of the charter commission shall constitute a quorum. The commission may adopt such other rules for its operations and proceedings as it deems desirable. Members of the commission shall receive no compensation but shall be reimbursed for necessary expenses pursuant to law.

(2)   Expenses of the charter commission shall be verified by a majority vote of the commission forwarded to the board of county commissioners for payment from the general fund of the county. The charter commission may employ a staff, consult and retain experts, and purchase, lease, or otherwise provide for such supplies, materials, equipment and facilities as it deems necessary and desirable. The board of county commissioners may accept funds, grants, gifts, and services for the charter commission from the state, the Government of the United States, or other sources, public or private.

125.63 Proposal of county charter.

The charter commission shall conduct a comprehensive study of the operation of county government and of the ways in which the conduct of county government might be improved or reorganized. Within 18 months of its initial meeting, unless such time is extended by appropriate resolution of the board of county commissioners, the charter commission shall present to the board of county commissioners a proposed charter, upon which it shall have held three public hearings at intervals of not less than 10 nor more than 20 days. At the final hearing the charter commission shall incorporate any amendments it deems desirable, vote upon a proposed charter, and forward said charter to the board of county commissioners for the holding of a referendum election as provided in s. 125.64.

125.64 Adoption of charter; dissolution of commission.

(1)   Upon submission to the board of county commissioners of a charter by
      the charter commission, the board of county commissioners shall call a
      special election to be held not more than 90 nor less than 45 days sub-
      sequent to its receipt of the proposed charter, at which special election
      a referendum of the qualified electors within the county shall be held to
      determine whether the proposed charter shall be adopted. Notice of the
      election on the proposed charter shall be published in a newspaper of
      general circulation in the county not less than 30 nor more than 45 days
      before the election.

(2)   If a majority of those voting on the question favor the adoption of the
      new charter, it shall become effective January 1 of the succeeding year
      or at such other time as the charter shall provide. Such charter, once
      adopted by the electors, may be amended only by the electors of the
      county. The charter shall provide a method for submitting future charter
      revisions and amendments to the electors of the county.

(3)   If a majority of the voters disapprove the proposed charter, no new ref-
      erendum may be held during the next 2 years following the date of such
      disapproval.

III. THE CONTENT OF CHARTERS

Although each charter is somewhat different, they follow the same general
format. That makes it easy to compare them and to identify differences, small
though they often are. Generally, the charters are concerned with institutional
matters that have consequence for all activities. Within this general scheme, it is
important to be alert to ways in which directives are provided for the fulfillment
of the three basic roles of the county: handling of traditional functions, providing
urban services where they are not available through a municipality; and serving as
the leader and regulator for countywide services and policies.

Typically, little specific guidance is provided in the charter on the traditional
county role. Its nature is implied in the various institutional provisions. That is
not the case with the other two roles, however. It is necessary to be on the lookout
for statements that legitimate the urban services role and establish the parameters
of the regional leadership role.

The framework of the Charlotte County charter, which took effect in 1986,
indicates what is generally found in these documents.

The Charlotte County Charter 1986

Preamble

Article I
Creation, Powers, and Ordinances of Home Rule Charter Government
Sec. 1.1 Creation and general powers of Home Rule Charter Government
Sec. 1.2 Relation to state law
Sec. 1.3 Relation to municipal ordinances
Sec. 1.4 Relation to independent special districts

Article II
Organization of County Government
Sec. 2.1 Elected commission and appointed county administrator form of government
Sec. 2.2 Legislative branch
A. County Commission
B. Redistrictimg
C. Salaries and other compensation
D. Authority
E. Vacancies
F. Recall
G. Initiative
H. Municipal service taxing or benefit units
I. Economic impact of ordinances
J. Debt policy
Sec. 2.3 Executive Branch
A. County administrator
    (1) Responsibility
    (2) Appointment process
    (3) Salary
    (4) Removal provisions
B. County department heads
C. Noninterference with employees
D. County attorney
F. Administrative code

Article III.
Elected Constitutional Officers
Sec. 3.1 Relation to home rule charter
Sec. 3.2 Residency requirements

Article IV
Home Rule Charter, Transition, Amendments, Review, Effective Date
Sec. 4.1 Home rule transition
Sec. 4.2 Home rule charter amendments
A.   Amendments proposed by board of county commissioners
B.   Amendments proposed by initiative
C.   Amendments and revisions by charter review commission
Sec. 4.3 Home rule charter effective date

Forms of Government and Charters

The Florida statute establishing the conditions for adopting a charter by ordinance suggests that the State considers the most important element of a county charter is its form of government. Where a charter adopted by public referendum allows essentially any type of government, three specific forms are permitted under the ordinance arrangement. These are:

County Executive, where there is a separation of powers between an elected board of county commissioners and an elected head of an executive branch. It is essentially the system that has operated in Jacksonville for nearly 40 years and was recently adopted in Miami-Dade.

County Manager, where an elected board of county commissioners holds ultimate responsibility for the government. It appoints a manager who provides leadership to the administrative operations but who serves at the pleasure of the governing board. A key requirement of this system is that there be a formal separation between the legislature and the administrative arms of the government. This is a form that has been adopted almost uniformly by the charter counties.

County Chair-Administrator, which draws its inspiration from Orange County. This is the unique situation where the chair of the board, elected at large, also assumes responsibility for managing the government. Since Orange County voted a change in title in 2004, the idea of the Mayor as legislative and executive head should be incorporated into the title.

In effect, the adoption of a charter by ordinance involves no significant constraints. The three forms of government permitted encompass all those found in the charter governments.

Only three counties (Miami-Dade, Jacksonville, and Orange) have deviated from an approach that places strong reliance on an appointed administrator. The same arrangement is found overwhelmingly in the non-charter counties. It shows a healthy and strong commitment to professional management, dating back several decades.

There is one major difference between the non-charter and charter arrangements, however. While boards of commissioners in non-charter counties can delegate authority to an appointed manager, they remain responsible for administration. The extent of delegation is a function of personalities and custom, not of formal rule. In the charter counties, on the other hand, there is the opportunity to get very formal about things and to assign full authority and responsibility to the manager.

Formal Separation of the Legislative and Administrative

As we have already explained in considerable detail, such a separation of the tasks of the legislative body and of the manager is central to the Council-Manager idea in municipal government, where this structure originated. It is critical, too, that the entire administrative structure fall under the authority of the manager.

Thirteen of the 14 "other" counties make a formal separation of the legislative and executive branches. Only Sarasota does not; but, as will be seen, it provides for an implicit separation through its strong non-interference provision. In effect, all 14 meet this test for qualifying as Council-Manager governments. The statements providing for separation will vary among charters, but that of Charlotte County is a good example:

> Charlotte County shall operate under an elected county commission and appointed county administrator form of government with strict separation of legislative and executive functions in accordance with the provisions of this home rule charter. (Article II, Sec. 2.1)

Non-Interference Provisions in Charters

A second requirement for qualification as a Council-Manager government is a specific prohibition against involvement by legislators in administrative matters. They are required to work through the manager, thus to preserve the integrity of the chain of command. Eleven of the 14 counties, according to the Florida Association of Counties, include such a ban in their charters. The Sarasota County charter provides a good example of a detailed proscription:

2.6H Employee Supervision. Except for the purposes of inquiry and information, the members of the Board of County Commissioners shall not interfere
with the performance of the duties of any employee of the County who is
under the direct or indirect supervision of the County Administrator.

2.6I Board Instructions. Board instructions or directives to any employee of
County government under the jurisdiction and control of the Board shall be
issued only through the Administrator, with the exception of those persons
employed in the Office of the County Attorney, who shall receive instructions
solely from the County Attorney. Individual members of the Board shall not
issue directives or orders to employees. It is the express intent of this section
that recommendations for improvement in County government operations by
individual Board members be made to and through the Administrator, so that
the Administrator may coordinate efforts to achieve the greatest possible savings through the most efficient and sound means available. Nothing in the
foregoing is to be construed to prohibit individual members of the Board
from closely scrutinizing, by questions and personal observations, so as to
obtain independent information to assist the members in the formulation of
sound policies to be considered by the Board. *(Added 11/5/1995; Amended
3/14/2000.)*

These two tests indicate that the other "14 counties" have many of the features
of a Council-Manager form of government.

A Third Test: Integration of the Organization Structure

However, they basically flunk on a third criterion. It requires that the manager
have control over the entire administrative apparatus, thus to give the structure an
integrity and responsiveness to a single authority. The tradition of row offices in
the counties violates that principle, and the fact that the "other 14" have generally
retained this feature makes them less than full Council-Manager governments.

Since the Constitutional officers perform major administrative functions,
there can be no doubt that the authority of the manager over the structure is
seriously compromised. The elective clerk of the court constitutes a particularly
important assault on the manager's authority. That is because of the very peculiar
Constitutional provision that puts the clerk in charge of finances in the non-charter counties. If there is anything that is critical to the manager's capacity to exercise control over a system, it is finances. Such data are basic to the budget process
through which the manager exercises control over an array of highly varied functions. It is important that financial information be organized and be processed in

ways that give the budget the greatest possible reality. If a manager lacks control over such vital processes, he can no longer be held fully responsible for administrative performance.

Yet 12 of the 14 counties made no change in the clerk's role when the charter was formulated and adopted. An example of the extent of the clerk's financial responsibilities is seen in Pinellas County where the organization chart shows three major sections in this office: finance accounting, finance reporting, and financial information services.

Only Clay and Osceola Counties separated the clerk from county finances. Both have brought these functions into a department directly responsible to the manager. The finance department in Osceola County describes its role in these terms: "The Office of Finance is a service department of the Board of County Commissioners, its departments, and the public. It is responsible for financial reports, vendor and payroll disbursements, accounts receivable, banking, investments, fixed assets, tax collection, and audits."

There is the further complication that the other elected Constitutional officers, with their major administrative responsibilities, operate outside the ambit of the manager in all 14 counties. Effectively, they are beyond the administrative reach of the manager. In reality, then, all the "other 14" have significantly compromised his/her capacity to manage the enterprise. The Council-Manager system prevails in only a part of the total county operation.

While there can be no doubt that the counties have made great strides in providing professional leadership to operations under the control of the boards of county commissioners, the tradition of row offices leaves the "14" still open to the charge that they operate an assemblage of independent organizations. Further, the reluctance to lodge the finance operation firmly under the manager poses important problems even within that part of the organization under his/her authority.

IV. SPITZER'S BASIC OPTIONS IN DEVELOPING A CHARTER

Kurt Spitzer, long involved with county governments and much respected as a consultant, has prepared a "Basic Options" list of the questions with which a charter study commission will inevitably be involved. It is a highly useful contribution because it provides a helpful summary of the issues involved in developing a charter. With one exception we will follow the sequence with which he addresses these questions.

1. *Legislative branch.*

    A. *Districting*

- *All elected at-large*
- *Single member*
- *Mixed-combination of single and at-large*
- *Number of Commissioners*

    B. *Elected on what basis?*

- *Partisan vs. non-partisan*

    C. *Length of term*

- *4 years vs. some other number of years?*

    D. *Limits of terms*

- *No limitations*
- *Two terms, three terms, etc.*

    E. *Salaries*

- *As in state law*
- *Set by charter*
- *Set by Board of County Commissioners*

The Florida Association of Counties maintains a data base that is very helpful in securing a picture of the practices in the various charter counties. However, the data are incomplete and thus can provide only an approximate picture. We have used the Association's information in summarizing the ways in which the counties have approached the questions raised by Spitzer.

Most of the "other 14" have continued with five person boards of county commissioners. The number with this pattern is 10; and the other four have a slightly increased body of seven. In most cases the election arrangement for the boards is a combination, with most commissioners coming from districts and the others elected at large. Eleven follow this pattern; two elect from districts exclusively. None of 13 elects solely at large. There is no information on one county.

Every county elects its representatives for four years, and the mode is to have a limitation of two terms. One county (Alachua) has no term limits. There are no data, however, for six counties.

The Association data base provides no information on how commissioners' salaries are set.

2. *Executive Branch*

   A. *Appointed Administrator*

- *Selection process*

- *Termination*

- *Qualifications—in charter or by ordinance*

- *Noninterference clause-in charter? Penalties?*

   B. *Elected Position*

- *Elected "weak chairman" example, Tallahassee*

- *Elected chairman—example, Orange*

- *Elected executive—example, Tampa, Miami-Dade, Jacksonville/Duval*

   C. *Major departments*

- *Specify in charter? Which ones?*

- *Department head appointment and termination—Commission concurrence or administrator's decision?*

As has been previously reported, the administrators in all 14 of the "other" chartered counties are appointed by the board of county commissioners. There is typically a statement defining the process of appointment, but it will vary from one charter to another. The statement in the Charlotte County charter is common: "The County Administrator shall be appointed on the affirmative vote of four (4) members of the Board of County Commissioners on the basis of administrative ability and qualifications, pursuant to requirements specified by ordinance, and shall reside within the County while employed … The County Administrator's salary shall be set by the Board of County Commissioners." (Article II, Sec. 2.3 (2,3)

In the Association database, there is information on eight of the 14 counties, the mode (5) providing for appointment of the administrator by a majority of the board. The other three require a super-majority, four of five in one case and five of seven in two. The data on termination practice is too limited for generalization, though it appears those who appoint on the basis of a majority are likely to fire in the same way.

Charlotte County provides two patterns of dismissal. One is by the vote of a super majority at a single meeting, with or without cause. The other is by a 3-2 majority at two separate board meetings held at least two weeks apart. Charlotte is the only county which provides an option; Hillsborough and Sarasota require votes at two separate meetings.

Qualifications for appointment to the county administrator position were not included in the database of the Association of Counties, but it may be assumed they are addressed in some way in the charters. Sarasota's charter carries considerable detail:

Table 8
Government Features in the "Other 14" Charter Counties

Name	Board Size	How Elected	Admin- istrative Head	Selection Vote	Non-** Interference	Consti- tutional officers+	Finance Functions	Charter Review Freq.
Alachua	5	District/ At Large	Appointed	Majority	No	All	Clerk of Court	10 years
Brevard	5	District/ At Large	Appointed	Majority	Yes	All	Clerk of Court	6 years
Charlotte	5	District/ At Large	Appointed	Majority	Yes	All	Clerk of Court	6 years
Clay	5	District	Appointed	Majority	Yes	All	Not clerk; Manager	4 years
Columbia	5	District	Appointed	Not in charter	Yes	All	Clerk of Court	10 years
Hills- borough	7	4 District 3 at large	Appointed	*Super- Majority	No data	All	Clerk of Court	5 years
Lee	5	District/ At Large	Appointed	Majority	Yes	All	Clerk of Court	4 years
Leon	7	5 District 2 at large	Appointed	Not in charter	Yes	All	Clerk of Court	8 years
Osceola	5	District/ At Large	Appointed	Majority	Not in charter	All	Not clerk; Manager	4 years
Palm Beach	7	District	Appointed	Not in Charter	Yes	All	Clerk of Court	Not in Charter
Pinellas	7	4 District/ 3 atlarge	Appointed	Super- Majority	Yes	All	Clerk of Court	6 years
Polk	5	District/ At Large	Appointed	Majority	Yes	All	Clerk of Court	8 years

Name	Board Size	How Elected	Admin-istrative Head	Selection Vote	Non-** Interference	Consti-tutional officers+	Finance Functions	Charter Review Freq.
Sarasota	5	District/ At Large	Appointed	Super-Majority	Yes	All	Clerk of Court	4 years
Seminole	5	District/ At Large	Appointed	No data	Yes	All	Clerk of Court	6 years

* A Super-Majority requires four votes in a five-person board and five votes in one with seven members.

** Charter contains a clause prohibiting legislators' involvement in administration.

+ The five Constitutional Officers are sheriff, property assessor, tax collector, supervisor of elections, and clerk of court. Columbia and Polk provide for non-partisan elections of these officers (and Columbia also for commissioners); Palm Beach for the sheriff, appraiser, and supervisor of elections; and Leon does so for its board of commissioners and its supervisor of elections.

2.6c **Qualifications.** The County Administrator shall be appointed solely on the basis of his or her executive and administrative abilities and qualifications, and he or she shall meet one or more of the following requirements:

(1)   A master's degree from an accredited college or university, and have a minimum of two (2) years experience as an appointive city manager or county administrator.

(2)   A bachelor's degree from an accredited college or university and at least ten (10) years * of progressively responsible professional management experience.

He or she shall maintain residency within the County during his or her tenure of office and shall not engage in any other business or occupation. *(Amended 11/5/1996 and 3/14/2000.)*

Non-interference by legislators into administrative matters, a matter of extreme significance in the Council-Manager form, was discussed earlier. The election of administrative leaders has also been considered and is somewhat less relevant because all of these counties have opted for appointed leaders serving under an elected board of county commissioners.

The Association of Counties database reveals that it is relatively common for an administrator's appointment of department heads to require the approval of the board of commissioners. That prevails in eight of the 12 cases where information is available. The other four delegate the responsibility to the administrator. Boards are more inclined to allow the administrator more freedom, however, when the dismissal of a department head is involved. In nine cases the administrator is free to fire without board concurrence. In two, board approval must be obtained; and in one the board will entertain an appeal.

3. *Constitutional Officers*

    A.   *Leave as in current practice*

    B.   *Revise status*

        Uniform support services

- *Budget*
- *Personnel*
- *Data processing*
- *(Independent) performance audit/reviews*
- *Purchasing*
- *Risk management*
- *Legal services*

        Salaries

        Partisan/ Non-partisan

        Recall

        Selection Method

- *Elected charter officers?*
- *Appointed charter officers?*

    C.   *Leave some offices untouched but examine revisions to others*

4. *Legal Services—County Attorney*

    A.   *Selection*

    B.   *Qualifications*

    C.   *Provides services to which departments/offices*

The treatment of the Constitutional officers will be highly important in constructing a charter for a county.

Thus, the first item on this list, "leave as in current practice," will certainly be a major issue in charter deliberations.

Despite county traditions, there appears to be considerable feeling in Florida that local officials ought not to have party affiliations. While the overwhelming preference for partisan elections remains, three counties have opted for a major degree of non-partisanship. Palm Beach, which was chartered in 1985, requires that three of its Constitutional officers run in a non-partisan election, Sheriff, Property Assessor, and Supervisor of Elections. Polk county, chartered in 1995, requires all its Constitutional offices be non-partisan. More recently, the two counties who were the latest to charter displayed a strong disposition toward non-partisanship. Columbia county insists on non-partisan elections not only for its Constitutional officers but also for its Board of County Commissioners. Leon county declared that its Board of County Commissioners, as well as its Supervisor of Elections, should run as non-partisans. It is not possible to say there is an overwhelming move toward non-partisanship but certainly there is some tendency in that direction.

Spitzer also raises a question about charter officers. Since a charter gives the county the opportunity to specify the terms of appointment for its officers, there is certainly no requirement they maintain Constitutional status. Their functions can, of course, be transferred to appointive positions within the county. Where there is a large commitment to elective officers, a compromise is to leave them elective but make their offices a part of the charter government. They become elective charter officers, as happened with the Sheriff in Jacksonville. The advantage is that they clearly become a part of the charter government and are subject to all its rules and regulations.

While such an arrangement would appear to be appealing, it has generated very little interest. There has been a very modest tweaking of arrangements, notably in the transferring of the financial functions of the clerk of the court to the manager in two counties, as explained earlier.

6. *General Powers and Miscellaneous Provisions*
    (Note: We have skipped item 5 and will return to it later.)
    A. *Initiative (ordinances)*
        - *On what subjects*
        - *By what percentage of electorate*
    B. *Charter amendments*
        - *By board of county commissioners*
        - *By charter review commission*
        - *By electorate*

C.   *Charter Review Commission*
-    *Meets how often*
-    *Composition/membership*

D.   *Special districts/authorities/commissions*
-    *Left alone*
-    *Revised*
-    *Abolished and transferred to Board of County Commissioners*

Virtually all the charters provide a mechanism by which citizens can enact, amend, or repeal county ordinances. They differ only in some of their details. The Osceola statement is a good example of the way in which this matter has been handled. It says:

> Amendments to this Home Rule Charter may be proposed by petition signed by a number of electors equal to at least 10% of the number of qualified electors registered to vote in the County at the last preceding general election. Each such proposed amendment shall embrace but one subject and matter directly connected therewith. Each Charter amendment proposed by petition shall be placed on the ballot by resolution of the Board of County Commissioners for a special election called for that purpose occurring in excess of 90 days from the certification by the Supervisor of Elections that the requisite number of signatures has been verified.

The requirement that 10 percent of electors sign a petition is common in the charters, though that is at the high end. Brevard county demands only 4 percent, and six other counties ask for less than 10 percent.

Provision for a Charter Review Commission is also common in the charters. These groups often play a major role in amending the charters on a regularized, systematic basis. The frequency of the charter reviews varies considerably, with four counties (Sarasota, Lee, Clay, and Osceola) calling for an examination every four years. Two counties, Alachua and Columbia, require such an undertaking every 10 years, and the intervals for the others are 5, 6, and 8 years. A section in the Columbia charter suggests how these requirements are framed:

> Not later than July 1 of the year 2005 and of every tenth year thereafter, the Board of County Commissioners shall appoint a Charter Review Commission to review the Charter of the county. The Charter Review Commission shall be

appointed in the same manner as a Charter Commission under Section 125.64 of the Florida Statutes as that section now exists or may be hereafter amended. The commission shall be funded by the Board of County Commissioners and shall be known as the "Columbia County Charter Review Commission." It shall, within one (1) year from the date of its first meeting, present to the Board of County Commissioners its recommendations for amendment or revision of the Charter or its recommendation that no amendment or revision is appropriate. If amendment or revision is to be recommended, the Charter Review Commission shall conduct three (3) public hearings, at intervals of not less than ten (10) days, immediately prior to the transmittal of its recommendations to the Board of County Commissioners. The Board of County Commissioners shall schedule a referendum on the proposed charter amendments or revisions concurrent with the next general election. The Charter Review Commission may remain in existence until the general election for purposes of conducting and supervising education and information on the proposed amendments or revisions.

Special districts and various other entities operating in the county do require consideration in the charter. Their character, special features, and relations to the counties will be discussed in the next chapter.

V. ASSUMING THE URBAN SERVICES ROLE

The "other 14" chartered governments are one-tier agents for a very large part of their populations. Half of the counties are in situations where more than 50% of their populations live in unincorporated areas. Ninety percent of Clay is unincorporated; and the smallest population requiring urban services from the county is Pinellas, with 30%.

This circumstance is characteristic of Florida, where nearly 50% of the people in the state look to the counties for their city-type services.

It is clear that the "other 14" have a profound obligation to engage in role two, namely the provision of the services that a municipality, if it existed, would offer. While there is no doubt that these obligations must be met in all cases, the charter provisions for them vary. That occurs in substantial degree because the counties, charter or non-charter, perform such services. The Florida State Department of Community Affairs has the responsibility for tracking special districts and maintains a relatively small file on those established by counties solely to finance services or other projects in the unincorporated areas. That file shows a substantial portion of the financing mechanisms operating are in non-chartered counties. Apparently, there is not a necessity for a special charter provision to deliver urban services in the unincorporated parts of a county.

An underlying requirement is that the county not use its general funds to provide services to only a part of its population. General funds are to go for general county purposes. The financing arrangement, then, becomes critical in establishing the means by which counties serve their unincorporated areas. Two vehicles are employed in Florida, one for services and the other for various kinds of capital projects. The first is the MSTU, municipal service taxing unit, which sets boundaries for the area and then taxes residents for special services rendered. The second is the MSBU, the municipal service benefit unit, which involves a special assessment for a capital improvement. It can involve a bond issue.

Charters have handled the urban services responsibility differently. In some there is no mention of the task and the obligation involved, since obviously it exists in both charter and non-charter counties. More typically, it is treated instrumentally, as in Charlotte county:

> *Municipal service taxing or benefit units.* The board of county commissioners shall, upon the petition of thirty (30) or more electors residing within a municipal service taxing unit (MSTU) or municipal service benefit unit (MSBU), establish by ordinance an appointed board of advisors to consist of five (5) qualified resident electors of such MSTU or MSBU. The ordinance shall provide for the terms of the board of advisors and for the responsibilities of the board of advisors to request such services and facilities as deemed necessary to serve the residents of the MSTU or MSBU. The board of county commissioners may abolish a board of advisors by ordinance after a public hearing, and, upon abolition of the board of advisors, no new petition for the creation of a board of advisors, shall be considered for a period of two (2) years.

Sarasota county, in contrast, deals more generally with its role:

> The Board of County Commissioners shall have all powers to accomplish County and Municipal purposes within the unincorporated areas of the County. Such powers shall include, but not to be limited to, the creation of Special Districts, Municipal Service Taxing Units and Municipal Service Benefit Units. Real Property situated outside a Special District, Municipal Service Taxing Unit or Municipal Service Benefit Unit shall not be subject to taxation or assessment for services provided by such entity exclusively for the

benefit of the property or residents of such Special District, Municipal Service Taxing Unit, or Municipal Service Benefit Unit.

VI. THE ROLE OF REGIONAL LEADER AND REGULATOR

Spitzer's list includes a fifth category:

5.   *Municipal Relations*
    A.   *Conflict with municipal ordinances*
        - *City prevails*
        - *County prevails*
        - *County sets minimal policy in certain areas, city may exceed*
          (e.g., planning or environmental matters)
        - *What subject areas?*
    B.   *Functional consolidation of services*
        - *What subject areas?*

This list raises a broader set of questions. It concerns the third, and crucially important, role of the county, namely to function as the arbiter of regional needs and priorities. As we have noted earlier, this role is inherited because the county is always the largest unit of government, in terms of land, within what may be a highly complex set of institutions. Spitzer has headed the section, "Municipal Relations," and that is appropriate. The crucial question is how the county will impose itself on its municipalities.

There is no issue in the non-charter counties. They operate under a Constitution that specifically prevents them from exercising a regional role. Their ordinances are simply not observed within municipal boundaries. The situation can be greatly different, though, in the chartered county. Depending on the desires of the electorate, the county has the flexibility to construct a major regional role.

However, the Charter Counties have taken relatively little advantage of this opportunity. Five have chosen to accept no regional role. They have simply continued the practice that existed when they were non-charter and have opted for no countywide powers.

Of the 13 who have recognized a regional responsibility, the charter provision has often been quite limited. It has concentrated on planning and land development and the environment, including such natural sites as the beaches. There is a frequent preamble that municipal ordinances shall prevail except ... The Charlotte statement is fairly typical:

> Municipal ordinances shall prevail over county ordinances to the extent of any conflict, except that county-wide ordinances relating to the following subjects shall prevail over municipal ordinances to the extent of any conflict:
>
> A.   Impact fees on new development to pay the cost of providing county public facilities required by such development.
>
> B.   A county-wide comprehensive plan or county-wide elements of a county comprehensive plan and county-wide land development regulations as defined by Chapter 163, Part II, Florida Statutes, as the same may be amended by the Florida legislature.

Hillsborough County established County-wide organizations for planning and environmental protection, thus securing regional perspectives for these important functions without direct County involvement.

While proclaiming that municipal ordinances prevail, a few counties have been more inclusive in identifying areas where there is a greater regional role for the county. The Association of Florida Counties has maintained a rather extensive analysis of these countywide powers:

Columbia. Adult entertainment, protecting environment by regulating air or water pollution, outdoor burning, hours of sales of alcoholic beverages, animal control, firearms, weapons, and protection of standards on County-maintained roads.

Palm Beach. Protection of wells and well fields; matters relating to schools, County-owned beaches, district parks and regional parks, solid waste disposal, County law enforcement, and impact fees for County roads and public buildings; County fire-rescue and County library impact fees in those municipalities whose properties are taxed by the County for library and/or fire-rescue services; adoption and amendment of County-wide land use element; matters related to establishment of levels of service for collector and arterial roads which are not the responsibility of any municipality.

Table 9
Charter Counties and Their County-wide Policy Authorities

County	Population	Number Cities	Countywide Authority	Policy Areas
Alachua	236,174	9	very limited	environmental protection when more stringent than municipalities
Brevard	521,422	15	no	
Broward	1,729,131	30	yes	land use planning, minimum standards to protect environment
Charlotte	156,985	1	yes	impact fees for county facilities; countywide comp plan and land development regulations
Clay	163,461	4	no	
Columbia	60,453	2	yes	minimum countywide standards for adult entertainment, environmental protection, outdoor burning, animal control, others.
Duval	840,494	4	yes	consolidated government
Hillsborough	1,108,436	3	yes	has consolidated planning and environmental organizations
Lee	521,253	5	no	
Leon	263,896	1	no	
Miami-Dade	2,379,818	34	yes	metro government
Orange	1,013,937	13	yes	minimum standards for regulating adult entertainment; environment
Osceola	225,816	2	no	
Palm Beach	1,242,270	37	yes	protection of wells and well fields, impact fees for schools, county parks, solid waste disposal, law enforcement, county roads
Pinellas	943,640	24	yes	large group of areas in which county controls
Polk	529,369	17	no	

County	Population	Number Cities	Countywide Authority	Policy Areas
Sarasota	358,307	4	yes	comprehensive plan and land development
Seminole	403,381	7	yes	land use planning
Volusia	484,281	17	yes	minimum standards for environment, beach access, and unified beach code

Pinellas. Development and operation of 911 emergency communication system; development and operation of solid waste disposal facilities, exclusive of municipal collection systems; development and operation of regional sewer treatment facilities, exclusive of municipal systems; acquisition, development and control of County-owned parks and buildings; public health or welfare services or facilities; operation, development and control of St. Pete-Clearwater airport; design, construction, and maintenance of major drainage system in both the incorporated and unincorporated areas; design, construction and maintenance of County roads; animal control; civil preparedness.

Volusia. The Growth Management Commission has County-wide power; minimum standards for environment, including tree protection, storm water management, river and waterway protection, hazardous waste disposal, wetlands protection, beach and dune protection, air pollution. Standards shall apply in all areas of the County; County ordinances prevail, except when municipalities may have adopted stricter standards. Unified beach code—County has jurisdiction over coastal beaches and approaches (specifically including municipal areas) and exclusive authority to regulate the beaches and public beach access.

Aside from Jacksonville and Metro-Dade, it appears that Pinellas and Volusia have shouldered their regional responsibilities to a greater degree than other Florida counties.

VII. INCREASING CONFLICT WITH MUNICIPALITIES

It is one thing to say that counties should assume a regional role, but it is quite another to secure such authority within the complex of municipal governments that frequently prevails. It is in terms of the regional role that a collision with municipalities and their interests is likely to occur. Municipalities also take home rule seriously; and so intervention by the county as a higher level of government is certainly not welcome. In recent years issues between the cities and the charter counties have increased in frequency and become more pressing, notably in the planning and land use areas. There is no problem with the non-charter counties, of course, because municipal ordinances always prevail.

While the view has been taken in this book that the counties have been slow to assume their regional roles, the cities feel the counties have already gone too far. Rebecca O'Hara, the deputy general counsel of the Florida League of Cities made this comment: "If charter counties are allowed to continue on this path, they will strip municipalities of the very things that make a city a city."[66]

The battle is being waged in the corridors of the Florida State Legislature and also in the courts. One of the most significant court cases was decided in the Fifth District Court of Appeals in January 2006. It pitted Seminole County against the city of Winter Springs, which is located in that County. Seminole is a relatively large county, with a 2005 estimated population of about 410,000, about half of whom live in the unincorporated area. It contains seven cities, all over 7,000 population and therefore considered full service. Sanford is the largest, with about 49,000 people and Lake Mary and Longwood are the smallest, both with about 13,000 people. Winter Springs, the contestant in the case, had a 2005 estimated population of 33,321.

The County had been concerned about its eastern, rural area that was largely unincorporated. In 1994 it established a boundary to protect the territory from urban development. However, the charter operated in traditional terms and had effect only in the unincorporated areas. As the Court noted, all a municipality needed to do was work out a voluntary annexation, after which the zoning could be changed to allow for high density development.

The triggering event in this case was a dispute over the development of a subdivision on the eastern edge of Winter Springs, known as Battle Ridge. There was litigation, but it was settled when Seminole County withdrew its challenge with the "implicit understanding" that this development would represent the easternmost urban expansion of Winter Springs. But this agreement did not hold up. Winter Springs increased its utility lines, originally planned to serve 110 dwelling units, to handle 1300. Further, it annexed three more areas immediately east of Battle Ridge within the County-designated rural area.

Seminole's Board of County Commissioners then proposed a charter amendment that would put the County firmly in charge of the eastern area, regardless of the jurisdiction. It said that the County could pass necessary implementing ordinances, and "municipal ordinances ... are superseded to the extent of such con-

66 Rebecca O'Hara, "Father Knows Best: The Charter County Assault on Municipal Home Rule," *Quality Cities* (January/February 2007), p. 31

flict." In another paragraph, there is the declaration that, "The Board of County Commissioners must approve all changes to the future land use designations of all rural lands, regardless of whether some or all of the rural lands are located within a municipality."

The proposed amendment certainly threw down the gauntlet to Winter Springs and the other municipalities. They would no longer control the zoning in newly annexed areas in the east. The proposal generated considerable public interest. We were able to search the Internet and found some references, all of which supported the County. They are not necessarily representative of the debate at the time, but they do indicate that the County had supporters, and the issue of planning was considered significant.

These statements were made before the election:

> Recognizing the negative effects of unchecked urban expansion, the Seminole County Board of Commissioners implemented the rural area boundaries over 10 years ago in the Seminole County Comprehensive Plan, to guide growth responsibly and protect sensitive lands.

> On Tuesday, November 2, Seminole County voters will be asked to vote on an amendment to the County Charter which will reaffirm this boundary around the eastern rural portion of the County and will give the Board of County Commissioners oversight over land use changes within this boundary. There are only three cities that this has any affect on, Oviedo, Winter Springs and Sanford. They are the only municipalities adjacent to the Rural Boundary and rural lands in east Seminole.

> Unfortunately, not all of these cities have adhered to the Comprehensive Master Plan, instead developing methods of circumventing it for their gain without regard to others. They dodge the Comprehensive Master Plan by annexing property within the rural area boundaries for the sole purpose of increasing the size of their city. Under our current charter, once a tract of land is annexed by a City, that City can change land use as they see fit. For example, Winter Springs recently annexed a Suburban Estates property and re-zoned what was once 1 dwelling per acre in the county, changing to 10 dwellings per acre in the city. A YES vote for the Home Rule Charter amendment would provide responsible oversight on land use within Rural Seminole County, regardless of land annexation by a city.

On this Internet site, it was later reported that the Seminole county charter amendment passed by a 56–44% margin. It declared that citizens were "fed up" with municipal zoning that led to poorly planned growth and had therefore established a rural area in the east county where it would be difficult for the cities to annex property.

In the subsequent trial, the Appeals Court declared that the Trial Court had "… issued a detailed and well-reasoned order rejecting most of the Winter Springs arguments." However, the Trial Court found two flaws that caused it to declare the County amendment invalid: (a) the ballot summary language was misleading and (b) the amendment violated the charter's "single subject" rule.

In its consideration of the case, the Appeals Court was particularly careful to draw a distinction between charter and non-charter counties. It concluded that the Florida constitution did mean to provide broad home rule powers to the counties. "The most significant feature of charter counties," the court declared, "is the direct Constitutional grant of broad powers to self-government, which includes local citizens' power to enable their charter county to enact regulations of county-wide effect which preempt conflicting municipal ordinances … the power which may be granted to county governments under a charter is the power to have county ordinances take precedence over municipal ordinances."[67]

The explanation for the charter amendment on the ballot was called misleading by the city because the Board of County Commissioners was given the power to create ordinances for the east county. It was claimed that this arrangement made the initiative provisions of the charter moot. The court wrestled with this question and concluded that, particularly in the area of comprehensive planning, the Board had to be the authority. There were so many state requirements that it would be impossible to work with citizen initiatives. It concluded that the initiative could be "harmonized" as an exception to the general rule that authority rests with the Board.

As a result, the Court decided that the power given the Board was fully compatible with the charter provisions for initiative and referendum. It also found that the amendment did not violate the charter's "single subject" requirement. Thus the amendment stood and Seminole County had the right to control land use in the east county.

There was one other matter addressed. It involved a piece of property in the east county annexed to Winter Springs. There was the question whether a dual referendum was required in the County and the City to legitimate the County intrusion. The Court declared emphatically that a dual referendum was not required,

---

67 Opinion, 5th District Court of Appeal, Seminole County, Florida v. The City of Winter Springs, Florida, Case no. 5D05-81 (January Term 2006), p. 3.

specifically observing that there is a difference between the transfer of functions or powers relating to services and to regulation. Here is what the Court said:

> ... We find that the electorate of a charter county may preempt a city's land use regulation by charter, without a dual vote of the city's electorate. As held by our Supreme Court in *Broward County,* 480 while section 4 requires dual referenda to transfer functions or powers relating to services (Emphasis in original) Land use regulation is just that—regulation. Therefore dual referenda are not required. *id.* This obvious conclusion is also memorialized in the Act itself, which expressly recognizes that: "In the case of chartered counties, the county may exercise such authority over municipalities or districts within its boundaries as is provided for in the charter." 1673.3171(2), Fla. Stat. (2005)

The final statement of the court summarizes the disposition of this case and makes the further point that regulation allows great flexibility in the charter county's discharge of its regional obligations.

> When it comes to charter counties, the Constitution expressly grants the electorate a right to determine by charter which government they desire to vest with preemptive regulatory power ... The voters of Seminole County have made that election. With respect to the "rural area" of Seminole County the people have chosen to grant preemptive land use regulatory power exclusively to the County. Their decision to do so constituted a perfectly valid election under the Florida Constitution.[68]

No doubt this battle will be waged further in the State Legislature. The Florida League of Cities identified the issue with the counties as one of its 2007 priorities. O'Hara reported that the League supported two bills in the 2006 session designed to remedy the problem. The dual referendum would have been required under these bills, thus insuring that a municipality would have the right of veto. O'Hara reported a favorable response from legislators, but they were worried about retroactivity language that would have undone existing charter provisions. She declared that the League was unable to reach a compromise with the counties and that even a temporary moratorium that would provide time for reaching a compromise was unacceptable to the counties. It was likely that the debate in 2007 followed familiar lines.

O'Hara, likely speaking for the Florida League of Cities, made these arguments in her January article in *Quality Cities.*

---

68 Ibid., p. 14

- The irony is that most growth these days occurs not in cities but in the unincorporated areas of the state.

- Land use planning, zoning and water services are essential municipal functions that determine the basic personality of a city and the overall quality of life of its residents.

- County charter amendments take this power away from city residents, thereby undermining the decision to incorporate and form a city in the first place.

- These piecemeal transfers of municipal power to county government will, over time, result in defacto consolidated governments.

- There is no question that charter counties will continue their assault on municipal home rule unless the Florida Legislature acts.[69]

VIII. SUMMARY

Five counties in Florida have used home rule either to develop significantly different ways of doing their business or have struggled to achieve change. Their experiences have been treated in previous chapters.

That leaves 14 of the 19 chartered counties uncovered. They are the subject of this current chapter, and it also seems appropriate to consider the more general question of the chartering process, where the "Basic Option" list prepared by Consultant Kurt Spitzer is used as a guide.

There can be no doubt that the 1968 Florida Constitution opened a new era for the state's counties. Through the home rule provisions included in the Constitution, the counties were granted tremendous freedoms to construct a system that would most effectively meet their needs. The extent of that grant of autonomy was dramatically emphasized in a 2006 opinion of the Florida 5th District Court of Appeals which declared that the counties received "... a direct constitutional grant of broad powers for self-government ..."

The 14 counties were grouped together in this chapter, however, because they have taken relatively little advantage of the home rule opportunities available to them. Both in their leadership arrangements and in their continued commitment to a traditional row officers structure, they have displayed relatively little interest in significant institutional change. They are all governed by plural bodies of five to seven members. And they all have elective officials in

---

69   O'Hara, *loc.cit.*

the traditional positions-sheriff, property assessor, tax collector, supervisor of elections, and clerk of the courts. Further, all but two have continued the long-honored practice of placing the clerk of the courts at the center of the county's financial operations.

What is most encouraging is the strong movement toward professional management in the other parts of the county organization. A review of the biographies of several of the administrators revealed impressive education and experience. It is apparent that the boards of county commissioners have sought to place qualified, able people in the top administrative slots.

The charters in the "other 14" have reinforced this tendency. All of them make it clear that a separation of the policy and administrative functions must be honored. The boards of county commissioners are restricted to policy formation and to oversight of administration, while the appointed administrator has authority and responsibility for policy execution. There is typically a statement in the charter announcing this formal separation; and there is also a "non-interference" requirement, either placed in the charter or ordered to be established by ordinance, that prohibits authoritative contact between board members and administrative personnel.

The one shortcoming in all this is that a substantial portion of the administrative establishment in all the 14 counties lies outside the control of the boards or their appointed administrators. All retain the row offices, whose incumbents are elected and therefore enjoy virtually full independence from any hierarchical authority in the county. This arrangement weakens the power of the administrator, of course, and makes it less possible to hold him/her accountable for the system as a whole. In 12 of the 14 counties the clerk of the court continues to play an important role in financial matters, weakening the hand of the administrator further.

The "other 14" typically have large unincorporated areas, with the result that they all perform municipal-type services. Many of the charters do not contain provisions specifically permitting these kinds of activities. That is because they are characteristically performed by all counties, charter or non-charter. With so many people living in unincorporated areas, such a county service obligation is inevitable. It appears that the only requirement is the ability to raise money to perform such particular services, and that comes through special districting arrangements.

With regard to the discharge of a regional role, the "other 14" are less uniform. Six have not diverged from their non-charter moorings, where the enactments of the municipalities are supreme. In the other eight, the authorization to legislate countywide is limited. It appears that Pinellas and Volusia have granted more countywide authority in their charters than the other 12.

The assumption of regional responsibilities places the counties on a collision course with the municipalities, who still enjoy a kind of sovereign immunity in the non-charter counties. Conflict has tended to rise most particularly in land use where the counties have limited the municipalities in re-zoning land.

These issues are being confronted both in the courts and in the State Legislature. The Florida League of Cities made restricting such countywide authority a 2007 priority in Tallahassee.

A significant case was decided in the 5th District Court of Appeal in 2006. It supported the counties' effort to strengthen their regional role. The opinion emphasized the idea of home rule for the counties and took the position that the Constitutional grant was broad. It specifically stated that county ordinances could take precedence over those of municipalities. Finally, there was the opinion that, in the regulatory area, the grant of authority was particularly great.

CHAPTER NINE

SPECIAL DISTRICTS

In addition to the 412 municipalities operating in the counties, there are over 1500 special districts that occupy various roles. They differ greatly in their character; but the important thing is that they are recognized as units of local government. As such, they function alongside and in association with the counties and the municipalities. The formal definition states that they are "… a local unit of special government, except district school board and community college districts, created pursuant to general or special law for the purpose of performing prescribed specialized functions, including urban service functions, within limited boundaries."

The Florida Department of Community Affairs has assumed responsibility for monitoring the special districts of the state. As part of that obligation, it has created a *Florida Special District Handbook*. In it there is a characterization of the special district and how it is to be distinguished from other governmental units.

Special Districts are somewhat similar to counties and municipalities. However, special districts are units of *special-purpose* government as opposed to units of *general-purpose* government. Florida's laws generally treat them alike.

A special district …

- is a unit of local special-purpose government (board has policy-making powers)
- operates within limited boundaries
- is created by general law, special act, local ordinance, or by rule of the Governor and Cabinet.

A special district is not a …

- General-purpose government (City or County)
- School district

- Community college
- Municipal Service Taxing or Benefit Unit
- Seminole and Miccosukee Tribe Special Improvement District
- Board providing electrical services that is a political subdivision of a municipality or part of a municipality.

Though the schools and community colleges are highly important parts of the local government scene, they operate within quite a different state framework. Thus their presence is to be noted, but they are sufficiently separated from the other units of local government that they will receive no further attention in this chapter.

The Handbook includes a short history of, and rationale for, special districts in Florida. Because it provides a brief and synthetic view of these relatively unique parts of the local government whole, its first section is reprinted here in its entirety.

I. A BRIEF HISTORY OF SPECIAL DISTRICTS

Benjamin Franklin established the first special district on the 7th of December 1736, when he created the Union Fire Company of Philadelphia, a volunteer fire department. Residents in a certain neighborhood paid a fee to receive fire protection services. Any resident not paying the fee had no fire protection services. Soon, many volunteer fire departments formed throughout Philadelphia. This prompted Franklin to boast that his city had the best fire service in the world.

In Florida, the first special districts were created more than 180 years ago. Then, Florida was a territory of log settlements scattered between the only two cities, Pensacola and St. Augustine. The entire territory consisted of two large counties, Escambia and St. Johns, whose contiguous border was defined by the Suwanee River. Because no roads existed, the Territorial legislators had to make the long, difficult sea voyage between the co-capitals, Pensacola and St. Augustine. In 1822, the legislators voted to establish a capital in a more convenient location. A year later, two men met on a pine-covered hill, halfway between Pensacola and St. Augustine, and chose the site of a new capital. Within a year, Florida's first Capitol, a small log cabin just big enough for all six legislators, was built in what is today Tallahassee.

Early, Floridians realized that the transportation needs of a growing territory could be effectively managed by a group of local citizens organized into a district with vested powers. During the same session that the decision was made to move the capital, the Territorial Legislature also authorized the creation of the first special districts in Florida by enacting the Road, Highway, and Ferry Act of 1822.

Created to establish and maintain public roads, the first road districts had no taxation authority and solved their labor needs by conscription. Men failing to report to work were fined one dollar per day.

In 1845, soon after Florida became a state, the Legislature went a step further and established the first special district by special act. Five commissioners were empowered to drain the "Alachua Savannah." To finance the project, the first special assessments were made on landowners based on the number of acres owned and the benefits derived.

The popularity of special districts to fund public works continued throughout the end of the 19th century as more settlers came to Florida. By the 1920's, the population had increased substantially in response to Florida's land boom. Many special districts were created to finance large engineering projects. Some of these special districts are still in existence today, such as the South Florida Conservancy District and the Florida Inland Navigation District. By the 1930's, the surge of new residents created the need for the first mosquito eradication district and other very specialized districts. After World War II, the baby boom and Florida's growing popularity created the need for a variety of new special districts, such as aviation authorities and hyacinth control districts. Soon, beach erosion, hospital, and fire control special districts grew rapidly along with the traditional road, bridge, and drainage special districts.

The Uniform Special District Accountability Act of 1989

In 1989 the Florida Legislature passed Chapter 189, *Florida Statutes* (also known as the *Uniform Special District Accountability Act of 1989*). This Act sets forth the general provisions for all special districts, although it excludes certain types of special districts from some sections. The Act addresses such provisions as the creation, operation, financial reporting, taxation/assessments, elections, definitions, compliance with general law provisions (e.g., Government-in-the-Sunshine), and comprehensive planning of special districts.

Special District Advantages

The Legislature, counties, and municipalities recognize the following advantages of creating new special districts to address Florida's growing public service needs. They:

- Provide for projected growth by focusing on those benefitting from its services without overburdening other taxpayers and governments.

- Operate to provide specific, essential public services that address community needs.

- Can manage, own, operate, construct, and finance basic capital infrastructure, facilities, and services, which provides assurance to property owners and the community that infrastructure maintenance and other services will continue helping to protect property values and quality of life.

- Ensure accountability of public resources, since special districts and their governing boards are held to the same high standards as municipalities and counties.

- Save money because they do not pay sales tax on goods and services, may be able to finance with tax-exempt bonds issued at reduced interest rates, and are eligible to participate in state term contracting.

- Can be set up so that their governing board is comprised of appointed and/or elected members who have the expertise to manage its specialized functions.

- Have Sovereign Immunity Protection.

From the county perspective, there are two categories of special districts that have significance. One of these categories distinguishes between districts that cover two or more counties and those that operate in a single county. Hence we have the multi-county and the single county districts. Another category is found in the single county district and involves a distinction between those that are "independent" units in the sense that they operate quite separately from a host government, either county or city, and "dependent" ones. These latter types are closely tied to a host government in determining their leadership and/or in terms of controlling their finances. The separation of the two is important because the independent districts are obviously much freer to operate on their own terms than are the dependent ones.

A tally by the Florida Department of Community Resources, as of February 7, 2007, showed a total of 1530 special districts in the state, of which 67 are multi-county. That leaves 1463 single districts dispersed among the 67 counties of the State. As Table 11 indicates, the largest number of districts are found in the counties with the greatest populations. Five of the six biggest counties have the most special districts, ranging from 89 to 131. The exception is Pinellas, which has only 41. Hillsborough outstrips all the counties with 131, followed by Lee (sixth in population size) with 93. Two counties have only two special districts each, Charlotte and Hamilton, but the disparity in their population size suggests that the numbers of districts in a county are more than a matter of the volume of people.

II. MULTI-COUNTY DISTRICTS

All the counties are involved in at least one multi-county district, with Monroe having the minimum affiliation. Its single attachment is to the South Florida Water Management District. On the other hand, there are two counties who have associations with 11 multi-county districts, Sarasota and Hendry. Again, the population discrepancies are to be noted. Sarasota is fairly large, with more than 365,000 people, but Hendry is quite small, about a tenth the size of Sarasota. Hendry's district memberships suggest that location is a highly important determinant of involvement. Hendry is a member of these multi-county districts: Barron Water Control, Cow Slough Water Control, East County Water Control, Disston Island Conservancy, Everglades Agricultural Area Environmental Protection, Flaghole Drainage, Port Labelle Community Development, Ritta Drainage, South Florida Conservancy, South Florida Water Management, and Sugarland Drainage.

Florida Inland Navigation District

One of the largest and the oldest of the multi-county districts in Florida is the Florida Inland Navigation District, which associates with 11 counties. Its responsibility is a well-recognized physical landmark, the inland waterway. The development and maintenance of the waterway has long been an interest of both the Federal and the State governments. The Rivers and Harbors Act of 1927 established the Inland Navigation District and spelled out how the national and the state governments would associate. In effect the national government constructs and maintains the waterway and the District (as an agency of the State) provides the land needed for development. Legislation in 1965 gave authorization for the District to levy a tax up to 0.1 mill to discharge its responsibilities.

At the time the District was created in 1926, eleven counties agreed to participate but in 2007 there were 12 (Brevard, Broward, Duval, Flagler, Indian River, Martin, Miami-Dade, Nassau, Palm Beach, St. Johns, St. Lucie, and Volusia). They are arrayed along the east coast of Florida from Miami-Dade through Duval and up to Nassau in the north. The District is governed by a board with a representative from each of the member counties, appointed by the Governor.

Water Management Districts

While the Inland Navigation District is older, by far the most major of the multi-county districts are those involved in the water management of the state. Every county is a member of at least one of these districts. All five districts were established by the Water Resources Act of 1972.

The largest is the South Florida Water Management district, which includes 16 counties, covers a population of nearly nine million, and embraces a territory of nearly 20,000 square miles. With one exception, the five districts are organized in the same way. A board, appointed by the Governor and confirmed by the Senate, holds basic responsibility and depends on an executive director for the management of the undertaking.

Table 10
The Largest Special Districts Operating in More Than One County*

Name of District	Population of Counties Served	Area of Counties Served
South Florida Water Management District	About 8,907,000	19,856 square miles
Florida Inland Navigation District	about 8,180,000	12,486 square miles
St. Johns River Water Management District	about 5,140,000	14,026 square miles
Southwest Florida Water Management District	about 5,000,000	12,365 square miles
Northwest Florida Water Management District	about 1,390,000	11,305 square miles
Northwest Florida Regional Housing Authority	about 1,340,000	15,802 square miles
Suwanee River Water Management District	about 620,000	9,961 square miles

* Totals are higher than the population of the State because a number of counties are in more than one district.

The South Florida District is the oldest, having begun as the Central and Southern Florida Flood Control District in 1949. It gained its new name and responsibility in the Water Resources Act of 1972. In 1976 South Florida and the other districts were given the authority to levy property taxes via a Constitutional amendment. Subsequent legislation has added responsibilities in such areas as land acquisition and management, permitting, and environmental restoration and protection.

The Northwest Water Management District identifies its goals as: (1) to ensure an adequate supply of water; (2) to provide for the protection and enhancement of natural systems through integrated land and water resource management programs: (3) to minimize harm from flooding ; (4) to protect, maintain and improve the quality of the water resource; (5) to enhance public awareness, understanding and participation in comprehensive water resource management; and (6) to develop the District's overall water management capabilities, expertise and abilities to provide technical assistance for local needs.

The Southwest Florida board differs from the others in one significant way. It has established "basin boards" in eight of the nine drainage basins in its area of responsibility. This move has introduced an additional 44 leadership posts in the District and has provided more grass roots involvement. Each of the basic boards includes one person from each county within the basin; and they identify key issues and priorities in four areas of responsibility: water supply, flood protection, water quality, and natural systems.

Although each of the seven districts in Table 10 includes more than 10 counties, the numbers of counties participating in a specific district are generally small. Nearly fifty percent of the multi-county districts (30) involve just two counties. Another 14 include only three; and nine affiliate with four counties. Nearly 80% of the multi-county districts enroll four or fewer counties.

The multi-county districts cover a wide variety of functional areas. Some indication of the scope of their activities is seen in the categories into which they are placed in the Florida Department of Community Affairs listing: community development, conservation and erosion, distribution pipelines, economic development, expressways and bridges, fire control and rescue, hospital, housing, infrastructure provision, inlet maintenance, library, navigation, research and development, solid waste, subdivision, transportation, utility, water control, water management, water supply, and water and sewer.

The multi-county districts occupy a more significant place in the inter-governmental system of Florida than their numbers indicate. The involvement of two counties in eleven different districts is certainly indicative. Indeed, the 66 multi-county districts have engagements with 170 counties. That works out to an average involvement per county of about 2.7 districts. Furthermore, it should be remembered that multi-county districts are independent units, generally with control over their management and finances. They are entities with which negotiation is a requirement.

III. SINGLE COUNTY DISTRICTS

The picture for the single county districts is far more mixed. They are, of course, much more numerous, with the number in February 2007 at 1439. The complications they present for the counties depend very much on their status and function. The distinction between an independent and a dependent special district becomes very important because the amount of independence will dictate how free a district is to come into conflict with a county. The *Florida Special District Handbook* takes great care to identify the characteristics of the dependent district as a way of determining independence. If a district has none of the features of the dependent unit, it is, *ipso facto,* independent.

Independent and Dependent Districts

The dependent district will have one or more of these characteristics, according to the *Manual:*

- Its governing body members are identical to the governing body members of a single county or a single municipality.

- Its governing body members are appointed by the governing body of a single county or a single municipality.

- During unexpired terms, its governing body members are subject to removal at will by the governing body of a single county or a single municipality.

- Its budget requires approval through an affirmative vote by the governing body of a single county or a single municipality.

- Its budget can be vetoed by the governing body of a single county or a single municipality.

In effect, if a district has the freedom to decide who is in charge and how money is to be spent, it likely has independence. The governing body of the independent district will either be elected or appointed from outside the county or city government, and the budget will be established independently of the local governing body. Multi-county districts are almost always independent because it would take a special arrangement to put them under the control of a single county. In assessing the inter-governmental complexities a county may face, it is therefore useful to take a look at the distribution of the independent and dependent districts with which it deals. Generally speaking, the greater the number of dependent units the fewer the inter-governmental problems; and the more independents in the system, the more tension and required negotiation.

Municipalities, as well as counties, are involved with special districts. Indeed, many special districts have their basic association with a city and not a county. Unfortunately, however, we have found no inventory that identifies the districts specifically within the cities. Obviously, those that are allied closely with the incorporated areas become less of a burden for the counties.

A review of the Department of Community Affairs data shows that special districts apparently tied to the cities are those concerned with community redevelopment, housing, and downtown development. There were 25 of the community redevelopment districts (out of 187) where "city of" was in the district name; and there were many others that carried the city's name. A similar situation prevailed with housing authorities, where 17 of 81 had "city of" in the name. Virtually all the downtown development authorities were related to a municipality. In most other cases, however, the counties tended to be more heavily involved.

Table 11 is a detailed picture of the district situation (including the numbers of dependent and independent units) in each county in the state. The Table is long and occupies several pages, but there is really no simple way to generalize on the manner in which the districts impact on the various counties. It is necessary to examine the particular county and draw inferences on the data found there. As much care as possible has been exercised in preparing this lengthy and detailed Table, and it is generally consistent with the February 12, 2007, Internet file on the Department of Community Affairs web site. Yet it is very easy to make minor mistakes, and so the author vouches for the general contours of the data but not for each little turn in the road.

Of the 1463 districts located in a single county, 867 are independent, about 60% of the total, and the other 596 are dependent. Counties must, of course, cope with the 67 multi-county districts, which are all independent. The counties with the highest number of special districts are also the ones with the largest populations, as might be anticipated: Hillsborough (1,131,546), 131; Miami-Dade (2,422,075), 95; Lee (549,442), 93; Palm Beach (1,265,900), 90; and Broward (1,740,987), 89. However, three of the largest counties in the state did not follow this trend: Duval (861,150) with 28 districts; Volusia (494,649) with 34 districts; and Pinellas (947,744) with 41 districts. These three were 20th, 17th, and 15th in the number of districts they had.

An overwhelming number of the counties are required to deal with more independent districts (50 of the 67) than dependent, generally presenting more intergovernmental problems for them. Twelve of the 67 counties face independent districts over 80% of the time, with Walton County contending with the largest percentage of independents, 20 of 21 districts within its boundaries. Of the large counties Lee has 83 independents out of 93 special districts, or 89%.

There are relatively few counties, eight, where the dependent special districts outnumber the independents. It is interesting, though, that four of the eight are large population counties (Broward, Brevard, Pinellas, and Volusia). Indeed, Volusia has the highest percentage of dependent counties, 71%, in Florida. Thus there seems nothing that requires the establishment of independent special districts, with their greater problems, in a particular county.

Nine counties have managed a "break even" circumstance, where they split the number of independent and dependent districts. The nine are among the smallest in the state, with Okeechobee (37,765) the largest and also the one with the most special districts in this group, 20.

The pattern of independent and dependent districts in a county will obviously depend on the functions they perform. A county with a substantial number of community development, fire and rescue, hospital, soil and water conservation, and water control districts is destined to have a great many independent ones. On the other hand, a county with a weighting toward community redevelopment, housing, and library districts will likely have more dependent units. It is important, therefore, to examine the structure of districts in a particular county to establish their importance inter-governmentally

Table 11, covering the next several pages, provides detail on the number of special districts in each of the 67 counties.

Table 11

Numbers of Special Districts in Each of the 67 Counties

County Name and Population	Com. Dev. Districts (1)	Com. Redev. Districts (2)	Fire Ctrl., Rescue Districts (3)	Hospital Districts (4)	Housing Authorities (5)	Soil, Water Districts (6)	Library Districts (7)	Water Control Districts (8)	Multi-County Districts	Other Single Districts	Total Districts in County
Alachua 240,764	1 0 active	4			Dep. 2	Ind. 1	Ind. 1 Dep. 1		2	Ind. 1, Dep. 4	17—Ind. 6 Dep. 11
Baker 23,953				Ind. 1	Dep. 1	Ind. 1			5	Ind. 1	9—Ind. 8, Dep. 1
Bay 101,721	2 1 active	4		Ind. 1	Dep. 2	Ind. 1	Dep. 1		4	Dep. 2 Ind. 2	19—Dep 9, Ind. 10
Bradford 28,118		1				Ind. 1			4	Ind. 1 Dep. 2	8—Ind 6, Dep. 2
Brevard 531,970	7 3 active	10		Ind. 2	Ind. 1 Dep. 3	Ind. 1	Ind. 1 Dep. 4	Dep. 1	4	Ind. 8, Dep. 13	55—Ind. 24, Dep. 31
Broward 1,740,987	15 8 active	8		Ind. 3	Ind. 1 Dep. 7	Ind. 3		Ind. 10 Dep. 7	5	Ind. 4, Dep. 26	89—Ind. 41, Dep. 48
Calhoun 13,945		1							5	Ind. 1, Dep. 1	8—Ind. 6, Dep. 2
Charlotte 154,030	6 2 active	2			Dep. 1	Dep. 1		Ind. 4	9	Dep. 6	29—Ind. 19, Dep. 10

County and Population	Comm. Dev.	Com. Redev.	Fire Ctrl., Rescue	Hospital	Housing Authorities	Soil, Water	Library	Water Control	Multi-County	Other Single	Total in County
Citrus 132,635	3 0 active	2	Dep. 1	Ind. 1					4	Ind. 3, Dep. 1	15—Ind. 11, Dep. 4
Clay 169,623	10 2 active					Ind. 1			3	Ind. 1, Dep. 3	18—Ind. 15, Dep. 3
Collier 317,788	19 9 active	2	Ind. 5		Ind. 1	Ind. 1		Ind. 1	3	Ind. 3, Dep. 10	45—Ind. 33, Dep. 12
Columbia 61,466		1		Ind. 1	Ind. 1		Ind. 1		3	Dep. 1, Ind. 1	9—Ind. 7, Dep. 2
De Soto 32,606	1 0 active			Ind. 1	Dep. 1			Ind. 1	3	Ind. 1	8—Ind. 7, Dep. 1
Dixie 15,377		1				Ind. 1			6	Dep. 1	9—Dep. 2, Ind. 7
Duval 861,150	11 0 active	1				Ind. 1	Dep. 1		4	Ind. 5, Dep. 4	28—Ind. 21, Dep. 7
Escambia 303,623	1 1 active	1			Ind. 1	Ind. 1	Ind. 1		5	Dep. 6, Ind. 1	17—Ind. 10, Dep. 7
Flagler 78,617	2 2 active	4			Ind. 1	Ind. 1			2	Ind. 4	14—Ind. 10, Dep. 4
Franklin 10,845		2		Ind. 1 Dep. 1	Dep. 1	Ind. 1			5	Ind. 4, Dep. 1	16—Ind. 11, Dep. 5

County and Population	Comm. Dev.	Com. Redev.	Fire Ctrl., Rescue	Hospital	Housing Authorities	Soil, Water	Library	Water Control	Multi-County	Other Single	Total in County
Gadsden 47,713		1		Dep. 1	Dep. 1	Ind. 1			2	Ind. 1, Dep. 2	9—Dep. 5, Ind. 4
Gilchrist 16,221		1			Ind. 1	Ind. 1			4	Dep. 1	8—Ind. 6, Dep. 2
Glades 10,729	·					Ind. 1			7	Dep. 3 Ind. 2	13—Ind. 10, Dep. 3
Gulf 16,479			Dep. 3						6	Dep. 3, Ind. 2	14—Dep. 6, Ind. 8
Hamilton 14,315						Ind. 1			3	Ind. 6	6—Ind. 6
Hardee 27,333		1				Ind. 1			2	Ind. 1	5—Ind. 4, Dep. 1
Hendry 38,376				Ind. 1	Ind. 1	Dep. 1		Ind. 2, Dep. 1	11	Dep. 2 Ind. 6	25—Ind. 21, Dep. 4
Hernando 150,784	5 1 active	1	Dep. 1		Ind. 1, Dep. 1		Dep. 1		4	Dep. 5	18—Dep. 8, Ind. 10
Highlands 93,456		4		Dep. 1	Dep. 1 Ind. 1	Ind. 1		Ind. 2, Dep. 1	3	Dep. 5 Ind. 1	20—Dep 12, Ind. 8
Hillsborough 1,131,546	56 16 active	3		Dep. 1	Dep. 1	Ind. 1	Dep. 1		4	Dep. 51 Ind. 13	131—Ind.74, Dep. 57

County and Population	Comm. Dev.	Com. Redev.	Fire Ctrl., Rescue	Hospital	Housing Authorities	Soil, Water	Library	Water Control	Multi-County	Other Single	Total in County
Holmes 19,157				Ind. 1	Ind. 1	Ind. 1			4	Dep. 1	8—Ind. 7, Dep. 1
Indian River 130,043		1	Dep. 1	Ind. 1		Ind. 1		Ind. 6	3	Dep. 2 Ind. 2	16—Ind. 13, Dep. 3
Jackson 49,691				Ind. 2	Dep. 1	Ind. 1			4	Dep. 3	11—Ind. 7, Dep. 4
Jefferson 14,233						Ind. 1			5		6—Ind. 6
Lafayette 7,971						Ind. 1			3		4—Ind. 4
Lake 263,017	10 4 active	9		Ind. 3 Dep. 1		Ind. 1		Ind. 1	3	Dept. 3, Ind. 1	30—Ind. 17, Dep. 13
Lee 549,442	45 9 active	9	Ind. 16	Ind. 1	Ind. 1, Dep. 1	Ind. 1	Ind. 2	Ind. 3	7	Dep. 7,. Ind. 9	93—Ind. 83, Dep. 10
Leon 271,111	3 3 active				Dep. 1				2	Dep. 6. Ind. 3	15—Dep. 7, Ind.8
Levy 37,985		1			Ind. 1	Ind. 1			5	Dep. 1 Ind. 1	10—Ind. 8, Dep. 2
Liberty 7,581									3		3—Ind. 3,

County and Population	Comm. Dev.	Com. Redev.	Fire Ctrl., Rescue	Hospital	Housing Authorities	Soil, Water	Library	Water Control	Multi-County	Other Single	Total in County
Madison 29,696		1		Dep. 1		Dep. 1			3		6—Dep. 3, Ind. 3
Manatee 304,364	27 5 active	5	Ind. 8, Dep. 1		Dep. 1 Ind. 1	Ind. 1	Dep. 1		10	Dep. 7 Ind. 7	69—Ind. 54, Dep. 15
Marion 304,926	5 2 active	1		Dep. 1	Dep. 1	Ind. 1			5	Dep. 4, Ind. 3	21—Ind. 14, Dep. 7
Martin 141,059		2			Dep. 1	Ind. 1	Ind. 1	Ind. 1	4	Dep.3, Ind. 1	14—Dep. 6, Ind. 8
Miami-Dade 2,422,075	48 1 active	11	Dep. 1		Dep. 1, Ind. 1	Ind. 1	Dep. 1		4	Dep. 21, Ind. 6	95—Ind. 60, Dep. 35
Monroe 82,413		2	Ind. 1	Ind. 2	Dep. 1. Ind. 1				1	Dep.3, Ind. 3	14—Dep. 6, Ind. 8
Nassau 65,758	5 0 active				Dep. 1 Ind. 1	Ind. 1		Dep. 1	3	Dep. 1, Ind. 3	16—Ind. 13. Dep. 3
Okaloosa 188,939	1	2	Ind. 9		Dep. 2				5	Dep. 5 Ind. 6	30—Ind. 21. Dep. 9
Okeechobee 37,765						Ind. 1		Ind. 2	3	Ind. 4	10—Ind. 10
Orange 1,043,437	18 4 active	7		Ind. 1	Dep. 2	Ind. 1	Ind. 1	Dep. 2 Ind. 2	6	Dep. 9	49—Ind. 29, Dep. 20

County and Population	Comm. Dev.	Com. Redev.	Fire Ctrl., Rescue	Hospital	Housing Authorities	Soil, Water	Library	Water Control	Multi-County	Other Single	Total in County
Osceola 235,156	19 8 active	3				Ind. 1	Dep. 1		4	Ind. 2, Dep. 10	44—Ind. 26, Dep. 18
Palm Beach 1,265,900	23 5 active	10			Dep. 4	Ind. 1	Dep. 1	Dep. 1 Ind. 16	9	Ind. 9, Dep. 14	90—Ind. 60, Dep. 30
Pasco 406.89	37 10 active	4			Ind. 1	Ind. 1			3	Ind. 4 Dep. 5	55—Ind. 46, Dep. 9
Pinellas 947,744	3 2 active	10	Ind. 4		Dep. 2 Ind. 1			Ind. 1	4	Ind. 5, Dep. 11	41—Ind. 18, Dep. 23
Polk 541,840	16 3 active	10			Dep. 5	Ind. 1	Dep. 1	Ind. 4	3	Ind. 5, Dep. 8	53—Ind. 29, Dep. 24
Putnam 73,764		3			Dep. 1	Ind. 2			4	Dep. 2, Ind. 6	12—Ind. 6, Dep. 6
St. Johns 157,278	41 2 active	1			Dep. 1	Ind. 1			4	Ind. 6, Dep. 5	43—Ind. 36, Dep. 7
St. Lucie 240,039	31 4 active	1	Ind. 1		Dep. 1	Ind. 1	Ind. 1	Ind. 2	2	Dep. 6 Ind. 5	51—Ind. 43, Dep. 8
Santa Rosa 136,443	1	23	Ind. 3		Dep. 1				7	Dep. 4 Ind. 2	20—Ind. 13. Dep. 7
Sarasota 367,867	6 2 active	2	Dep. 1	Ind. 1	Dep.2	Ind. 1	Dep. 1	Dep. 1 Ind. 1	11	Dep. 7 Ind. 1	35—Ind. 21, Dep. 14

County and Population	Comm. Dev.	Com. Redev.	Fire Ctrl., Rescue	Hospital	Housing Authorities	Soil, Water	Library	Water Control	Multi-County	Other Single	Total in County
Seminole 411,744	1 1 active	3			Ind. 1 Dep. 1	Ind. 1	Dep. 1		3	Dep. 6 Ind. 1	18—Ind. 7, Dep. 11
Sumter 74,052	10 3 active	1		Ind. 1		Ind. 1			2	Dep. 1	16—Ind. 14, Dep. 2
Suwanee 38,174					Dep. 2	Ind. 1			2	Dep. 2 Ind. 1	7—Ind. 4, Dep. 3
Taylor 21,310						Ind. 1			3	Dep. 2 Ind. 1	7—Ind. 5, Dep. 2
Union 15,0146		1			Ind. 1	Ind. 1	Dep. 1		4		8—Ind. 6, Dep. 2
Volusia 494,649	2 1 active	9	Dep. 1	Ind. 3	Dep. 4	Ind. 1			2	Dep.10 Ind. 2	34—Ind. 10, Dep. 24
Wakulla 26,867						Ind. 1			5		6—Ind. 6
Walton 53,525	5 1 active		Ind. 4		Dep. 1	*Ind. 1*			5	Ind. 5	20—Ind. 20, Dep. 1
Washington 23,097				Dep. 1		Ind. 1			4	Dep. 4	10—Ind. 5, Dep. 5

(1)   We count a total of 491 Community Development Districts, all of them Independent. Our figure in adding all the counties differs from the tally reported in the Department of Community Services database. In one place the number is 465 and in another 509.

(2)   We count a total of 187 Community Redevelopment Districts, all of which are listed as Dependent. The Department of Community Affairs reports 179.

(3)   We count a total of 60 Fire Control and Rescue Districts, 51 Independent and 9 Dependent. 86% are Independent. The Community Affairs figure is 68.

(4)   We count a total of 36 Hospital Districts, 29 Independent and 7 Dependent. 80% are Independent. The Community Affairs figure is 35.

(5)   We count a total of 81 Housing Authorities, 21 Independent and 60 Dependent. 75% are Dependent. The Community Affairs figure is 93.

(6)   We count a total of 58 Soil and Water Conservation Districts, 55 Independent and 3 Dependent. 95% are Independent. The Community Affairs figure is 64.

(7)   We count a total of 26 Library Districts, 9 Independent and 17 Dependent. 62% are Dependent. The Community Affairs figure is 32.

(8)   We count a total of 74 Water Control Districts, 59 Independent and 15 Dependent. 80% are Independent. The Community Affairs figure is 96.

(9)   The "Other Districts" are in the following function categories, with the numbers of them in parentheses: Airport/Aviation (26), Conservation and Erosion (9), County Development (11), Distribution Pipelines (3), Downtown Development (17), Economic Development (8), Education/Research/Training (1), Educational Facilities (Higher)(12), Educational Facilities Benefit (2), Emergency Medical Services (6), Environmental Protection (7), Expressways and Bridges (21), Health Care (6), Health Facilities (33), Historic Preservation (1), Housing Finance (28), Industrial Development (26), Information Systems (1), Infrastructure Provision (6), Inlet Maintenance (3), Juvenile Welfare (7), Lighting (3), Mobile Home Parks (4), Mosquito Control (18), Municipal Services/Improvements (21), Navigation (12), Neighborhood Improvement (35), Nursing Home (1), Parking, (1), Personnel (2), Planning and Zoning (2), Port (15), Recreation/Parks (24), Research and Development (5), Solid Waste (8), Sports (4), Subdivision (54), Transportation (14), Utility (7), Wastewater Treatment (3), Water Management (5), Water Supply (16), Water and Sewer (24).

(10)   A few districts were not included in the analysis. They are: Affordable Housing (1), Aquatic Plant Control (1), Arts (2), Beach and Shore (5), Beautification (1), Capital Finance (4), Children/Welfare (9), and Civic Center (6).

(11)   A number of districts have more than one function. Addition of numbers above will not yield a correct number for the total special districts in the state.

In Table 11 the most common special districts in Florida are identified, with an indication of the numbers of each to be found in the 67 counties.

The Community Development districts are a special case, and we will return to them. Whatever their number and status, however, they are always and inevitably independent. The Community Redevelopment Districts, of which we count 187, appear always to be dependent. Along with the multi-county districts, these two are the only ones whose type is usually known. The Soil and Water Conservation Districts are 95% "pure" independents, with only three out of 58 dependent.

Aside from Community Development, the most common single county district is Water Control, of which there are 74. However, these are concentrated in only 19 counties, with Broward and Palm Beach Counties each having 17. The Water Control Districts are overwhelmingly independent, with 80% of them having such a structure. In Palm Beach County 16 of 17 are independent and in Broward 10 of 17.

Fire Control and Rescue Districts are reasonably prevalent. There are 60 of them in 17 counties. The general profile is one of independence, with 51 of 60 in this category, 86%. However, these figures are heavily skewed by the presence of 34 districts in three counties, all but one of which is independent. Lee County has 16 independent districts; Okaloosa 9; and Manatee has eight that are independent and one dependent.

Hospital districts are arrayed more broadly among the counties, both large and small. There is no concentration of districts in a county, as with Water Control. Lake has the most, with four (3 independent and 1 dependent) and Broward and Volusia each have three independent Hospital Districts. Overall, the 36 Hospital Districts reside in 26 counties and are heavily independent, 29 to 7.

Two other of the predominant special districts, housing authorities and libraries, usually hold dependent status. Of the 81 housing authorities, 75% (60) are dependent. The authorities are spread over 45 counties, with Broward having the most (7 dependent, 1 independent). There are seven counties which have one independent and one dependent housing authority. We tallied 26 library districts, 62% of which are dependent. In 16 of the 19 counties in which library districts are found, there is a single one. Brevard has the largest number of library districts, 5 (4 dependent, 1 independent).

IV. COMMUNITY DEVELOPMENT DISTRICTS

The Community Development Districts are a kind of "wild card" in the general analysis of the special districts in the counties. That is because it is unclear just how many CDDs are really operating. In the listing of these districts in the Department of Community Affairs database, our count shows 491. That differs from numbers found at various places on the Department of Community Affairs website, where we identified 465 at one place and 509 at another. Further confounding things, the Department reports that only 116 Community Development Districts are "active." Also, a State Senate report in 2003 put the number at 203; and an essay posted on the Internet in February 2007, declares the total "more than 250."

In assessing the significance of the special districts in the inter-governmental world of the counties, it is obvious that the number of CDDs actually functioning has immense consequence. It is one thing if they constitute about a third of all special districts in the state and quite another if the total number of districts is reduced to about 1100 and the Community Development Districts are only about 15% of that total. Hillsborough County, which has the most special districts in the state, would reduce its total by 40, simply by accepting the Community Affairs "active district" count. Its CDDs would drop from 56 to 16; and it would also change the balance of total independent and dependent districts. The recalculation would leave Hillsborough with 57 dependent districts and 34 independents, for a total of 91.

It has been observed that deactivating a Community Development District is a time-consuming process. The State requires information, often difficult to obtain, on these evidences of continued operation: (1) a recorded action by the district in the last two years: (2) a governing board with the required quorum; (3) the filing of required reports to the Department of Community Affairs; (4) payment of special assessment fees to the Department in the last two years. A shortfall on any one of these four requirements is sufficient for deactivation. The list of 161 "active districts" therefore is likely composed of those who have met all these obligations.

Whatever the number, the Community Development Districts are an important part of the Florida inter-governmental system. Begun when the Uniform Community Development District Act of 1980 was passed, they provide a financial incentive to large developers and can give homeowners assurance that basic infrastructure improvements are made, with provisions for their maintenance.

The essential vehicle for all this is the tax-free bond, which must be issued by a government. It means that a developer can borrow money at a lower rate of interest; but it doesn't necessarily provide a financial break for the homeowner. The capital improvements financed by the bonds are paid back over a period of time, typically 20–30 years, by the homeowners. Thus developers can offer attractive amenities from the outset without furnishing the money for them. The CDD may also provide a means for maintaining the facilities through a working capital fund, replenished by fees. In many cases, though, the maintenance is taken on by a Homeowners' Association, whose organizational integrity is established by deed or covenant restrictions and which operates within the framework of the Community Development District.

The Districts have a broad freedom to provide specialized services within their territorial confines. They are authorized to engage in the following activities: water management and control, water supply, sewer and waste management, reclamation and reuse, bridges and culverts, roads, street lights, parks and other outdoor recreational, cultural, and educational facilities, fire prevention and control, school buildings, security, mosquito control, and waste collection and disposal.

The initiative to create a CDD typically comes from a developer with a large piece of land. If the size of the development is more than 1,000 acres, it can be authorized by the Florida Land and Water Adjudicatory Commission. A Capital Region CDD in the city of Tallahassee including an unincorporated area of Leon County of 3,241 acres, was approved by the Commission, with the St. Joe Company as developer. It has subsequently emerged as the community of Southwood. Properties of less than 1,000 acres are established by an ordinance enacted by a city or a county. There is a requirement that 100% of property owners within the proposed district approve, but that is seldom a problem for a major developer.

Community Development Districts continue to be created, though perhaps at a lessened pace than has been true in the past. An announcement for the Longleaf CDD in the Tampa Bay area suggests how the advantages of this arrangement are marketed:

> Longleaf is one of many fine, master-planned communities which operate as a Community Development District (CDD) for the purpose of protecting the future of the community and the quality of life enjoyed by its residents. By overseeing basic infrastructure amenities and community operations, the CDD helps ensure the maintenance of the community and preservation of property values long after the developer has left. How will I benefit?
>
> Because of the Longleaf CDD, amenities like recreational facilities are constructed early in the development rather than later. So you can enjoy many of the special benefits of Longleaf without waiting years for them to be complete. In addition you enjoy the pleasures of a well-maintained and managed community while you live in Longleaf and have the peace of mind of knowing that your community will show well should you decide to sell sometime in the future.

Joe Kollin, writing for the *South Florida Sun-Sentinel*, posted an article on the Internet May 5, 2007, in which he reported that the city of Pembroke Pines [Broward County] had created a "mini-government" for a residential developer. He wrote that the firm will pay at least $10,000 less per lot for the construction of roads and water and sewer systems. The price of the 208 townhouses involved was to be proportionately reduced in price. Kollin also reported on two other developments:

> Two other Community Development Districts in the city are Meadow Pines, which includes the Cobblestone community, and Walnut Creek.
>
> The city in 2003 created the Meadow Pines Community Development District for the 850-home Cobblestone development on the west side of I-75 between Pines Boulevard and Pembroke Road. The developer, Westbrooke Cos., Inc., of Miami, borrowed $17.4 million and was to charge each Cobblestone homeowner $700 a year for 30 years to repay it ...
>
> The commission in 2000 created the Walnut Creek Community Development District for Lennar Homes' 1,112-unit subdivision east of University Drive between Taft and Sheridan streets. Each owner pays $40 a month to the District to pay off the loan.
>
> The preliminary estimate of costs for Pembroke Harbor is $3.5 million. Each homeowner's payment to the district, which will be for 30 years, hasn't been announced.
>
> A five-member board of representatives of the developer governs each Community Development District for the first five years. Then the homeowners, generally through their homeowner associations, begin taking over the board.
>
> The districts cease to exist when bonds are repaid ...

V. INCREASING SCRUTINY OF SPECIAL DISTRICTS

Special districts have generally attracted little public attention, despite the fact that the majority of them are independent and have the capacity to levy taxes. With the continuing concern in Florida for the costs of government, it is not surprising that the special districts are attracting their share of attention. An article by Steve Bousquet in the *St. Petersburg Times*, posted on the Internet February 10, 2007, was titled, "Special Districts Nibble at Taxpayers." Here is part of what Bousquet wrote:

Which local government has been raising your property taxes the fastest?

Is it the county? city? school board?

Guess again. The answer is those overlooked but important creatures known as special taxing districts.

They are local governments created by the Legislature that have specific missions that may matter to you. Health care for kids, mass transit, water quality, mosquito and fire control.

Many of them collect only user fees or assessments. But more than 200 of them collect property taxes, and they are largely ignored by the public and the media.

Statewide, their collective tax take has increased 136 per cent since 2001, according to the Governor's office. It's true that they tax at a much lower rate than cities or counties, which is why you probably don't notice them in the fine print on your annual tax bill …

… taxing districts are multiplying in this state.

Florida has 1,494 special taxing districts.

Hillsborough County has 129, more than any other county …

Miami-Dade is second with 91. Pinellas has 41, Pasco 54 and Hernando 19 …

… Rep. Ron Saunders, a Key West Democrat, wondered why the property taxers with the "highest growth rate" wouldn't be made to do with a little less, like counties and cities.

Rep. Kevin Ambler, R-Lutz, said it would be wrongheaded for the state to protect special taxing districts from a tax cut others must endure.

"We don't want to encourage more special districts," Ambler said.

A former Republican state legislator, Stan Bainter, wrote an article for *Florida Taxwatch* saying that there needs to be more public attention paid to these districts.

In a year in which property taxes is front and center as the state's dominant political issue, it's a good bet that will happen.

"Our legislators need to know exactly what they have created," wrote Bainter, who voted to create more than a few of them when he was in the House.

VI. FINANCING DISTRICTS BUT NOT UNITS OF GOVERNMENT

The *Florida Special District Handbook* makes it very clear that a Municipal Services Taxing or Benefit Unit is not a special district, in the sense that it has its own organization integrity. Yet such financing arrangements, which are particularly common in the unincorporated areas of the counties, are often referred to as special districts, As a result, it is easy to become confused about their place in the structure of government arrangements.

Essentially, the taxing and benefit units are vehicles used by the counties to finance projects and services in the unincorporated areas, where there is a concern that money collected from the entire county not be used to benefit a piece of it, particularly one that pays no municipal taxes. In a very real sense the units are a guard against the charge of double taxation by city dwellers. They want to be assured county taxes go for county purposes and not for municipal-type services in the unincorporated areas.

The Municipal Services Taxing Unit is basically characterized by its reliance on property taxes for its revenue. The unit has specific geographical boundaries, and the assessment levied against a particular property is its proportionate share of the total assessed valuation within the unit. A Collier County statement notes that taxing districts (or MSTUs) may be established to finance such capital projects as drainage improvements, sidewalk construction, road improvements, landscape beautification, and decorative lighting.

Typically, these financing arrangements are administered by the county government. In Collier, however, there is a practice of establishing advisory committees composed of community members from within the MSTU area, appointed by the Board of County Commissioners.

A particularly noteworthy example of these arrangements is the International Drive Master Transit and Improvement District in Orange County. Created in 1992, the District is a unique amalgam of three distinct parts of the International Drive tourist area in Orlando. It operates a transit service and also provides various promotional and marketing services.

Actually, the District is composed of three different Municipal Services Taxing Units and levies property taxes cooperatively to support the area-wide services. Unlike most MSTUs, this one does have a governing board, composed of two representatives from Orange County and one from the City of Orlando. The District regards itself as "… an outstanding example of cooperation between three distinct entities … as the first district of this type established in Florida … and is now used by other regions as a model."[70]

The Municipal Services Benefit Unit (MSBU) differs from the MSTU in one fundamental respect. It does not levy a property tax. Its revenue comes from other sources, such as fees. As Charlotte County describes the process, a determination is made of the number of assessment units within the service area, and a charge is made for each of the units. A residential lot is typically an assessment unit.

Seminole County declares that the MSBU program has been particularly established for residents of the unincorporated areas, providing an opportunity to acquire public health and safety improvements or services. It identifies four types of community improvements and services that are funded through Municipal Service Benefit Units:

1. *Aquatic weed control,* which also includes re-contouring improvements for retention ponds.

2. *Construction,* which includes road paving, drainage, sidewalks, water services, and sewerage services.

3. *Solid waste,* which includes curbside collection and disposal of household garbage, recycling and yard waste, and access to County disposal facilities.

4. *Street lighting,* which includes residential street lighting fixtures, poles, and utilities.

Declaring that an MSBU requires the approval of the County Commission and is governed by statutory regulations, Seminole County specifies that three conditions must be met to establish such a financing arrangement:

1. The benefitting property is located in unincorporated Seminole County.

2. The property upon which the improvement is to be made is publicly owned (or subject to qualifying easements).

3. Two or more parcels benefit from the improvement of service.

VII. SUMMARY

The understanding of Special Districts in Florida government has been greatly facilitated by the work of the Department of Community Affairs. It maintains a

---

70 "What Is the International Drive Master Transit and Improvement District?" Ride Trolley, website, itrolley.com/idmtid.asp> Posted May 28, 2007

data base that will answer most of the factual questions people may have about their operations.

It is important that there be such citizen concern and that information be easily available. That is because special districts are important elements of government in Florida, with significant roles to discharge. They have particular consequence for the counties, whose responsibilities often intersect with them.

Since special districts come in many forms, it is somewhat difficult to describe and categorize them definitively. However, it is possible to identify three universal characteristics. First, they are recognized as formal units of government, just as the cities and counties are, and there is an established body of law that governs their conduct. The Uniform Special District Accountability Act of 1989 currently sets the terms for their operations. Second, they operate within a defined territorial framework, thus setting limits on where they may function. And third, their responsibilities are specific in terms of the tasks they are established to perform. In this sense, they are different from cities and counties, which are often called "general purpose" governments, free to engage in any activity that is not specifically prohibited.

It is largely within the framework of this specific assignment of duties that Special Districts were developed and achieved popularity. Long before counties were operating in any more than a minimal sense and there were no cities, Florida's Road, Highway, and Ferry Act of 1822 was passed. It set in motion the first effort to provide the state with a system of public highways.

There are basically two types of special districts, and the defining distinction is how they affect the counties. Sixty-six operate in more than one county and are labeled multi-county districts. The Department of Community Affairs lists another 1439 which are found in a single county and are predictably called single county districts. Essentially all the multi-county districts have a high degree of independence; and, in effect, they function quite separately from the counties in which they are located.

One of the oldest and still one of the largest of the multi-county districts is the Florida Inland Navigation District, whose roots date back to the time when much of the transportation in Florida was by river and canal. The District is basically a collaboration between the Federal and State governments, with 11 counties on the eastern side of Florida as participants. Its purpose is to develop and maintain the inland waterway.

By far the biggest venture in multi-county districts, however, involves water management. The Water Resources Act of 1972 built on efforts which had been under way in South Florida and created water management districts in the five major watersheds of the state. They embrace all the counties of Florida and operate in roughly similar ways, with their main objectives to assure a water supply for the state, to protect the sources of water, and to limit the damaging effects of flooding.

The South Florida Water Management district is the largest, covering 16 counties, serving nearly nine million people, and spread over a territory of nearly 20,000 square miles. The smallest is the Suwanee River Water Management District, covering 13 of the smaller Florida counties in the north, serving about 620,000 people, and having a territory of 9,961 square miles.

The other multi-county districts perform a variety of functions, ranging from economic development to solid waste to transportation.

There is one complexity and also a distinction that is important in the analysis of the single county districts. The complication is that we are not sure about the total number of operating districts in the state, a problem that can have its effect on the analysis of the special district situation in a particular county. The issue has to do with Community Development Districts, of which the Department of Community Affairs reports there are 509, roughly a third of the total. Ascertaining the status of the CDDs, however, is difficult because they are usually established as a means of obtaining tax-free bonds for infrastructure improvements. When a subdivision is well established and the bond servicing is a customary part of housing payments, there may be little interest in maintaining the organization. Thus the Department of Community Affairs shows only 116 CDDs fully active. How to think about the rest, and more significantly, how to conclude about their place in county affairs becomes a problem.

The key point of analysis for the single county district is its status as an independent or dependent unit. The distinction is highly important in ascertaining a district's relationship either to a county or to a city. In one aspect or another, a dependent district is subordinate to its host. This may be in terms of the ways its leadership is identified or constructed, or it may be that the host controls the purse strings. If, on the other hand, a district may decide how it is to be led and how much money it has and where it is to be spent, it is independent. It is free to run its own show.

Obviously, status as dependent or independent will be a determining factor in the nature of a district's relationships with its host, either a city or a county. Our assumption is that the larger the number of independent districts in a county the more complications for the governing body. Walton County, for example, where there are 20 independent districts out of 21, is likely to find special districts more troublesome than Highlands County, where 12 of its 20 districts are dependent. This is "one factor" reasoning, of course, and many other considerations may influence how district dynamics occur in these two counties.

We have taken great pains to construct Table 11, which provides a view of the structure of the special districts in each of the counties. We have included the special districts which appear in the Department Community Affairs data base, but not always the most frequently. We were interested in seeing, for example, where the library districts were and whether they were dependent or independent. (It turned out they were most frequently dependent.)

We did go through the entire DCA data base, and districts not included in the chart are found in the "Other Single Districts" column. Paragraph 8 at the bottom of Table 11 lists the districts analyzed with their numbers in parentheses. The districts are organized according to the classificatory scheme of the Department of Community Affairs.

Overall, we came out with numbers roughly similar to, but certainly not the same as, those in the DCA database.

The chapter concludes with a brief discussion of Municipal Services Taxing Units and Municipal Services Benefit Units. As we have taken pains to point out, these are not special districts in the terms of this book, though they have often been given that name. They are not governed by State special district law and they are not regarded as units of government.

Rather, they are very handy funding mechanisms developed particularly by the counties to finance the many urban services required in the unincorporated areas. They have become an important means by which counties have discharged their urban service responsibilities

CHAPTER TEN

REVENUE SOURCES AS A FACTOR IN HOME RULE

However much formal authority may be assigned to a level of government, the reality is that its exercise depends on money. It takes cash to hire people to carry out tasks, to provide them the necessary facilities, and to fund the many other expenses that are part of the management of any large organization. Counties in Florida are no exception.

Indeed, it is fair to say that much of the authority assigned to the counties by the State is largely symbolic, precisely because such delegations have often not been accompanied by appropriate financial arrangements both in relationship to expenditures and to revenues. The State may impinge on the authority of a county by requiring it to spend specified amounts for prescribed purposes; and it can also limit the ways in which a county may secure revenues to support its many activities.

At the time of this writing, Florida is involved in a major conflict over the financing of local government, particularly in relationship to the property tax. Such clashes occur periodically, and they tend to be couched in economic terms. People don't like to spend money. While taxes in general are frequently at issue, the property tax is a particular target. There is a reason for that, as will be discussed later. Here it is sufficient to note that politicians and citizens alike descend on it both because it is highly visible and its local character makes it easier to control.

The emphasis on money and economics is unfortunate because there is more at stake. Some taxes are supportive of local governments and their freedom to operate; others are not. We therefore need to consider taxes not just from a money standpoint but what they do to keep local governments strong and viable.

This chapter is consequently concerned with the place of revenues in constructing a positive, supportive set of relationships between the State and its counties. It seeks to establish a framework for appraising revenue sources in terms of their institutional impacts, rather than in terms of economics. Unfortunately, such an orientation receives relatively little attention in these days of the economists' hegemony. And the perspective unfortunately gets lost during a heated campaign when politicians want to make citizens feel good by lowering their taxes. Yet the freedom of a community to choose tax sources in terms of its value system and economic conditions, as well as to determine how to apportion costs among the various revenue sources, is a core element of any decentralized governmental system.

In this chapter we propose a way of thinking about the financial support for Florida's local governments, and counties in particular. The next and concluding chapter will present a picture of county finances in Florida as they existed before a major change that may occur in 2007 or 2008.

I. THE CONCEPT OF HOME RULE—AGAIN

Although we have already written a great deal about home rule, the concept is so important that a reminder is in order. The idea itself is quite simple. It is that a community should be free to deal with the problems that lie within its borders. Not only is it important for a democracy that people feel themselves participants in events that directly affect them, but home rule is an important energizing element. When people do feel they are in control and can make a difference, powerful motivations can be unleashed. Citizens are often willing to participate and tax themselves more because they do see direct benefits from such efforts. Interventions by higher levels of government lead to the familiar results of centralization: alienation, reduction in feelings of personal responsibility, and allocation inefficiencies. The absence of home rule, from the political standpoint, means that citizens tend to think of themselves more as subjects of government than as participants. Further, financing becomes more difficult because the benefits of State expenditures are less directly focused, making increased taxes less acceptable.

Assumptions of Home Rule

There is a number of assumptions about the consequences of home rule that become an important point of orientation for this chapter. They are:

1.   There is a correlation between the exercise of political accountability and the institutional level, particularly in terms of population, at which the activity occurs. The smaller the institution the greater the accountability.

2. There is a correlation between political accountability and effective government. Services will be delivered more effectively when officials know that they are being held accountable at the polls.

3. Fiscal flexibility is a critical ingredient of "county home rule."

4. The intergovernmental system is more effective when there is a constructive and competitive relationship among the units in that system.

5. The property tax, as it is administered in Florida and many other states, is not as regressive or onerous as political figures, the media, and others suggest.

6. From a home rule perspective, the property tax is the most flexible source of revenue available to county governments.

7. The biggest problems with the property tax are the result of actions and decisions made by persons other than elected county commissioners.

8. The generally held belief that local government officials tend to avoid sensitive issues, especially of a fiscal nature, is incorrect.

9. Fiscal paternalism, as frequently expressed and exercised by State and national legislators, is detrimental to a constructive intergovernmental system.

With these assumptions in mind, it makes sense to consider revenue sources from a home rule (institutional) perspective, as well as an economic one.

Financing and Home Rule: The Source Does Matter

Here is a case which shows how differently issues of taxes are frequently handled at the various levels of government.

Several years ago, within a 60-day period, the citizens of Leon County experienced the following budgetary actions: the State of Florida (whose capital is in Tallahassee), held hearings on a budgetary increase of $635 millions; the City of Tallahassee held hearings on a hike of $3.5 millions; and Leon County conducted hearings on a raise of $900,000. At the State hearing, no local citizens appeared, and there were only lobbyists requesting more money. At the City hearing, 80 residents appeared, each seeking more funds for an individual or group program. At the County hearing, more than 400 residents appeared (in a courtroom with seating for 150). Six testified in support of specific programs; the remaining 400 angrily protested a tax increase.

Why the difference? The increased revenues were to come from the sales tax in the case of the State; utility charges in the City; and the property tax in the

County. In addition to normal growth, the County had to raise property taxes sufficient to cover the loss of a $350,000 reimbursement, which the State chose to discontinue. Also, it had to replace income which would have been generated by $130 millions of taxable property that had been removed from County rolls by State action. The cause was an increased homestead exemption, which rose from $15,000 to $25,000 over a period of three years, resulting in the total exemption of 1300 more homes from County property taxation. That was in addition to the more than the 2000 exempted in the previous year. Obviously, the burden had to be shifted to those remaining on the rolls.

In the five-hour County hearing, the demand was, "Cut something. We want our property taxes reduced.!" The public reaction to the property tax contradicted a generally positive attitude toward County services. Indeed there were several indicators of a "good government" climate in Leon County. There was little turn-over in elected officials; high turnout in local elections; a long history of honest public officials; and positive rankings in public opinion polls.

Yet all was not well on the fiscal front. While 400 citizens is a small percent-age of the total population, it was still 375 more people than normally attended a budget hearing. There was equal unrest among the County Commissioners, one of whom commented:

> Sometimes I'm not sure whether I'm a policymaker or simply an elected administrator. It seems like I spend far more time performing basic administra-tive functions than I do as a participant in the process of establishing public policy. I'm not so naive as to believe that an elected official can divorce him-self from administration. I do, however, find frequently that the policy which establishes the need for administrative action has already been determined by someone else. It seems like the only real policy questions arise around expen-diture of those revenues that come from the property tax; and when you think that only 25 percent of our revenue comes from property tax, it is frightening. When you couple that with the fact that approximately 75 percent of our *ad valorem* revenue is used to satisfy mandates, it is bewildering.

There is no doubt about the frustration that both elected officers and citizens experience in the County situation. While the problems prompting the property tax increase were complicated and difficult of resolution, one thing seems clear. The property tax provided an important vehicle for citizen participation in the County governance process. That did not seem to happen either in the State or the City situation, where other types of revenues were involved.

Economists have argued that the critical elements in tax and revenue discussions are: sufficiency of the source, ease of collection, equity incidence, and permanence. These are, of course, highly important. Yet most economists leave untouched the basic institutional questions which led to the Boston Tea Party. Who should decide what the taxes will be, who will be taxed, and how much will be paid?

II. CRITERIA FOR ASSESSING LEVELS OF HOME RULE IN TAXES

When examining revenue questions from the institutional (home rule) perspective, the questions become quite different.

1. How easy is it for the citizen to influence tax policy, i.e., have accessibility?
2. How easy is it for the citizen to understand the facts about the tax, i.e. visibility?
3. How easy is it for the citizen to identify the officials responsible for the tax policy, i.e. accountability?
4. How much control over a given tax source does a particular jurisdiction have, i.e. exclusivity?
5. How free is the jurisdiction to impose a particular tax within its jurisdiction, i.e. authority?
6. How free is a jurisdiction to use the product of its revenue sources, i.e. flexibility?

These six questions can be translated into a similar number of criteria by which to evaluate the institutional impact of various revenue sources. A discussion of each of these criteria follows.

Accessibility

In the representative system of government in the United States, individuals elect those people whom they feel most closely represent their perspectives. The larger the constituency an elected official serves, the more difficult it is for him/her to represent the interests of the single individual. Put another way, the larger the constituency, the harder it is to articulate the interests of each individual represented. In our present forms of representative government, we have moved a great distance from the direct democracy of the New England town meeting.

Accompanying the directness of representation is the concept of participation. When the community can gather in the town hall, involvement remains high. This reality suggests that convenience, logistics, and familiarity play a role in participation.

Taxes are, of course, a prime concern of most citizens. Thus the opportunity to have a direct contact with one's elected representative is particularly important. Yet the representatives of the Federal government, which takes the largest share of taxes, are the most distant from their constituents; and much of the same remoteness characterizes representative democracy in a state as large as Florida. It is at the local level that citizens have a real opportunity for participation, namely to exercise direct influence on their legislators. Ideally, then, a revenue source which encourages such direct participation has institutional advantages over one that does not.

Visibility

Directly related to accessibility is visibility, which is important in terms of two perspectives. One is the element of open government, in which the activities of public officials can be observed by individual citizens and are reported by the media. Florida has developed a strong tradition, and also a legal requirement, of government in the sunshine. Citizens do have the opportunity to "see" their government in action; and, obviously, such an observation is much easier in the case of local, close-to-home entities.

The second element is public information. Open government provides access to the media, but there is the need for a responsible press to bring such knowledge to the citizenry. With radio, over the air TV, cable, and the Internet, there are now many channels of communication beyond the print media. In considerable degree, however, governmental events at the local level are inadequately reported. In many cases citizens do get better information about their national government than they do about their county. Nevertheless, the 400 people who appeared at the Leon County hearing did have access to information; and, when there are critical tax matters to be decided at the local level, the necessary facts do tend to reach a concerned citizenry.

When officials and information are visible, access to decision makers is also made easier for the citizen. As people are informed and know how to obtain access to their public officials, their opportunities for influence in the best democratic sense are greatly increased.

Accountability

A citizen's expression of interest has no value unless there is a response from public officials. To insure a necessary level of responsiveness, there must be specific points in the decision process in which officials express their opinions. Casting a vote in the legislative body, taking an official "stand," and making public statements for the record all are means by which accountability is established. To the extent that public decisions are taken without specific expressions of preference on the part of public officials, the system of accountability is weakened.

Tax structures and processes that force the public official to take a position enable the citizen to know who supports a particular decision and who does not. The property tax, for example, promotes accountability because local legislators must set the rate each year. As in Leon County, legislators know such decisions are carefully scrutinized and can have their effect in the next election. And, as was being observed in Florida in early 2007, these decisions can have broader, longer-lasting consequences.

Exclusivity

The exclusivity of a revenue source involves the degree to which a particular political body has sole determination of its scale and administration. Ideally, a citizen's participation in the democratic process is eased by a separation of levies among jurisdictions, thus leaving decisions in regard to the amount and application of a particular tax the responsibility of a single government.

Again, the institutional problem is to simplify the governmental agenda with which the citizen must deal. When a number of governments are utilizing the same tax sources and very likely charging different rates, the problem for the citizen in ferreting out tax arrangements he/she either supports or rejects becomes very difficult. Like many others, the State of Florida has formally renounced any right to levy a property tax. That step was taken largely on grounds of exclusivity. While several local governments—the county, the city, the school district, and the various special districts—continue to utilize the tax, the withdrawal of the State has at least made it possible for the citizen to focus attention on the governments closest to home.

Flexibility

Earmarking is a familiar word in government financial circles; and it involves the restriction of revenues from a particular source to certain types of expenditures. The counties may levy, for example, an optional tax on gasoline. But the use of these monies is restricted to the improvement of roads. It is an earmarked tax, a fact which often makes it more attractive to voters.

From the standpoint of the general government, however, it is desirable to separate revenues and expenditures. Monies that carry no strings enable public officials to direct resources toward those programs and services where needs are greatest. Thus flexible sources of revenue are extremely critical to achieving a responsible and responsive government.

Authority

The issue of authority is closely related to flexibility; in fact, it may be regarded as the formal side of flexibility. The counties, for example, live with a financing scheme that is considerably complicated by their service responsibilities in the unincorporated, urban areas. Such services are financed by taxes levied in the districts served; and such revenues can be utilized rather flexibly within the unincorporated area. But the counties have no authority to reallocate such monies to other needs either in the broad county area (incorporated and unincorporated) or in the incorporated areas. The authority to use such funds, then, is limited territorially. In contrast, the Federal income tax generates revenue that meets the tests of both flexibility and authority. Such revenues can be used for a huge range of purposes, suggesting high flexibility. At the same time, substantial authority is also provided to carry out tasks wherever needed by a jurisdiction. Taxes that permit financing of a wide range of activities are, of course, to be preferred.

III. APPLYING THE CRITERIA TO PRESENT REVENUE SOURCES

Because so little has been done to examine the institutional impact of the various revenue sources, an effort is made in the following pages to apply the home rule criteria described above to the numerous income possibilities available to governments. The concern in this section is with sources currently available to county governments in Florida; the succeeding section will examine other alternatives. At the end of the analysis, a chart will be presented that illustrates the comparative relationship of present and possible sources to the criteria.

Property Tax

The property tax has a special place in this analysis for three reasons: (a) it is the source from which Florida counties receive the greatest part of their revenue;

(b) from the county viewpoint, it is both administratively complex and has the largest number of decision makers involved in its usage; and (c) it is the tax which most frequently comes under attack and is subjected to various types of manipulation. That was the situation in Florida in 2007.

The property tax, which is also frequently known as the *ad valorem* tax, rates especially high in terms of two criteria: authority and exclusiveness. The State Constitution assures the source to county government, as well as other local governments. Exclusivity is provided, in that the Constitution states clearly that the tax is for county and city governments, as well as special districts, and is precluded from usage by the State or by quasi-governmental agencies. Many observers also contend that the election in the counties of the appraiser, collector, clerk of the board, and board of commissioners assures public accessibility. The assumption is that standing for election makes such individuals more accessible than appointed ones.

In terms of the visibility criterion, the data are mixed. The decision process by which rates are lowered or increased does provide maximum visibility. The rate cannot grow in real dollars without a formal notice published in the newspapers. Each taxpayer receives notice of proposed changes and hearing dates prior to any action being taken. However, because of the nature of the property assessment procedure, particularly through exemptions, there can still be extensive avoidance of property taxes without attendant publicity.

The several Constitutional officers, including the commissioners, are assumed to share responsibility for the tax and to be "looking over the shoulder" of the others. Theoretically, accountability is enhanced through this process. Property is also a hard asset that can be seen, measured, and compared with other physical assets. As a result, the assessment process can be monitored relatively easily. Such a responsibility rests with the State Department of Revenue, which thereby builds further accountability into the property tax.

Last, there are virtually no restrictions on the uses to which the tax can be put, so long as it meets general public purpose tests. Florida law is quite clear in stating that levies for general purposes are valid when the proceeds provide common and general benefits to the property within the district considered as a whole. The fact that one taxpayer's benefits are remote or non-existent does not therefore invalidate the tax. The general rule is that the question of benefit and of unlawful burden does not arise when the levy is uniform and collected for a public purpose within the power of a legislative body to pursue.

Despite all these advantages, the property tax was under great attack in 2007. Governor Charlie Crist's 2006 campaign platform called for property tax reform;

and Jeb Bush, the incumbent Governor in 2006, created a Property Tax Reform Committee. It made its preliminary report in December, 2006.

The issue was quite clear. Property taxes were said to have gotten too high. There was, of course, a reason for this. With the dramatic increase in property values in the period 2000–2005, assessments had also zoomed. One thing we have gotten right in the last decades is the linking of the selling prices of houses to their assessed valuations. The Florida State Department of Revenue serves as the enforcer on local assessors.

If this were all that were involved, we would have a beautiful system. Property owners could feel comfortable that they were paying only their fair share because assessed values were fairly and equitably computed.

But things are not that simple. The 2000–2005 housing bubble rose far too fast. Property taxes rates were cut, but not enough. As has happened in other cases in the past, there was not enough citizen involvement to institute the necessary correctives. It is a fact, of course, that there were plenty of needs for the extra money, and Pinellas County has reported it has laid away $15 millions in a disaster emergency fund.

In any case, the statistics are not good. According to the Governor's Property Tax Reform Committee, property tax income in the period 1999–2006 was up 80% while personal income growth was 39%. Inflation and population growth was calculated to have increased 32%. Further, the property tax as a percentage of personal income increased from 3.5% in1995 to 4.2% in 2006. It is likely, however, that the days of hyper-inflated prices are over; and so, also, are exalted assessed valuations. If nothing is done, it is likely that homeowners will find tax bills in 2007 that are not very different from those of 2006. We may already be in another cycle where we may be disappointed that housing prices and assessed valuations, and hence tax bills, go up so little.

It is also important to observe that the uproar over high taxes comes not from the property levy itself but from the structure of the assessment process and also from the way we set tax rates. Assessed values do not have to be put at 100 percent of market value; and a different level can be established without affecting the basic equity of the system. (State law, however, currently requires that appraised value recognize full market value.) Also, while the TRIM (Truth in Millage) process theoretically assures that citizens have the capacity to affect tax rates, it is obvious the system has not worked. It has to be asked what might have been done by citizens to make rates more consistent with economic conditions and needs.

While one of the great assets of the property tax is its capacity to bring equity to the system, much of the activity over the last years has made it more inequitable. The move toward unfairness began in Florida in 1934. That is when the first homestead exemption, $5000, was placed in the State Constitution. By the 1980s, a popular vote brought the exemption to $25,000, where it was in 2007. This tax relief is available to any resident of the State; and, in 2006, about half the property owners availed themselves of significant savings in their taxes. Over $100 billion in property value was protected from the tax collector.

It is significant, though, that about half the State's citizens don't enjoy this benefit. Businesses, renters, owners of second homes, and out-of-state owners have to pay the full freight. Obviously, the homestead exemption produces a major inequality in the incidence of the property tax in Florida.

Further, there are other exemptions identified in Department of Revenue material, worthy as many of them are, that further magnify the inequities. There are exemptions in relatively small amounts for widows and widowers, for the blind, disabilities in general, and disabilities connected with military service. For those who are totally and permanently disabled, full exemptions from the property tax are possible. And county governments can provide additional exemptions up to $25,000 for persons 65 and older.

It was not enough to tamper with assessments in these relatively accustomed ways. A Constitutional amendment, passed in 1992, implemented in 1995, and labeled Save Our Homes, further corrupted assessments, on the dubious theory that the longer a person lives in a house the lower the tax should be. It limited the growth in the assessed value of a homestead property either to three percent per year or to the consumer price index, whichever was lower. In the bubble years, when housing prices were often rising by 20 percent and inflation was less than three percent, homestead residents were exempted from virtually all the tax increase and may even have gotten a small rate reduction.

The Governor's Property Tax Reform Committee reported that in 2006–2007, Save Our Homes protected over $400 billion from the property tax, compared to the slightly more than $100 billion sheltered by the homestead exemption. The Committee also observed that about 4.3 million homeowners were covered by Save Our Homes. Further, if this coverage were eliminated, it would result in an instant 24.5% increase in the statewide property tax base. The average tax rate could fall by 19.6% and still deliver the same amount of revenue. The Committee estimated that, for the average Save Our Homes owner, property taxes were reduced $1,130 annually.

It is almost humorous that many recipients of the Save Our Homes largess felt themselves "locked in" by this generous arrangement. They said they could not consider moving because the benefits from Save Our Homes were so great.

These many assaults on the property tax have left it with little credibility in Florida. Its virtues are its accessibility, its visibility and its accountability. Yet all the things that have moved the property tax from a highly equitable to an inequitable levy have been imposed from above. The people who must pay the tax at the local level no longer have control over it. And it is likely they are only vaguely aware of what is happening. There is enough visibility to prompt a general realization that the burden of the tax is not falling equally on everyone. But the devil may be in the details. The extent of the differences, and their widespread prevalence, may have escaped general notice. There is need for reform, but its purpose should be to give the property tax back its good name.

User Fees

From a home rule perspective, user fees rate positively. The authority has been clearly established for counties to use this source of revenue, though typically with narrow restrictions. They are an important source of revenue for the counties. In an analysis of 20 large counties, 10 chartered and 10 not chartered, we found that user fees averaged about 20% of total revenue. Interestingly, they were slightly more heavily utilized in the non-chartered counties.

Because there is a direct relationship between benefits received and costs paid, the criterion of accountability is particularly observed. User fees also have a high level of visibility. Individuals have an opportunity on an almost daily basis to experience the costs of particular projects or services. From an accessibility standpoint, the rate of the fee structure is normally set by county ordinance within legislative parameters. The discussion of fee increases typically must occur in a public forum by amending an ordinance.

This source does not hold up well on the criterion of flexibility. It is a generator of significant revenue, but such levies are not capable of producing income much beyond the cost of performing the service. As a source of revenue to support the needs of other obligations within the county, it is unproductive.

Fees have a high degree of exclusivity for local governments. Generally speaking, the State government is not a provider of services and therefore does nothing which would justify such charges. A lack of exclusivity comes about, however, through competition among various entities at the local level. Many fee-oriented activities can be, and frequently are, provided by private and not for profit organizations. Only when a government has a monopoly over the use of a revenue source can it be said that the exclusivity criterion has been fully honored.

Intergovernmental Revenues

Although there has been a substantial curtailment in Federal funds available to counties in the last two decades, a pattern of Federal involvement has been established over a longer period. As the parties in power change in Washington, the reliance on inter-government transfers will ebb and flow. Although they currently appear to be at a low point, it is important to recognize them as sometimes highly important sources of revenue for Florida's counties. A review of the 2005 revenue profiles in 26 counties, including all but one of the chartered ones, indicates that Federal monies still account for two to three percent of revenues on average, and there are a few counties in which they are much higher. In Miami-Dade, for example, Federal subventions account for seven percent of income.

Since the U.S. Congress has been very specific in assigning authority for the disbursement of Federal funds, there are highly complex and inter-related problems in setting responsibilities for their use. Such programs as saving cities, reducing unemployment, and promoting economic development require new and highly specialized technical knowledge. This necessary specialization, however, has made it increasingly difficult to manage program interactions, as occurs when environmental activities impact efforts in the economic development and employment areas. These complications confuse the accountability for these revenue sources.

Also, the authority picture is complicated by varying degrees of Federal control over the administration of programs. Some require approval of plans; others are accompanied by close, on-site monitoring. The result of the confusion is that there is an increasing frequency of assistance-related disputes. These conflicts between Federal agencies and recipients disrupt what should be close working relationships in order to bring all governments together in the achievement of national objectives.

From a visibility standpoint, the channeling of funds to a variety of agencies within counties (not to mention other governments) often tends to obscure any understanding of their end use. On the Federal side, the Congress and the agencies appear to act and think primarily in terms of single programs, with little regard for the effects of their uncoordinated actions on multi-source recipients. An increasing number of not for profit organizations, quasi governments, and other entities have become participants in receiving these funds. Grants and cooperative agreements are frequently used to fund activities in the private sector.

Such a lack of accountability and visibility is further compounded by the tendency to impose an increasing number of national socio-economic objectives (such as preventing discrimination, protecting the environment, and providing for the handicapped) as a general condition for receiving assistance.

The visibility of Federal aid, which might normally be provided by the news media, is extremely difficult because of the technical specialization required in these programs. In effect, the system is incomprehensible. Further, the requirement of annual re-financing leads to the conclusion that there is no exclusivity for the source.

In the last analysis, the application of the criteria suggests that Federal funds have been far from an ideal source of income for local governments.

While the State-shared revenue system is more readily understood in terms of both amounts and recipients of monies, it has many of the problems of the Federal. Authority remains outside the control and, for the most part, even the influence, of local officials. Program definitions and regulations are established by the State Legislature and executive agency leaders.

Overall, the State accounts for a significant amount of the counties' income. The analysis of 20 large counties, 10 chartered and 10 non-chartered, revealed that State monies provided 8–9% of the counties' revenues. The range in the chartered counties was 5% to 17%, with a mean of 7.8%. In the non-chartered counties the range was 6% to 12%, with a mean of 9.1%.

There are many components of the state revenue sharing system. The most prominent of these is the sales tax. A major reform occurred in 1982 when the State tax was increased from four to five percent, and a half-a-cent of that was allocated to the counties and cities. Each was to receive a quarter of a cent. The main reason for the tax share arrangement arose as a result of the Constitutional mandate in 1968 that limited each of the governments to a 10 mill cap on the property tax. The shortfall was particularly acute in the smaller, rural counties; and the State shared taxes continue to be a more significant share of their income.

This particular subvention rates low, however, on the six criteria of a desirable tax from an institutional perspective because the State has retained almost total control. Most crucially, a hike in the levy to six percent in 1987 left the local governments no better off. They got no share of the increase. The Fiscal Resource Committee of the State Senate reported in 1999 that the city-county share of the sales tax income averaged 8.5 percent annually for the decade beginning in 1988.[71] While the failure to share in the 1987 increase accounts for most of the decline in share from a theoretical 10 percent in 1982, there have been other kinds of nit-picking, such as service charges and contributions to a solid waste fund, as well as charges for emergency distribution to qualified counties.

Still, the counties have fared better than the cities. Where it was originally assumed that the funds would be distributed more or less equally between the two local government types, it was estimated in the Senate report that in 1999–2000 the cities would get 2.9 % of the total pie and the counties 6%.[72]

---

71 Fiscal Resource Committee, Florida State Senate, *Revenue Sharing with Local Governments: Examination of Alternatives*, August 2000. Report No. 2000-46, p. 12

72 Ibid., p. 13.

While the sales tax has been the major contributor to local government finances, revenue sharing actually began earlier. The first significant move appeared to occur in 1941 when intangible tax income was divided between the State (75%) and the counties (25%). Similarly, the State began sharing cigarette tax revenues with the cities, in a rather cumbersome way, as early as 1949.

Revenue sharing trust funds were established for the counties and the cities in 1972, with the monies coming largely from the intangible tax and cigarettes. That led to "guaranteed entitlements," for the cities and counties, specifying that the amount shared in the future would not be less than that in 1972. A second guaranteed entitlement was provided the counties in 1982, this time specifying that the amount in the revenue sharing trust fund would not be reduced in the future. In effect each of the counties was promised two pots of money, the first set by the amount received in 1972 and the second by the sum available in 1982. By 2006 the amounts received from these two sources differed dramatically. Pasco County reported, for example, that the first guaranteed entitlement amounted to $310,426 in that year and the second guaranteed entitlement was $1,782,481.

The experiences with these funds reveals that they are very much dependent on State decisions and therefore do not meet the standards of an institutionally desirable tax. Very productive for a considerable length of time, the intangible tax yielded varying amounts to the counties, depending on State whim. At one point the share was 55%, at others much lower. The tax was completely abandoned in 2006. A somewhat similar fate befell the cigarette tax, of which the cities were the prime beneficiary, essentially because of the decline in smoking. Despite the reduction in these basic sources of income, the State continued to honor its commitment to the Revenue Sharing Fund for the Counties. But flexible these sources were not. Pasco County reported that its receipts from the two entitlements were exactly the same for 2004, 2005, and 2006.

There is another aspect of revenue sharing in Florida that is much more consistent with the standards of a good institutional tax. In the last several decades the State Legislature has regularly expanded the capability of the counties to impose local sales tax levies. The counties are free to levy these new taxes for specific purposes, and they are generally called local option taxes The arrangements vary, though their pattern is very much in a home rule mode, where local people decide whether they want to be taxed. As a result, these are taxes where the authority is local, the accountability is local (with specific time limits in many cases), the visibility is clear, and exclusivity is high. Flexibility varies according to the tax; and, in general, it will vary with the economic situation in the county.

At least 17 different taxes may be levied by the counties, with a few available only to particular jurisdictions. The State Department of Revenue has summarized them:

Local Discretionary Sales Surtaxes: charter county transit system surtax, local government infrastructure surtax, small county surtax, indigent care and trauma center surtax, county public hospital surtax, school capital outlay surtax, voter approved indigent care surtax.

Tourist Development Taxes: 1 or 2 percent tax, additional 1 percent tax, high tourism impact tax, professional sports franchise facility tax, additional professional sports franchise tax.

Others: Local option food and beverage taxes, local option fuel taxes, municipal resort tax, tourist impact tax, convention development tax, consolidated convention development tax, charter county convention development tax, and special and sub-county convention development tax.

The Legislative Committee on Intergovernmental Relations has estimated that, were all counties to levy a 1% local option tax, the total receipts would amount to $3,105,903,128. In 2004 eleven counties levied no local option taxes; still, the total income to the 56 others was $1,304,021,648. The amount shared by the State from the half a penny sales levy was $2,078,223,349, which suggests how significant local option taxes are in county budgets and the potential that still exists for further support. This type of fiscal home rule, though limited in the sense that these funds are not available for general purposes, does much to enhance the viability of county governments in Florida.

Debt Mechanisms

The general obligation bond, not surprisingly, has full visibility and accountability. As the bond must be voted by the citizens, it requires action by the county board to place the issue on the ballot. It must also adequately and thoroughly document exactly where the proceeds of the bond sale will be directed. Thus, there is a mechanism for providing the public with necessary information upon which to vote for or against the bond. The source has exclusivity because, once the bond is sold, the money received may be used only for the purpose stated.

Because its proceeds are limited only to the purposes for which the money was borrowed, such a debt mechanism has little flexibility. Once passed, there is no way in which citizens or elected officials can re-allocate funds. There are essentially no more decisions to be made. The government's only responsibility at this point is to assure integrity in the use of the monies and to provide an accounting system that forecloses any misuse of the monies.

As with the general obligation instrument, the revenue bond cannot be used as a general county revenue. It also must be directed to a specific project and therefore has little flexibility. The key decision for the county, then, is the determination whether a debt should be incurred. Within this framework, choices are made to borrow or to go on a pay-as-you-go basis. Clearly, both general obligation and revenue bonds do make it possible to free up current monies in the budget for purposes other than capital projects.

Because the approval of general obligation bonds is so lengthy and also because they are instrumental in determining the credit rating of a county, revenue bonds are finding increasing favor. Originally, they were used to finance enterprises, where fees for services provided a steady stream of income. Today, however, the emphasis is on the steady stream of income, not its source. Pasco County, for example, reported that it is using essentially all its monies from the State Revenue Sharing Funds (the two guaranteed entitlements) to provide for its debt service. In effect, it is using fixed income to cover fixed costs.

IV. APPLYING THE CRITERIA TO POSSIBLE NEW REVENUE SOURCES

The dramatic changes in approach at both the State and Federal levels may force the discovery and adoption of new revenue sources for local governments. For that reason, it seems appropriate to analyze two sources, the sales tax and the income tax. The Florida Constitution prohibits use of the income tax; and State statutes generally reserve the sales tax for use by the State. Even though the State did agree to share half a cent of sales tax with local governments in 1982 and did permit the counties to adopt local option taxes for specific, earmarked purposes, the abolition of the sales tax on services and the one cent increase in the tax on products in 1987 has greatly reduced the political viability of the source.

In 2007 the State had a six percent sales tax which applied to most consumer products and a few services. Certain necessities, such as food and medicines, were exempted; and the tax did not apply to motor fuel products, which were covered by earmarked Federal and State sales taxes. In a growth state like Florida, the sales tax is extremely productive. Perhaps its greatest advantage is that it is exportable to Florida's tourists, who pay about 30 percent of the total received.

The sales tax can generate significant new revenue without a change in the rate. For example, if inflation drove prices 10 percent higher, sales tax income would rise at roughly the same rate. Similarly, an increase in purchases of products will result in more revenue. Unfortunately, however, sales tax income does not fully correlate with population expansion and needs for urban services. Further, the mix of economic activity in this tourism-oriented state continues to shift away from products toward services, which are generally not taxed. As a result, it has been concluded that the present State approach to this source of revenue will make it a less significant element in the financing of the State's governments in the future. As the yield to the State proportionately declines, further sharing with local governments will be less likely.

Also, it is not clear how far the State will bend to the counties' interests. There is no doubt, for example, about who will be the collector of these levies. All the local option taxes identified above are collected by the State Department of Revenue and sent back to the counties. In this sense the tax is "owned" by the State. The other question is how far the State will allow the counties to go in increasing the size of local option taxes. In 2004 the local option taxes represented about 0.8% of the total sales tax collections in the State. If it were two percent, how would the State respond?

There is really little reason to discuss the income tax. If voters were, by some turn of fate, to allow the income tax to be levied, it would be taken over by the State. The National Association of Counties has reported that the income tax is a significant source of county revenue in only two states, Indiana and Pennsylvania. Florida is not likely to be another. The best that can be anticipated is that sales tax income might be more generously shared.

V. SUMMARY

Taxes are generally considered only in terms of their economic dimensions. While considerations of yield and equity have highly significant consequences for the individual citizen, the quality of the institutions central to the functioning of a democratic society can also be greatly affected. Put another way, tax arrangements impact heavily on the ability of governments within the system to perform tasks, to maintain viability as a part of the overall political framework, and to be valued as institutions by their constituents.

One of the most important of institutional considerations is home rule. The American system is unique in its commitment to decentralization and the provision of a consequent opportunity for local people to handle those public problems that are essentially local in nature. The principle of home rule, then, is that local governments will be left free to deal with matters that are purely local. Much of the philosophizing about home rule, however, has concentrated on issues of power and authority. Often left unsaid is the great importance of commanding the necessary finances to take advantage of powers that have been formally granted by higher levels of government. In short, local governments must have the capacity to generate income sufficient to finance those undertakings desired by their constituents.

Table 12
RELATIONSHIP OF INSTITUTIONAL CRITERIA TO
COUNTY TAX SOURCES

Criteria	Property Tax	User Fees	Revenue Sharing	Local Option Tax	Debt
Authority	high	high	low	med**	high
Accountability	high	high	low	high	med
Visibility	high	high	med	high	low
Exclusivity	high	high	med	high	low
Accessibility	high	low	low	high	low
Flexibility	med*	low	low	med**	low

* There is a 10 mil limit on the rate of the property tax that can be imposed
** The local option tax can be imposed only for certain purposes, thus also limiting its flexibility.

In this chapter an attempt has been made to examine the institutional dimensions of various types of revenue sources. Six institutional criteria were suggested by which these sources could be evaluated. Table 12 summarizes the narrative analysis of the previous pages in a single matrix. The measurement is subjective; and it would not be justifiable to do more than apply the criteria in very broad terms. High refers to those items which promote a major degree of home rule, based on the previously stated assumptions.

The institutional gains from a particular revenue source can be negated in two ways. One is through the demand for expenditures regardless of local needs and interests, i.e. the mandate problem. Usually, the higher authority will specify only the activity to be performed; and the revenue source is left out. Thus, while a particular tax may rate high on the home rule scale, its flexibility may be destroyed by the insistence that it be used to fund specific, required programs.

The other force that may countermand institutional gains through specific tax sources is inflation. While inflation has been low in the last decades, earlier experience cannot be overlooked. Dollars produced by a tax must keep pace with inflation and allow for maintenance of "real" effort, thus to secure consistency with institutional criteria.

CHAPTER ELEVEN

FINANCES AND MANDATES IN THE COUNTIES

I. A FURTHER REPORTING ON PROPERTY TAX REFORM IN 2007

As 2007 opened, the relatively comfortable situation of Florida's counties came under severe attack. Some likelihood that change was in the air appeared in 2006 when Governor Jeb Bush established a committee to study property tax reform and when the successful candidate for Governor, Charlie Crist, made property tax reform an important feature of his campaign.

The most major and dramatic attack came on February 27, 2007, when the office of the House Whip, Ellyn Bogdanoff, issued a policy brief, *The House Proposal for Property Tax Relief and Reform*. Proposed was a two-phased attack, the first involving legislation and the second a Constitutional amendment.

The assault was aimed at the counties, the cities, and the special districts. School districts were exempted. It was further pointed out that the units included in the reform got their money from many sources, with the property tax providing 31% of the income to counties, 18% to cities, and 20% to special districts.

Key to the legislative move was a rollback of property tax rates to 2000–2001, on the theory that far more money had been pulled in by local governments in the succeeding years than was needed. From that point forward (2000–2001), the taxes "really" due were to be restricted to cost of living and population increases. In 2007 the property tax would be a result of the 2000–2001 levy plus the cost of living and population increases over the previous five years. The prediction was that this move would reduce the average property tax by 19%, a decrease the legislators felt the local governments could handle without a decline in service.

If a county board did believe that such a decrease would result in service declines, tax rates could be imposed at a higher level by a majority plus one or a two-thirds vote of a board of commissioners. Since most counties have a five-person board, that meant four had to support a higher tax rate.

Failure to conform to the tax reduction demand would bring a significant penalty. The recalcitrant county would lose its share of the State sales tax, which in Miami-Dade would have meant a loss of $275 million (as of 2004) and in small Union County $274,000. These sanctions were clearly conceived as imposing big costs for resisting.

The Constitutional amendment would eliminate the property tax on all homestead property, roughly half the homeowners in the State. It was estimated this group would save an average of $2,300 annually. The other half of taxable properties would continue on the rolls, though paying at the reduced rates established by the rollback system.

At the same time the State sales tax would be increased 2.5%, bringing the effective rate to 8.5%. While a major share of these funds would be provided local governments, the State government would also be a beneficiary. The Constitutional amendment would include the restriction that the State's revenues could increase only to the extent that the cost of living and the population did.

It was estimated that the taxpayers of the State would experience a net reduction of $5.77 billion. Elimination of the property tax would result in a saving of $13.55 billion but would be offset by an additional sales tax of $7.78 billion.

After this reform proposal emerged, there was a burst of activity. The House Budget and Policy Council passed its own version of reform the next month, strictly on a party line vote. It, too, focused on reducing the property tax; but it introduced even more complexity. A proposed Constitutional amendment would eliminate the share of property taxes that finance public schools, thus removing one of the local units that rely most on the levy. It was estimated this move would take 30% off the average homeowner's bill. The schools' loss would be financed by a 1% increase in the State sales tax, making it 7%.

Further, a bit of home rule philosophy was introduced. Each of the 67 counties would be free to reduce its property taxes by adopting, through a referendum, additional sales taxes up to 1.5%. In effect, a local option sales tax would function as a means of reducing property taxes.

Many other variants have been offered, essentially all within the context of reducing property taxes. Though he did not get involved in the legislative discussions, Governor Charlie Crist made it clear such reform was high on his agenda. In his campaign he proposed doubling the homestead exemption to $50,000 and permitting Save our Homes owners to transfer their exemptions when they moved.

He abolished former Governor Jeb Bush's Property Tax Reform Committee, noting that he was committed to the issues on which he campaigned and could not wait for the findings of the Committee, scheduled to be delivered in December 2007.

Governor Crist called a special session of the Legislature to meet June 12–22, 2007, with one of the agenda items the reform of the property tax. Unfortunately, this event came too late in the preparation of this book to include its decisions and any actions that ensued.

II. COLLIER COUNTY FINANCES

Concerned about its financial future, Collier County contracted with the Anderson Economic Group of East Lansing, Michigan, to make an exhaustive examination of its economic situation, identify problem areas, and indicate economic options for the future. The study was completed and presented in 2004; and it provides a useful contrast to the 2007 demand in Florida for property tax reductions.

The essential conclusion of the Anderson Group was that Collier's revenues would fall behind its expenditures in five years. No later than 2009, Collier County would either have to find more money or cut its services, a far different future than that foreseen by State legislators.

The Anderson Group pointed out that gross budget figures are often misleading in determining the actual financial status of a county. In Collier the total budget was considered to be $1.3 billion but 60% of that did not involve regular, recurring revenues and expenditures. Over $400 million were bond proceeds, which constituted a one-time outlay and were obviously funded by debt. They should be characterized as capital expenditures, not current ones. There was another major element in the Collier budget, also more than $400 million, which contributed to a distorted picture of the reality. Like a number of other governments, Collier included in the budget inter-fund transfers as revenues and then charged them off as expenditures. In effect, they were a wash and were simply an internal accounting event. As a result, Anderson concluded that the "real" revenues available for continuing expenditures in Collier County were about $370 million, less than 30% that set forth in the budget. We have found that these accounting approaches often occur in counties' reporting to the State. As a result, the figures on revenues and expenditures can be distorted and must always be treated with care.

With Anderson's recalculation of the true structure of revenues in Collier, the property tax takes on far greater importance. It contributes 60% of recurring revenue, dwarfing other sources. Sales and gas tax sharing with the State provide 10% of revenues, service charges 9%, licenses and franchising fees 8%, miscellaneous (including impact fees) 5.3%, tourist taxes 6.4%, and fines and forfeitures 1.7%. (As will be observed later in Table 14 in this chapter, the Anderson analysis of Collier revenues differs from the figures reported to the State of Florida.)

In its analysis the Anderson Group emphasized the importance of a revenue arrangement that is sustainable. The need is for taxes whose yield is recurring, ones that can be counted on to produce revenue year and year out. As a result, Anderson looked at the sustainable taxes and their performance over the next several years. The Group predicted the property tax would rise by 56% over five years; inter-governmental tax sharing by 36%; tourism taxes by 29%; service charges by 17%; fines and forfeitures by 17%; and miscellaneous income (including impact fees) by 21%.

Four reasons for pessimism about revenue growth in the future were identified by the Anderson Group:

(1)   An inevitable slowdown in population growth. Collier County's growth at 41% between 2000 and 2005 was one of the fastest in the State, and Anderson commented it "… could not last indefinitely."

(2)   A small fraction of the budget from sustainable sources. This is the point previously made that including one-time items in the budget masks the absence of recurring revenues, which will be badly needed, when things slow down. It was estimated that only about one-fourth of the budget was from sustainable revenues.

(3)   Over-reliance on income from impact fees. These levies, which have been used rather heavily in Collier County, depend on new development. If housing starts decline, impact fees suffer a similar descent.

(4)   The economic cycle. There are inevitably good times and bad times. Since Collier County has grown, just as all Florida has, the impact of lessened economic activity will be greater and result in a smaller tax take.

Only two new tax sources were identified by Anderson, one the local option surtax and the other more tourist taxes. Both have a defect. They generally require that the money be spent for a specific purpose and therefore do not add to the County's ability to finance its highest priority needs.

The recurring taxes (which were calculated to cover only about one-fourth of budget outlays) were judged insufficient to keep up with expenditures. The Anderson Group wrote: "Our quantitative analysis provides the same number as our qualitative one: some time over the next 5 years or so, the County is likely to discover that it cannot afford to continue to grow its budget, as revenues will grow much more slowly than recent expenditure growth. This is likely to occur even if the expenditure growth slows to about 70% of its recent pace."[73]

The analysis in Collier reveals further limitations on a county's resources. The gross amount of money in a county's till may seem large, but the purposes for which it can be used may be very narrow. This occurs even with the property tax, which is generally lauded because of the many ways in which its monies can be used. In Collier, as elsewhere, there is a large unincorporated area that must be provided municipal-type services. These undertakings are required to be financed separately, however, from the general government. The result is a separate property levy applicable to the unincorporated area, the recipients of the services. The total of $237 million reported in property tax for 2005 suggests, erroneously, that it is all "free" money. It is not. Nearly 25% was collected from the unincorporated area specifically to provide municipal-type services, or nearly $60 million. Such a restriction on the use of tens of millions means that policy makers in Collier are far more limited in their choices than would first appear.

A similar situation exists in many other Collier revenue sources. The gas tax share must go for roads, and in Collier much of it is further pledged to service the 2003 Gas Tax Revenues Bond Fund, which is a 20 year commitment.

Charges for services, as we have previously pointed out, are typically levied to support a specific activity. The money is, in effect, earmarked. It is also a fact that fees often cover only part of the cost and general funds are required. That is true with respect to the ambulance service in Collier, for example, and very likely also true in parks and recreation. Other areas in which Collier imposes fees are not likely to contribute substantially to the general fund: building permits, water and sewer services, landfill facility, and county airports, where revenues are derived from fuel sales and the rental of hanger space.

Much the same picture is seen with respect to impact fees, a significant source of revenue in Collier but whose utilization varies among the counties. The Anderson Group expressed reservations about the use of this source because it was seen as discouraging building and development. Further, it is not clear how successful the fees have been in providing the monies necessary to reduce the community facilities deficit which new development has brought. But it is apparent the fees have been imposed to deal with a specific problem and therefore should be considered earmarked funds. In Collier there are levies made for six road districts, community and regional parks, libraries in order to maintain a 1.10 books per capita ratio, water and sewers, correctional facilities, certain fire units, emergency management services, and general government building facilities.

---

73 Anderson Economic Group, *Fiscal Stability Analysis for Collier County, Florida.* East Lansing, Michigan: Sept. 3, 2004, p. 34-35, processed. (Total pages, 38)

In the detailed revenue records submitted to the State's Department of Financial Services for 2004, Collier reported an impact fee income of nearly $40 million, all of which was assigned to the Capital Projects account.

III. GENERAL AND SPECIAL ACCOUNTS: THEIR SIGNIFICANCE

Collier County is not alone in facing limitations on the use of the money it does have. As has been noted, the State Department of Financial Services maintains detailed records on the revenue picture in each of the counties. These data cover a wide range of revenue sources (Collier has 81, the smaller Columbia 76) and assigns the monies received to eight different account areas, including general revenue, special revenue, debt service, capital projects, enterprise, and three others. The majority of revenues is placed either in the General Revenue or Special Revenue columns. The Collier property tax is divided, as might be expected, with the bulk of it placed in the general account but with a substantial amount in the special account, thus reflecting the County commitment to municipal-type services in the unincorporated area. (The figures also are not exactly the same as those found in the Anderson document.)

The separation between the general and special accounts has great significance. It establishes the difference between money a county may use for most pressing needs and money that must go to prescribed purposes. As Table 13 reveals, Collier County has a total of $467 million of income in its general and special accounts. Though it has nearly twice as many special (57) as general accounts (30), the greater share of its money is in the general account, about 60%. The happy aspect is that these monies can be spent on general purposes; the negative is that 40% are restricted funds.

Table 13 contains information on 11 counties, most of them large, and seven cities of various sizes. It is impossible to generalize about the cities from this very limited sample, but our scan of a broader range of data suggests that these seven are fairly typical of the larger population.

The key insight is that the counties have many more special accounts than the cities, and a far greater percentage of their revenues flows in this direction. Six of the eleven counties have more special accounts than general, whereas six of the seven municipalities have far more general accounts. Six of the seven cities also have much more money in their general accounts than in the special. In the counties there is a far greater tendency to place money in special accounts. Indeed three of the 11 in Table 13 have greater amounts in special accounts; and, in six there is a difference in the size of the two types of accounts of less than 10%, all of them with the larger amount in general funds. Two counties, Broward and Collier, put a major share of their income in general accounts.

A sharp contrast is to be seen in a comparison between Broward County and the City of Melbourne, each with a high percentage of general accounts. Seventy percent of Broward's accounts are general; and 60% of its income is invested in them. In Melbourne 83% of its accounts are general and nearly 90% of the money is invested in them. In reviewing these figures, it should be remembered that there are eight accounts in the State Department of Financial Services reports, and we are working with only two of them.

If these data are reasonably reflective of the situation, a city like Melbourne has a far greater discretion in the use of its resources. It is restricted in the use of only about 10% of its revenues and can put the other 90% to their wisest and best use. The counties are much more constrained; they cannot apply as many dollars to areas of greatest need.

Why would the cities and counties experience such a great difference in their levels of discretion in financial matters? One explanation may be that the cities tend to be more integrated organizationally, with essentially all units reporting to the governing body. Hence there may be less interest in sequestering money for special purposes. The counties, on the other hand, have a history of wide organizational dispersion, and the frequent presence of special accounts may be an outcome of that background.

It is also true that cities have no unincorporated area. Their revenues are typically utilized in the interests of the whole community. That is not the case for the counties. They must establish separate financing arrangements for the areas to which they provide municipal-type services, and that means placing money in special accounts.

Table 13
A FINANCIAL PROFILE OF 11 COUNTIES AND SEVEN CITIES WITH SPECIAL REFERENCE TO THE NUMBERS OF GENERAL AND SPECIAL ACCOUNTS

Counties	% Income from property tax	No. General Accounts	No. Special Accounts	Totals in General Accounts ($millions)	Totals in Special Accounts ($millions)
Brevard	38%	42	38	$249	$233
Broward	48%	75	31	$1,206	$845
Charlotte	26%	60	57	$181	$189
Collier	54%	30	57	$284	$183
Columbia	56%	33	53	$23	$34
Miami-Dade	35%	49	70	$1851	$1765
Pasco	37%	45	83	$181	$207
Pinellas	42%	61	59	$520	$513
Polk	32%	64	47	$280	$207
Sarasota	40%	49	75	$233	$225
Seminole	36%	56	39	$319	$288
Cities					
Pensacola	17%	20	20	$49	$74
Panama City	22%	29	10	$3.4	$1.3
Perry	24%	14	4	$4.1	$.95
Tallahassee	21%	39	23	$119	$23
St. Petersburg	31%	30	29	$200	$147
Melbourne	13%	45	9	$37	$4.4
Neptune Beach	30%	24	11	$4.6	$.95

+ Cities depend less on the property tax than counties.

++Generally, there is a significant difference between cities and counties in the numbers of general and special accounts. The raw numbers don't matter because the counties are bigger but the distribution of general and special accounts is significant. The cities have proportionately fewer special accounts. Note Columbia County (56,000) which has both more special accounts and also more money in them and compare with Melbourne (75,000), which has very few special accounts and little money in them.

In any event, it seems apparent that considerably less than the gross income of a county can be used for a jurisdiction's most urgent needs. In some degree this absence of discretion over substantial amounts of money means some revenue must be discounted in determining just how affluent a particular governmental unit is.

IV. FINANCES IN THE COUNTIES IN 2005

As we reported earlier, the Florida Department of Financial Services maintains comprehensive records on the finances of local governments. The file which we found particularly useful is titled, "Summarized County Data, State of Florida, Fiscal Year Ended 2005."

It lists information on the revenues and expenditures for each county in 10 categories. In this sense it is really a summary because we have found that the general fund accounts may number 60 or 70. Nevertheless it provides a capsule picture of the financial situation in each of the 67 counties. Because the counties vary so much in size, the comparison of the raw figures is fairly meaningless. It was necessary to compute percentages of revenues and expenditures to gain any real sense of the differences among the jurisdictions.

It is within these terms that we constructed several tables as a means of gaining greater perspective on county finances. The first of these tables (Table 14) shows, in percentage terms, the revenue sources for 25 of the largest counties. Included are all but three of the chartered counties, Columbia, Jacksonville-Duval and Volusia. The second table (Table 15) provides a comparison of the revenue sources in eight chartered and eight non-chartered counties. A third (Table 16) indicates the principal revenue sources in the 10 smallest counties; a fourth (Table 17) presents the frequencies of the three major revenue sources in 64 of Florida's counties; and a fifth (Table 18) provides an expenditure profile for the same 25 counties covered in Table 14.

In Table 14, only six sources of revenue are specifically identified. The Department of Financial Services records contain an "other sources" category, and we have included in that "other miscellaneous revenues" and "court related revenues." both of which are relatively small. It is also important to remember that inter-fund transfers are included under "other sources." These are transactions which have no revenue or expenditure significance but are included for accounting purposes. Because they are often very large, they tend to distort both the revenue and expenditure profiles. Broward, Collier, Hillsborough, Leon, Palm

Beach, and Seminole Counties report large percentages of their income in "other sources," likely signifying the presence of inter-fund transfers.

The 25 counties reveal a considerable diversity of income sources, which is a reassuring sign for the future. The property tax is dominant but not overwhelmingly so. It is the largest single source of income in more than half the counties; but, in most cases, it is around 25% of the total. Leon and St. Lucie counties appear to rely on it the most, with the property tax accounting for 28% of income.

In three counties service charges provide a third or more of revenues: Manatee (38%), Miami-Dade (37%), and Okaloosa (31%). As has been observed earlier, these are monies with little flexibility. They go to perform the services for which the fees are being charged; and they do not provide help in meeting the broader needs of a county.

The Anderson Group's warning to Collier County that impact fees are not a "sustainable" source of revenue may apply particularly to four counties where they are the third highest income producer: Pasco (13%), Marion (12%), Lake (11%), and Hernando (9%). The concern is that these fees produce large amounts of money only as long as new housing and development are present. The building slowdown that began in 2006 and continued in 2007 will bring lower impact fee income, it may be assumed.

Despite that the counties enjoy a fairly wide range of funding sources, it is clear that three sources consistently and continually provide the biggest share of income. The three are the property tax, state tax sharing, and service charges. That pattern was true in 2005 and very likely persisted to the time this book was finished in 2007. The future structure of revenues will undoubtedly be much affected by actions of the Florida Legislature.

A further analysis of Table 14 shows that the three sources (property tax, state revenue sharing, and service charges) provided roughly half the income in the 25 counties listed. The percentage of revenues provided by these sources varied from 68% in Polk County down to 39% in Seminole and Escambia Counties. Thus the range is 39% to 68%, with the median 49%.

A further examination of these three sources is undertaken in Table 15. Here we have calculated the frequencies of these taxes in 64 counties and have contrasted them with the frequency of all other sources. The property tax appears far more frequently, 60 times as one of the top three revenue producers. The frequency of state revenue sharing is 43; and service charges appear 41 times. All the other revenue sources are grouped together and have a frequency among the top three choices of 36.

Table 14
2005 REVENUE PROFILES IN 25 COUNTIES

(Includes all chartered counties except Columbia, Jacksonville-Duval, and Volusia)

County Name	% Property Taxes	% other taxes, fees, licenses	% Federal Grants	% State, other govt. sources	% Service Charges	% Special assessments, impact fees	% Other sources, inter-fund
Alachua	27%	9%	2%	8%	14%	2%	28%
Brevard	22%	6%	4%	9%	24%	4%	23%
Broward	24%	4%	2%	6%	25%	<1%	33%
Charlotte	13%	12%	8%	7%	20%	4%	18%
Clay	25%	16%	2%	10%	8%	2%	28%
Collier	21%	5%	1%	6%	18%	4%	41%
Miami-Dade	15%	9%	7%	5%	37%	1%	21%
Escambia	17%	12%	32%	12%	10%	2%	9%
Hernando	26%	6%	3%	8%	26%	9%	16%
Hillsborough	20%	10%	3%	6%	17%	1%	39%
Lake	26%	9%	9%	8%	15%	11%	12%
Lee	19%	4%	1%	5%	25%	4%	36%
Leon	28%	8%	1%	7%	11%	<1%	38%
Manatee	27%	5%	2%	10%	38%	2%	12%
Marion	22%	8%	6%	10%	14%	12%	20%
Okaloosa	19%	7%	7%	12%	31%	<1%	20%
Orange	24%	12%	3%	9%	22%	9%	14%
Osceola	20%	20%	5%	8%	14%	6%	17%
Palm Beach	23%	6%	3%	5%	20%	4%	35%
Pasco	25%	7%	3%	9%	24%	13%	12%
Pinellas	26%	8%	2%	6%	26%	<1%	25%
Polk	22%	9%	3%	17%	29%	3%	9%
St. Lucie	28%	4%	14%	6%	14%	3%	24%
Sarasota	21%	10%	2%	7%	26%	9%	19%
Seminole	20%	10%	6%	8%	11%	3%	35%

Table 15
FREQUENCIES OF COUNTIES' THREE MAJOR REVENUE SOURCES

(Covers 64 Counties from Florida Dept. of Financial Services Database)

Source	Greatest Revenue Producer	2nd Greatest Revenue Producer	3rd Greatest Revenue Producer
Property Tax	37	18	5
State Tax Sharing	9	14	20
Charges for Service	9	20	12
Other sources—other taxes, fees, licenses in most cases	4	9	23

+ The property tax is the biggest source of income in about 55% of counties.

+ State tax sharing and other sources is one of top three producers in 43 counties, 67% of 64 studied.

+ Service charges are one of top three producers in 41 counties, 64% of 64 studied.

+ Other taxes, fees, licenses, are important income sources, with Federal grants important in three cases.

Table 16
THE TEN SMALLEST COUNTIES AND THEIR REVENUE PROFILES

(Numbers are assigned according to the significance of revenue source. The highest producer is No. 1; 2nd highest producer No. 2; and 3rd highest producer No. 3.)

County Name	Property Tax	State Sources	Service Charges	Other*
Bradford (26,000)	1	2		3
Calhoun (13,000)	3	2		1 (Federal Grants)
Franklin (11,000)	1	2	3	
Gilchrist (14,000)	1	2	3	
Glades (10,500)	1	2		3
Gulf (13,000)	1	2	3	
Hamilton (13,000)	2	1	3	
Jefferson (13,000)	2	1		3
Lafayette (7,000)	2	1	3	
Union (13,000)	2	1		3

* In four counties the third highest producer of revenue was other taxes, fees, and licenses.

To determine whether there were any consequential differences between the structure of revenues in the larger, more urbanized counties and the smaller, more rural ones, an analysis of revenues in the 10 smallest counties in the State was made (Table 16). They ranged in size from Lafayette with about 7,000 people to Bradford with about 26,000. The property tax and state revenue sharing were the top two sources of income in nine of ten counties. In Calhoun, Federal grants provided the largest amount of money. The rural counties were also not likely to employ service charges as extensively. Still, they were the third highest source of income in five of the ten counties.

The extensive degree to which all the counties depend on the same revenue sources means that any changes by the State can have highly significant consequences. The property tax is clearly the most seminal tax, with 37 of 64 counties relying on it as the most important source of revenue. Again, it is critical to remember that the property tax and state tax sharing provide discretionary income, money that can be used where it is most needed. Generally, the property tax and state revenue sharing account for only about one-third of a county's income. It must be concluded that county boards of commissioners operate under severe constraints in uncovering other resources that can be directed to high priority areas.

Table 17 deals with a question that returns to issues of chartering and non-chartering. It is generally assumed that the charter counties enjoy a greater freedom of operation, and that would imply more financial flexibility. As a result, there is the expectation that they may have been able to exploit additional revenue sources and thus to diversify their income base. However, a review of the various taxes available to counties leaves one with the impression that charter counties have had few additional options.

The data occasion the conclusion that chartering does not lead to greater fiscal flexibility. Revenue structures in the chartered and non-chartered counties are very much the same. The same three sources of revenue dominate, contributing 51% of income to the chartered counties and 55% to the non-chartered. The small difference may reveal a slightly more diversified revenue system in the chartered counties, but nothing significant. Of the counties with the least reliance on the three sources, one (Seminole) is chartered and one (Escambia) is not. They each received 39% of their income from the property tax, State tax sharing, and service charges. Also, of the two who rely most on the three sources, one (Manatee 75%) is non-chartered and one (Polk 68%) is chartered.

Table 17
A COMPARATIVE REVENUE SOURCE PROFILE FOR 10 LARGE
CHARTER COUNTIES AND 10 LARGE NON-CHARTER COUNTIES

Charter Counties	% Property Tax of Total Revenue	% State Sources of Total Revenue	% Service Charges of Total Revenue
Palm Beach	23%	5%	20%
Hillsborough	20%	6%	17%
Pinellas	26%	6%	26%
Polk	22%	17%	29%
Lee	19%	5%	25%
Brevard	22%	9%	24%
Seminole	20%	8%	11%
Sarasota	21%	7%	26%
Leon	28%	7%	11%
Alachua	27%	8%	14%
Non-Charter Counties			
Pasco	25%	9%	24%
Collier	21%	6%	18%
Manatee	27%	10%	38%
Marion	22%	10%	14%
Escambia	17%	12%	10%
Lake	26%	8%	15%
St. Lucie	28%	6%	14%
Okaloosa	19%	12%	31%
Hernando	26%	8%	26%
Martin	33%	10%	20%

+ Measures for charter counties: property tax mean, 22.8%, median 21.5%; state share mean 7.8%, median 7; service charges mean 20.3%, median 22%.

+ Measures for non-charters: property tax mean, 24.4%, median 25.5%; state share mean 9.1%, median 9.5%; service charges mean 21.%, median 17.5%.

Table 18
2005 EXPENDITURE PROFILES IN 26 COUNTIES

(Includes all chartered counties except Columbia, Jacksonville-Duval and Volusia)

County Name	% General Govt.	% Public Safety	% Physical Environment	% Trans- portation	% Economic Environment	% Human Services	% Other uses, inter-fund
Alachua	18%	27%	7%	3%	1%	3%	34%
Brevard	17%	22%	16%	8%	2%	3%	17%
Broward	9%	21%	10%	12%	1%	4%	30%
Charlotte	22%	15%	15%	16%	1%	3%	21%
Clay	18%	26%	6%	7%	1%	2%	31%
Collier	15%	23%	14%	13%	<1%	1%	13%
Miami-Dade	10%	14%	10%	16%	<1%	23%	14%
Escambia	13%	58%	3%	5%	3%	1%	10%
Hernando	20%	31%	13%	13%	1%	2%	9%
Hillsborough	12%	16%	11%	4%	2%	8%	36%
Lake	16%	33%	11%	10%	3%	3%	12%
Lee	13%	12%	11%	17%	1%	<1%	30%
Leon	12%	22%	7%	7%	1%	3%	26%
Manatee	19%	21%	18%	10%	2%	4%	12%
Marion	18%	26%	13%	11%	<1%	3%	21%
Okaloosa	19%	21%	13%	12%	6%	2%	19%
Orange	8%	24%	11%	8%	9%	7%	22%
Osceola	24%	16%	6%	9%	9%	3%	17%
Pasco	21%	26%	17%	11%	3%	3%	8%
Pinellas	16%	22%	15%	4%	3%	4%	26%
Polk	17%	31%	12%	10%	2%	6%	5%
St. Lucie	16%	18%	9%	21%	1%	3%	15%
Sarasota	8%	20%	21%	9%	1%	2%	24%
Seminole	11%	19%	12%	12%	2%	1%	37%

County expenditures, shown in Table 18, reflect a strong commitment to public safety. Twenty-two of the 25 counties listed in the Table spent the largest share of their money in that area of activity. Percentages varied considerably, with a range of 12% to 58% and a median of 22%, nearly a quarter of total expenditures. The presence of an elected sheriff, sitting outside the hierarchy reporting to the board of county commissioners, may partially account for the significant portion of dollars devoted to public safety. In a somewhat contradictory way, the second highest percentage of expenditures was for general government. This spending pattern seems to reflect the rise of large bureaucracies reporting to the boards of county commissioners, quite the opposite of the forces triggering public safety spending, with the sheriff in the lead. As counties add new functions, their overhead costs grow, and these extra outlays are assigned to general government. They reflect growth in the size and complexity of county governments.

Debt service costs are not included in Table 18, primarily because they are not large. That is good news. It means that the counties have been cautious about taking on debt. The percentage of money that goes to debt service is, of course, reflective of the size of a county's general debt. Miami-Dade and Lake Counties spend less than one per cent of their funds on debt service; and Leon County pays the most in debt service, 15%.

V. MANDATES

Since counties are subordinate governments of the State, even the most strenuous efforts to introduce home rule for local governments cannot ease the tensions that are bound to exist between the two levels. It is inevitable that the State will seize the opportunity to tell the local governments, and particularly the counties, what to do. The passage of the Constitutional amendment establishing the homestead exemption in 1934 is an early example of the way in which the people of the State limited the capacity of local governments to raise funds from property taxes.

The name assigned to this kind of event is mandate. In the dictionary, a mandate is defined as an authoritative command, an order. That well describes how the mandate works in the State-local government relationship. In the Florida State context, it is an action taken typically by the Legislature, but many times arising from citizen initiatives, that "… substantially increases the expenditures of or reduces the revenue or revenue-producing ability of counties or municipalities."[74]

---

74 Florida Legislative Committee on Intergovernmental Relations, *2003 LCIR Intergovernmental Impact Report, Draft.* Tallahassee, FL.: February 2004, p. 1.. (This document is 16 pages, plus appendices and charts.)

The property tax exemptions, which were subject to heated debate in 2007, are perhaps the most flagrant examples of mandates. The $25,000 homestead exemption, which applied to about half the homes in Florida, removed over $100 billion from taxation by local government, as was reported in the previous chapter. Even more significant is the Save our Homes exemption which imposed strict limits on the amount that property taxes could be increased in a given year. It was calculated that this arrangement exempted over $400 billions in assets from full taxation. The Florida Association of Counties has estimated that these mandates deprive the counties of about $600 million in property taxes per year. If Governor Charlie Crist's campaign proposals to raise the homestead exemption to $50,000 and to allow homeowners to transfer their Save our Homes exemption to other properties, the amount of exempted property taxes would rise perilously close to a billion dollars.

In the course of the debate already underway over property tax reform, the great costs of mandates have been particularly noted. In one of its documents, the Florida Association of Counties has stated:

> In recent years, state leaders have added to counties' fiscal burden by mandating they help pay for programs, or fund them outright. For example, counties have paid for an increasing share of Medicaid costs, for state juvenile justice programs and for coverage for the uninsured. Likewise, the federal government also imposes mandates on county government ranging from environmental, landfill, and voter regulations to welfare disabilities and labor.[75]

The Association concluded that the counties were expending about $1 billion annually to respond to these many demands.

Also, in answering the charges made in the debate on property tax reform, the Pinellas County budget office included the following paragraph in a statement about the property tax:

> Another factor impacting the County budget began in 2004 when Article V, Revision 7 reorganized the court system. Under this act, the State assumed the cost of the "essential" court employees and made the Clerk of the Court a fee-supported office. However, the State left the counties with inadequate revenue streams to fund the most expensive responsibilities of the courts including court technology, CJIS, pre-trial juvenile incarceration, facilities, communications, furniture for the court system and local optional programs

---

75 From a set of papers of the Florida Association of Counties, *Key Messages*, 2007 Florida Legislative Session. No date, unpaged.

for which there were previously adequate revenues in collected court fees. As part of Revision 7, the State changed its revenue sharing formula as well. The net negative effect on Pinellas County from Article V, Revision 7 is more than $30 million per year.[76]

Although the problem of mandates persists, a Constitutional amendment in 1990 undertook to limit the imposition of mandates on local governments. It declared that a city or county did not have to abide by an enacted law unless funds for it were provided, with some significant exceptions: (1) a declaration of state interest; (2) the law is determined to apply to all citizens of the state in a similar situation; (3) there is a Federal grant that requires State and/or local participation; or (4) both houses of the State Legislature vote by a two-thirds majority to adopt the law.

The amendment also included a provision that the Legislature could not enact, amend, or repeal any general law, except by a two-thirds majority in both houses, where the effect would be to reduce the taxing authority of the local governments, as it existed on February 1, 1989.

Also, there was a guarantee that the State tax sharing levels existing in 1989 could not be reduced, except by a two-thirds vote of each house: "… the Legislature may not enact, amend, or repeal any general law if the anticipated effect of doing so would be to reduce the percentage of a state tax shared with counties and municipalities as an aggregate on February 1, 1989."[77]

Working within a legal framework that mandates can be employed only sparingly, the Legislature has developed a process whereby laws are screened for any potential violations of the Constitutional prohibition on mandates. A mandate is identified in Legislative procedures as one where an action requires the expenditure of funds, where the effect would be to reduce the authority to raise revenue, or where the effect would be a reduction in the State monies available to local governments.

The Legislative Committee on Intergovernmental Relations annually scrutinizes the number and nature of mandates that appear in the bills passed by the Legislature. We reviewed the report for 2003, assuming it is representative of the process and kinds of problems encountered. About 60 bills issued from the 2003 session that had a mandate dimension. More than half, with 39 mandates, applied to both cities and counties. There were 21, with 25 mandates, that applied only to counties, whereas there were only three pertaining to the municipalities alone. A

---

76   From a Pinellas County paper, "Where Does the Money Go?" Posted on the Internet, June 6, 2007.

77   Florida Constitution, Article VII, Finance and Taxation, Section 18, paragraph (c)

perusal of the LCIR report quickly establishes the reason for this imbalance. The counties administer the court system, and a substantial number of the mandates are directed toward some aspect of the justice system.

In 2003 there were three pieces of legislation that appeared to have significant financial implications. All of them were exempted from the mandate restrictions.

The most significant act involved the conversion of Florida's entire 911 network to wireless, with the Federal, State, and local governments expected to pick up parts of the cost. It was to involve major amounts of money, but it was unclear from the LCIR report what those amounts were. At the time about $12 million was provided by the Federal government, $5.5 million to be distributed to the counties; and there was a requirement that a surtax on certain wireless communications be established, with the proceeds deposited into the Wireless Emergency Telephone System Fund for later distribution. More ominous was the statement that the counties would install and operate the system, with $10–12 million required annually for continuing operations.

Though this legislation had great fiscal significance for the counties, it enjoyed no further mandate review. First, it received a two-thirds majority in both houses and second, it involved a major Federal grant that required matching funds. Either of these actions was sufficient to secure exemption from the mandate restrictions.

A second piece of legislation with substantial financial implications involved the Florida Retirement System. It had been concluded that higher payments would have to be made by the counties as employers in the system, which is non-contributory. That may have involved a considerable amount of money, but we did not discover the specific amount. This is a mandate, in the sense that the counties are required to provide the money. The legislation was exempted, however, from mandate review because the required payment applied to all persons similarly situated, in effect everyone who came under the Florida Retirement System.

The third mandate involving significant cost concerned the South Florida Regional Transportation Authority (SFRTA). The legislation required that three counties, Miami-Dade. Broward, and Palm Beach, contribute a total of $2.7 million annually "… for as long as obligated to secure federal funding for the SFRTA." The counties were also compelled to give $1.56 annually to SFRTA for operating expenses.

This case has interest because it seems to violate the Constitutional prohibition against mandates that provide no financial support. In this case the counties were given no additional sources of revenue but were specifically permitted to use gas tax monies for these purposes. What secured the exemption, though, was the passage of the bill in both houses by a two-thirds majority. The mandate prohibition was inoperative.

The Legislative Committee on Intergovernmental Relations has observed that most mandates are "procedural" and involve little or no financial burdens for local governments. Here are the kinds of procedural mandates that come down to the counties on a regular basis:

- In order to give veterans preference in hiring, counties must determine that the person served at least one day during a war.

- Counties must grant those taking time off for military service 30 days leave with pay.

- The sheriff will be subject to the Quality Assurance review of the State Department of Children and Family Services.

- The Clerk of the Court must make a $161 surcharge on certain offenders. $150 goes to the Rape Crisis Program Trust Fund, and the Clerk keeps $1.

- Counties are prohibited from using any of their powers to adopt any ordinance, resolution, regulation, rule, or policy to restrict or otherwise limit a bonafide farm operation on land that is classified as agricultural. (This is identified as a preemption.)

Procedural mandates tend to be imposed in substantial degree on Constitutional officers. The Clerk of the Court, as might be expected, is a particular target. In 2003 five bills with six mandates were directed to this office. The Sheriff also received a share, two bills and four mandates. Finally, the Supervisor of Elections, much more in the line of fire in recent years, was also hit with mandates in 2003, two bills and two mandates. The property appraiser and the tax collector got no mandates from the Legislature.

V. SUMMARY

2007 may turn out to be a highly important year for the counties, possibly as significant as when the home rule provisions were incorporated in the State Constitution in 1968 and when the revenue base was expanded with state sharing of the sales tax in 1982. The difference, of course, is that those were positive events. What lay ahead in 2007 seemed entirely negative.

Virtually all the reform proposals sought a reduction in the property tax, which is not only the most important revenue source for the counties but one which also produces a major amount of money without strings. It can be used for nearly any valid county purpose. A cut in this source of funding, then, is bound to affect the counties and their operations greatly.

In order to gain a "bottoms-up" view of county finances, we selected Collier County as a particular point of attention. Aside from Collier's being representative of Florida's large and rapidly growing urban counties, the Board of Commissioners had contracted for a major economic study by the Anderson Group, completed in 2004. It provided a factual picture of Collier's financial situation and thus offered a way of checking the assumptions made in the State Legislature and in the Governor's office in 2007.

One important insight provided by the Anderson Group is that the raw budget figures can be misleading. Instead of an amount over $1 billion, the recurring outlays of the County were more on the order of $370 million. Why the huge difference? Four hundred million dollars in debt was included as revenue and as expenditure, but we know this is a capital outlay and not a recurring expenditure. Also there was another amount of nearly $400 million that included inter-fund transfers, internal transactions that are listed as revenues and then again as expenditures. They are simply accounting mechanics.

When the budget is reconstructed to eliminate these amounts, it turns out that the property tax is a huge amount of the recurrent revenue, 60 percent of the total. [Note that this percentage computed by Anderson is much higher than reported to the State Department of Financial Services and shown in Table 17.] In any case, a reduction would have serious implications for the "sustainable" revenues of the County.

Overall, the Anderson Group painted a pessimistic picture of Collier's financial future. It predicted that, within five years, the County would either have to find new sources of revenue or cut services. It did not sound like Collier was awash with money in 2004.

Just as total budget amounts can be misleading, so too can the accounting structure. Most of a government's revenues are placed either in a general fund or in a special fund. In terms of the discretionary use of funds, the difference is significant. Money placed in the general fund is typically available for any valid public purpose. By its placement in a special fund, money is earmarked for limited, specific, and special uses. It is not to be directed to any good purpose. In effect, more money in the general fund frees a government to make the best possible use of money; on the other hand, big amounts in special funds constrain decision makers and make it more difficult to find money for priority items.

A rather limited comparison of cities and counties in Florida indicates that the counties typically have a more major share of their money in special funds than do the cities. The comparison between Broward County and the city of Melbourne showed a rather striking difference. Broward maintained 31 special accounts and put 40% of its income in them; Melbourne, on the other hand, had only nine special accounts, where 10% of its revenues were deposited. It may be that the organizational integration of the cities gives them greater freedom to classify their income for general purposes.

While the counties do appear to enjoy a substantial diversity of revenue sources, it is a fact that nearly all depend on the same three revenue sources: the property tax, the State sharing of taxes, and charges for services. We found this was true, irrespective of the size and character of the county. It also made little difference whether a county was chartered or not.

It will be no surprise that the property tax again was most prominent. In a frequency study, the property tax was the biggest income source in 55 of the 64 counties analyzed.

Mandates imposed by the State are a significant and continuing problem for the counties. They are orders from on high that must be obeyed, regardless of their fiscal consequences.

The property tax has been the most vulnerable to mandates, going back at least to 1934 when a $5000 homestead exemption was placed in the Constitution. Today the debate over property tax reform really involves mandates. If Governor Crist's effort to raise the homestead exemption to $50,000 and those with Save our Homes exemptions are permitted to transfer these arrangements to other properties, it is possible that the counties will be foregoing revenues of as much as $1 billion per year. Whether that amount is reached or not, the counties will be prohibited from collecting very substantial amounts of money in property taxes.

After a great deal of criticism of the State Legislature's tendency to pile new mandates on local governments, a Constitutional amendment was passed in 1990 that prohibited the passage of bills loading new costs on local governments or reducing their taxing capacity. The result has been a conscious effort to examine each bill for its conformity with these Constitutional requirements.

When anything is important, however, these mandate prohibitions don't work. That is to be seen in the campaign for property tax reform in 2007. Escape valves were instituted in the 1990 mandate arrangements that provide fairly easy avenues to exemption. If a bill passes by a two-thirds majority in both houses, for example, the mandate prohibition does not apply.

There is no doubt that mandates continue to be an extremely troublesome factor in the relationships between the State and its local governments.

SELECT BIBLIOGRAPHY

Much of the research for this book depended on the Internet. Nearly all—but not all—the 67 counties now have web sites. They provided easily accessible and generally informative material on their structure and operations. That certainly eased the task of accumulating data on Florida's counties that are dispersed over a very large geographic area. There is one negative, however. Websites are constantly being changed. Even within a space of a month valuable information can vanish. The same is true of other websites, most particularly those of newspapers. There seems little advantage, as a result, in providing references to materials that are really fugitive and not likely to be available even when this book is first published. I have chosen, therefore, to include in this bibliography primarily hard copy resources that should be available in most major libraries. You will find, though, a few footnotes that indicate Internet sites, largely because I think they may have some interest beyond just checking back on a reference.

Also not included in this Bibliography are certain Florida state and association resources that are adequately covered in the text. Important information bearing on the counties can be obtained from three State sources: the Florida Department of Financial Services, the Florida Department of Community Affairs, and the Joint Legislative Committee on Intergovernmental Relations. Both the Florida Association of Counties and the National Association of Counties maintain easily retrievable files that provide much information on the structure, functions, and operations of these governments.

Books and Articles

Benton, J. Edwin and Gamble, Darwin F., "A City/County Consolidation and Economies of Scale: Evidence from a Time-Series Analysis in Jacksonville, Florida," *Social Science Quarterly*, March, 1984.

Chackerian, Richard, editor, *The Florida Public Policy Management System: Discontinuity and Reform* (Tallahassee, Fl.: Florida Center for Public

Management,1995), 438 pp. A second edition was published in 1998 by Kendall-Hunt (Dubuque, Iowa).

Crooks, James B., *Jacksonville: The Consolidation Story, from Civil Rights to the Jaguars.* Gainesville, FL: University Press of Florida, Florida History and Culture Series 2004.

Hertz, David Bendel *Governing Dade County: A Study of Alternative Structures.* Coral Gables: University of Miami, 1984.

Horan, James F. and Taylor, Jr., G. Thomas, *Experiments in Metropolitan Government.* New York: Praeger Publishers, 1977.

Lotz, Aileen, *Metropolitan Dade County: Two Tier Government in Action.* Boston: Allyn and Bacon, 1984.

Martin, Richard,. *Consolidation: Jacksonville Duval County: The Dynamics of Urban Political Reform.* Jacksonville, FL: Crawford Publishing Co., 1968.

O'Hara, Rebecca "Father Knows Best: The Charter County Assault on Municipal Home Rule," *Quality Cities* (January/February 2007).

Public Administration Service, *The Government of Metropolitan Miami.* Chicago: Public Administration Service, 1954.

Report on the History and Status of Local Government Powers in Florida. Tallahassee: Committee on Community Affairs, Florida House of Representatives, 1972.

Rosenbaum, Walter A. and Kammerer, Gladys M., *Against Long Odds: The Theory and Practice of Successful Government Consolidation.* Beverly Hills, CA: Sage Publications, 1974.

Selznick, Philip, *Leadership in Administration.* Evanston, Ill., and White Plains, N.Y.: Row, Peterson, 1957.

Smiley, Nixon, *Yesterday's Florida.* Miami: E.A. Seeman Publishing Co., 1974.

Tebeau, Charlton, *A History of Florida.* Coral Gables: University of Miami Press, 1971.

Dissertations

Schluckebier, Jack M., *A Study of the 1992 Consolidation Charter Proposal for Tallahassee and Leon County.* A Dissertation submitted to the Reubin O'D. Askew School of Public Administration and Policy, Florida State University, in partial fulfillment of the requirements for the degree of Doctor of Philosophy, 1995, typescript, 214 pages.

Vogel, Robert Kenneth, *Decision Making in Broward County: A Political Economy Approach.* A Dissertation presented to the Graduate School for the PhD, University of Florida, 1986, typescript, 198 pages.

Newspaper Articles

Florida Times-Union, October 16, 1956.

Florida Times-Union, October 1, 1978.

Joseph Tampani, "New commission: zoning friend or foe?" *Miami Herald,* April 23, 1993.

Dexter Filkins, "Metro: New faces, new feuds," *Miami Herald,* April 23, 1993.

Miami Herald, March 12,1999.

Miami Herald, January 19, 2007.

New York Times, June 10, 1987.

New York Times, February 18, 2007.

New York Times, August 10, 2007.

INDEX

978-0-595-48160-6
0-595-48160-4

www.ingramcontent.com/pod-product-compliance
Lightning Source LLC
Chambersburg PA
CBHW030259290526
45785CB00001B/144